T0358378

GOAL-BASED INVESTING

THEORY AND PRACTICE

GOAL-BASED INVESTING

INVESTING

THEORY AND PRACTICE

Romain Deguest
Lionel Martellini
EDHEC Risk Institute, France

Vincent Milhau
EDHEC Risk Institute, France

 **World Scientific**

NEW JERSEY · LONDON · SINGAPORE · BEIJING · SHANGHAI · HONG KONG · TAIPEI · CHENNAI · TOKYO

Published by

World Scientific Publishing Co. Pte. Ltd.

5 Toh Tuck Link, Singapore 596224

USA office: 27 Warren Street, Suite 401-402, Hackensack, NJ 07601

UK office: 57 Shelton Street, Covent Garden, London WC2H 9HE

Library of Congress Control Number: 2021938828

British Library Cataloguing-in-Publication Data
A catalogue record for this book is available from the British Library.

ISBN 978-981-124-094-2 (hardcover)
ISBN 978-981-124-095-9 (ebook for institutions)
ISBN 978-981-124-096-6 (ebook for individuals)

For any available supplementary material, please visit
https://www.worldscientific.com/worldscibooks/10.1142/12386#t=suppl

Desk Editors: Jayanthi Muthuswamy/Daniele Lee

Typeset by Stallion Press
Email: enquiries@stallionpress.com

Printed in Singapore

Preface

Individual investors' investment problems can be broadly summarised as a combination of various wealth and/or consumption goals, subject to a set of dollar budgets, defined in terms of initial wealth and future income, as well as risk budgets such as maximum drawdown limits, for example.

The starting point of an investor-centric goals-based investment (GBI) approach consists in recognising that the success or failure of these goals subject to dollar and risk budgets does *not* critically depend upon the standalone performance of a particular fund nor that of a given asset class. It depends instead upon how well the investor's portfolio dynamically interacts with the risk factors impacting the present value of the investor's goals as well as the present value of non-tradable assets and future income streams, if any. In this context, the key challenge for financial advisors is to implement dedicated investment solutions aiming to generate the highest possible probability of achieving investors' goals, and a reasonably low expected shortfall in case adverse market conditions make it unfeasible to achieve those goals. The need to design an asset allocation solution that is a function of the kinds of particular risks to which the investor is exposed, or needs to be exposed to fulfil goals, as opposed to purely focusing on the risks impacting the market as a whole, makes the use of Modern Portfolio Theory or standard portfolio optimisation techniques mostly inadequate.

While the efficient management of all risk buckets, versus market risk alone, is a central component of the Wealth Allocation Framework (WAF) introduced in Chhabra (2005),[1] the practical implications of this insight have not been fully exploited to date. Most financial advisors still maintain a sole focus on market risks taken in isolation, with investors' preferences crudely summarised in terms of a simple risk-aversion parameter.

The focus of this book is to present a general operational framework that can be used by financial advisors to allow individual investors to optimally allocate to categories of risks they face across all life stages and wealth segments so as to achieve personally meaningful financial goals. One key feature in developing the risk allocation framework for goals-based wealth management includes the introduction of systematic rule-based multi-period portfolio construction methodologies, which is a required element given that risks and goals typically persist across multiple time frames. Academic research has shown that an efficient use of the three forms of risk management (diversification, hedging and insurance) is required to develop an investment solution framework dedicated to allowing investors to maximise the probabilities of reaching their meaningful goals given their dollar and risk budgets. As a result, the main focus of the framework is on the efficient management of rewarded risk exposures.

The framework should not only be thought as a financial engineering device for generating meaningful investment solutions with respect to investors' needs. It should also, and perhaps even more importantly, encompass a process dedicated to facilitating a meaningful dialogue with the investor. In this context, the reporting dimension of the framework should focus on updated probabilities of achieving goals and associated expected shortfalls, as opposed to solely focusing on standard risk and return indicators, which are mostly irrelevant in this context.

Broadly speaking, GBI strategies aim to secure investors' most important goals (labelled as "essential" — see the definition that

---

[1]Chhabra, A., 2005, Beyond Markowitz: A comprehensive wealth allocation framework for individual investors, *The Journal of Wealth Management*, 7, 5, 8–34.

follows), thereby delivering a reasonably high chance of success for achieving other goals, including ambitious ones which cannot be fully funded together with the most essential ones, and which are referred to as "aspirational". Holding a leverage-constrained exposure to a well-diversified performance-seeking portfolio (PSP) often leads to modest probabilities of achieving such ambitious goals, and individual investors may increase their chances of meeting these goals by holding aspirational assets which generally contain illiquid concentrated risk exposures, for example, under the form of equity ownership in a private business.

This book introduces a general operational framework, which formalises the goals-based risk allocation approach to wealth management, and which allows individual investors to optimally allocate to categories of risks they face across all life stages and wealth segments so as to achieve personally meaningful financial goals. Through a number of realistic case study examples, we document the benefits of the approach, which respects the individual investor's essential goals with the highest degree of probability, while allowing for substantial upside potential that leads to a reasonably high probability of achieving ambitious aspirational goals.

In addition to developing and analysing optimal portfolio construction methodologies, this book also introduces robust heuristics, which can be thought of as reasonable approximations for optimal strategies that can accommodate a variety of implementation constraints, including the presence of taxes, the presence of short-sale constraints, the presence of parameter estimation risk, as well as limited customisation constraints.

It is not an overstatement to say that the wealth management industry is about to experience a profound paradigm change, and it is our hope that this book will provide assistance to the next generation of financial advisors and wealth managers who will focus on satisfying clients' needs through a dedicated investor-centric goals-based investment solution approach.

About the Authors

 **Romain Deguest** is an Associate Professor of Finance at IESEG School of Management and a member of the LEM-CNRS 9221. He holds a PhD in Operations Research from Columbia University and a PhD in Applied Mathematics from Ecole Polytechnique. He is the co-founder of Fundvisory, a Fintech robo-advisor that develops digital financial services for financial institutions such as client and risk profiling, automated portfolio construction, simulation of future wealth, regulatory and financial monitoring, and detailed reporting. He was previously an Adjunct Professor of Finance at EDHEC Business School and a Senior Research Engineer at EDHEC-Risk Institute where he worked on numerous research projects sponsored by major financial industry players including goal-based investing, life-cycle investing, asset-liability management, risk-controlled investing, and Smart Beta. His research topics also include asset pricing, model uncertainty, model calibration, risk management, portfolio construction, and asset allocation. His work has been published in leading academic and practitioner journals such as *Management Science*, *Mathematical Finance*, *Quantitative Finance*, *SIAM Journal on Financial Mathematics*, *The Journal of Fixed Income*, and *Risk Magazine*.

Lionel Martellini is a Professor of Finance at EDHEC Business School and the founding President of EDHEC Scientific Retirement, a venture dedicated to assisting asset owners and asset managers in the design and implementation of welfare-improving forms of retirement solutions. Professor Martellini is the former Director of EDHEC-Risk Institute and a former member of the faculty at the Marshall School of Business, University of Southern California. He has also taught at U.C. Berkeley and at Princeton University, where he has been a visiting fellow at the Operations Research and Financial Engineering department. He holds Master's degrees in management, economics, mathematics, and statistics, as well as a Ph.D. in finance from the Haas School of Business, University of California at Berkeley. Outside of his activities in finance, he recently completed a Ph.D. in Relativistic Astrophysics (University Côte d'Azur). Professor Martellini is a member of the editorial board of *The Journal of Portfolio Management*, *The Journal of Alternative Investments*, and *The Journal of Retirement*. He leads research and education programs on a broad range of topics related to investment solutions for individual and institutional investors. His work has been published in leading academic and practitioner journals and has been featured in major European and global dailies such as *The Economist*, *The Financial Times*, and *The Wall Street Journal*.

Vincent Milhau is Head of Research at EDHEC Scientific Retirement and a former Research Director at EDHEC-Risk Institute. At the Institute, he has worked on many applied research projects supported by financial industry players in the areas of asset allocation and risk management with applications to institutional and individual money management. His research topics include asset-liability management for pension funds, life-cycle investing, target date funds, long-term investing under short-term constraints, goal-based investing, and retirement investing for individuals. He has also contributed to the Institute's research on portfolio construction in the equity and the fixed-income universes. He has co-authored articles that have appeared in leading academic and practitioner finance journals such as *Management Science, The Journal of Corporate Finance, The Journal of Portfolio Management,* and *The Journal of Fixed Income.*

Acknowledgements

This book has greatly benefitted from many discussions with a number of industry colleagues with great expertise about the subject of goal-based investing, including most notably Ashvin Chhabra for being the source of inspiration for this project, Anil Suri for most generously sharing his insights and visions all along the way, as well as Stefano D'Amiano, David Laster, Ravindra Koneru and Hungjen Wang for providing most useful comments and feedback.

Contents

Chapter 1

Introduction

Individual investors' investment problems can be broadly summarised as a combination of various wealth and/or consumption goals, subject to a set of dollar budgets, defined in terms of initial wealth and future income, as well as risk budgets such as maximum drawdown limits, for example.[1] It is important to note that the success or failure to satisfy these goals subject to dollar and risk budgets does *not* critically depend upon the standalone performance of a particular fund nor that of a given asset class. It depends instead upon how well the performance of the investor's portfolio dynamically interacts with the risk factors impacting the present value of the investor's goals. In this context, it becomes clear that the key challenge for financial advisors is to implement dedicated investment solutions aiming to generate the highest possible probability of achieving investors' goals, and a reasonably low expected shortfall in case adverse market conditions make it unfeasible to achieve them. In other words, what will prove to be the decisive factor is the ability to design an asset allocation solution that is a function of the kinds of particular risks to which the investor is exposed, or needs to be exposed to fulfil goals, as opposed to purely focusing on the risks impacting the market as a whole. These simple insights have far reaching implications, including on regulatory requirements such as the "prudent man rule", which is the requirement that investment managers or any fiduciary agents must only invest funds entrusted to

---

[1] See Chapter 2 for a detailed classification and analysis of investors' goals.

1

them with prudence. This prudent approach might actually become counterproductive if it is cast in an isolated context, that is, with a sole focus on market risks without a proper integration of the investor's goals. For example, a seemingly safe short-term investment strategy such as the roll-over of money market debt can prove to be very risky from the perspective of meeting long-term consumption needs.

From the academic standpoint, the recognition of the critical importance of investors' personal risks, in addition to market risks, was first emphasised in the seminal work by Merton (1971, 1973), and subsequent papers on dynamic asset allocation decisions in the presence of income and consumption risks (see the literature review in Section 3.2 of Chapter 3). In this paradigm, which extends the standard efficient frontier paradigm introduced by Markowitz (1952) to an intertemporal setting, the optimal allocation strategy is shown to involve, in addition to the standard mean–variance efficient PSP, dedicated hedging portfolios that are designed to hedge investors against unfavourable changes in the risk factors impacting their income and consumption streams. While this framework serves as the foundation for most of modern dynamic asset pricing theory, the key implications of this paradigm for the wealth management industry have not been recognised until recently, with financial advisors mostly maintaining a focus on the management of market risks in isolation. The need for financial advisors to focus on the proper management of *personal* and *aspirational* risks in addition to the management of market risks was clarified in the *Goals-Based Wealth Allocation Framework* proposed in Chhabra (2005) (see Wang *et al.*, 2011).[2] In a nutshell, the goals-based wealth management framework includes two distinct elements. On the one hand, it involves the disaggregation of investor preferences into groups of goals that have similar key characteristics, with priority ranking and term structure of associated liabilities, and on the other hand, it involves the mapping of these groups to optimised performance or hedging portfolios possessing corresponding risk and return characteristics (see Chapter 2). While Chhabra (2005) provides a thorough analysis at the conceptual level of the challenges to implementing a goals-based risk and investment allocation process

---

[2]See Section 3.2 of Chapter 3 for a detailed review of the related literature.

(see Wang *et al.*, 2011), it does not present, however, a fully operational framework for implementing this process.

In particular, a series of questions remain regarding what extension of existing financial engineering techniques, if any, is required to formally establish the goals-based allocation framework.[3] The main objective of this book is to introduce a general operational framework that can be used by a financial advisor to allow individual investors to optimally allocate to categories of risks they face across all life stages and wealth segments so as to achieve personally meaningful goals. One key feature in developing the risk allocation framework for goals-based investing (GBI) strategies includes the introduction of multi-period portfolio construction methodologies, which is a required element given that risks and goals typically persist across multiple time frames.

Broadly speaking, the framework will encompass two main kinds of ingredients, namely the identification of the suitable building blocks, on the one hand, and the identification of suitable decisions in terms of allocations to these building blocks, on the other hand. We note at this stage that the framework only involves rule-based strategies, based either on observable quantities or on estimated parameter values. This notably excludes the use of stochastic optimisation techniques, which are typically well-suited for the analysis of optimal decisions under uncertainty when the number of possible future states is limited, but suffer from a black-box aspect, and cannot easily accommodate a realistically rich description of uncertainty. It is also important to emphasise that the framework should not only be thought of as a financial engineering device for generating meaningful investment solutions with respect to investors' needs but also encompass a process dedicated to facilitating a meaningful dialogue with the investor. In this context, the reporting dimension of the framework should focus on updated probabilities of achieving goals, as opposed to solely focusing on standard risk and return indicators, which are not necessarily relevant in this context.

From the academic standpoint, one contribution of the work presented in this book is to extend the seminal analysis of Dybvig and

---

[3]Our chapter is also related to the literature on commitment-directed investing (see Mindlin, 2013; CDI Advisors Research, 2014).

Huang (1988) to the presence of non-portfolio income. It is well-known that the existence of a state-price deflator, or equivalently of an equivalent martingale measure, is not sufficient to avoid arbitrage opportunities. The classical counterexample is the "doubling strategy" of Harrisson and Kreps (1979), which generates a riskless gain from nothing in a finite time frame, but does so at the cost of potentially unlimited losses. One possible remedy to the presence of arbitrage opportunities in dynamically complete continuous-time markets is the introduction of an integrability condition on the strategy weights (see Harrison and Pliska, 1981), but this mathematical restriction lacks economic interpretation. As an alternative, Dybvig and Huang (1988) propose imposing a non-negativity constraint (or in fact any negative lower bound) on wealth, which admits a natural interpretation as a credit constraint. They show that this condition rules out arbitrage opportunities and that it is equivalent to an integrability condition. While it allows for consumption, their framework, however, does not include non-portfolio income. It turns out that adding this ingredient is not a straightforward extension of their work because it modifies the definition of feasible consumption–investment plans. In particular, non-negative wealth has to be required at all dates, not only at the final date as in their paper, in order to prevent investors from borrowing against their future income. In this book, we examine in detail the question of financing a given consumption plan in the presence of income, when financial wealth only, as opposed to financial wealth plus human capital, is restricted to be non-negative. An important result we obtain is a general "affordability criterion", which characterises feasible plans and extends the well-known criterion stating that a consumption plan is financed if the investor's initial wealth exceeds the present value of the consumption payments. We also show that the introduction of forward contracts leads, in general, to a further decrease in the minimum wealth required to secure a given consumption plan.

This book is organised as follows. In Chapter 2, we introduce a formal risk allocation framework for GBI strategies and we present a set of theoretical optimality results regarding affordable goals and the relationship with the efficient design of building blocks involved in such strategies. Chapter 3 examines the question of how to efficiently allocate across the risk buckets defined in the preceding section and discusses the implementation challenges in a real-world setting. Chapter 4 presents an application of the framework to three different case studies, representing three possible types of investors clustered in different groups, defined in terms of affluence and life stage. Chapter 5 presents a number of conclusions, and technical details and proofs of the main results are relegated to a dedicated appendix.

Chapter 2

Efficient Allocation Within Risk Buckets

In this section, we introduce a formal continuous-time framework for the goals-based investing (GBI) problem. We then present the various types of goals that will be considered in this book, we define the notion of the affordability of a goal, which corresponds to attainability, and we present formal necessary and sufficient conditions of affordability, which can be regarded as verification criteria to characterise affordable goals in practice. We next describe efficient composition of the building blocks, also known as risk buckets, which will be involved in GBI strategies, distinguishing between a safety risk bucket, a performance-seeking risk bucket and a risk bucket containing all non-tradable and illiquid assets, if any, that an investor may hold for wealth mobility purposes.

2.1. Notation and Assumptions

Following the seminal work of Merton (1971), we cast the intertemporal portfolio choice problem within a continuous-time framework. Uncertainty in the economy is represented by a filtered probability space $(X, \mathcal{F}, \mathbb{P})$, where $\mathcal{F}$ is a sigma-algebra on X, and $\mathbb{P}$ is a probability measure that represents investor's beliefs. Unless otherwise stated, the investment horizon is a finite quantity T (which for example can be time of retirement or time of death depending on the context), and the initial date is 0, so the time span is $[0, T]$. The probability space supports a d-dimensional Brownian motion $\underline{z}$, d being the number of independent sources of risk in the economy, and is equipped with the filtration $(\mathcal{F}_t)_{0 \leq t \leq T}$ generated by this Brownian motion: $\mathcal{F}_t$ is a sigma-algebra on X, which represents the information accumulated by the investor up to date t. All stochastic processes introduced in what follows are implicitly assumed to be progressively measurable with respect to this filtration. This technical assumption is not very restrictive, as it is satisfied as soon as all stochastic processes are adapted (i.e. the value of the stochastic process on a date t is a $\mathcal{F}_t$-measurable random variable) and right-continuous (see Proposition 1.13 in Karatzas and Shreve, 2000). These two conditions will be verified for all the processes that we consider in this book.

2.1.1. *Asset prices*

The nominal short-term interest rate on date t, for lending or borrowing on the infinitesimal horizon dt, is denoted by r_t. The investment universe is assumed to contain a locally risk-free asset, the price of which, S_{0t}, is the continuously compounded short-term rate

$$S_{0t} = \exp\left[\int_0^t r_s ds\right].$$

There are also n "locally risky" assets, the prices of which, $S_1, \ldots, S_n$, follow diffusion processes as in Merton (1971)

$$\frac{dS_{it}}{S_{it}} = [r_t + \sigma_{it}\lambda_{it}]dt + \underline{\sigma}'_{it}d\underline{z}_t \qquad (2.1)$$

Here, λ_{it} is the Sharpe ratio, $\underline{\sigma}_{it}$ is the $d \times 1$ volatility vector, and σ_{it} is the scalar volatility.[1] At this stage, no particular restriction is imposed on the risk and return parameters, beyond the progressive measurability. In particular, Sharpe ratios and volatilities can be stochastic. More restrictive assumptions will have to be made in order to derive utility-maximising portfolio strategies, but these will be specified later (see Section 3.2.2 of Chapter 3).

---

[1] We use underbars to denote vectors and matrices. For instance, the scalar σ_{it} is the norm of the vector $\underline{\sigma}_{it}$.

We let $\underline{\sigma}_t$, $\underline{\Sigma}_t$ and $\underline{\mu}_t$ denote the $n \times d$ volatility matrix, the $n \times n$ covariance matrix and the $n \times 1$ vector of expected excess returns of the risky assets

$$\underline{\sigma}_t = \left(\underline{\sigma}_{1t} \cdots \underline{\sigma}_{nt}\right),$$

$$\underline{\Sigma}_t = \underline{\sigma}'_t \underline{\sigma}_t,$$

$$\underline{\mu}_t = \left(\sigma_{1t}\lambda_{1t} \cdots \sigma_{nt}\lambda_{nt}\right)'.$$

All these moments are instantaneous; because of non-trivial term structure effects, the moments evaluated over a non-infinitesimal horizon may be different from the above ones.

A critically useful notion is that of "state-price deflator", which will be used to find the present value of claims with uncertain pay-offs at later dates. Formally, a positive process $(M_t)_{0 \leq t \leq T}$ is said to be a state-price deflator if for $i = 1, \ldots, n$, the deflated price $M_t S_{it}$ follows a martingale. The existence of one such price deflator is ensured by the condition of absence of arbitrage opportunities (see, for example, Duffie (2001)). As shown by He and Pearson (1991), there exist infinitely many state-price deflators if markets are dynamically incomplete, that is, if the number of sources of risk (d) exceeds the number of risky assets (n). Among these, one is of particular interest, namely the state-price deflator associated with the "spanned price of risk vector"

$$\underline{\lambda}_t = \underline{\sigma}_t \underline{\Sigma}_t^{-1} \underline{\mu}_t,$$

$$M_t = \exp\left[-\int_0^t \left(r_s + \frac{\|\underline{\lambda}_s\|^2}{2}\right) ds - \int_0^t \underline{\lambda}'_s d\underline{z}_s\right],$$

where $\|\underline{\lambda}_s\|$ denotes Euclidian norm of the vector $\underline{\lambda}_s$. The vector $\underline{\lambda}_t$ has size $d \times 1$, and is said to be spanned because it falls in the span of the volatility matrix.

To each pricing kernel is associated an "equivalent martingale measure" (EMM), which is defined by its Radon–Nikodym density with respect to $\mathbb{P}$

$$\frac{d\mathbb{Q}}{d\mathbb{P}} = \exp\left[\int_0^T r_s ds\right] \times M_T.$$

Since there is a one-to-one correspondence between state-price defla-tors and EMMs, the EMM is unique if, and only if, the state-price deflator is unique, that is, if the market is dynamically complete. The price at date t of a payoff P_T paid on date T can be obtained by two equivalent formulas

$$\mathbb{E}_t\left[\frac{M_T}{M_t}P_T\right] = \mathbb{E}_t^{\mathbb{Q}}\left[\exp\left(-\int_0^T r_s ds\right)P_T\right].$$

In this equality (which follows from Bayes's formula), $\mathbb{E}_t$ denotes the expectation operator conditional on the information available to date t under the probability $\mathbb{P}$, and $\mathbb{E}_t^{\mathbb{Q}}$ is the expectation under $\mathbb{Q}$.

2.1.2. *Portfolio strategies*

The investor is endowed with a positive initial capital A_0, which he invests in the n risky assets and the risk-free one. The portfolio is said to be *self-financing* if no cash is infused in or withdrawn from the portfolio. We let $\underline{N}_t = (N_{1t}, \ldots, N_{nt})'$ be the $n \times 1$ vector of numbers of shares of the risky assets held on date t. The number of shares of the risk-free asset is thus

$$N_{0t} = \frac{A_t - \sum_{i=1}^n N_{it}S_{it}}{S_{0t}}.$$

The budget constraint describes the evolution of liquid wealth. It reads

$$dA_t = \sum_{i=0}^n N_{it}dS_{it} = \sum_{i=1}^n N_{it}dS_{it} + \left[A_t - \sum_{i=1}^n N_{it}S_{it}\right]r_t dt. \qquad (2.2)$$

Equivalently, the strategy can be described in terms of the dollar amounts invested in the risky assets. Let $\underline{q}_t = (q_{1t}, \ldots, q_{nt})'$ be the $n \times 1$ vector of these amounts. They are related to the numbers of shares through

$$q_{it} = N_{it}S_{it}, \quad \text{for } i = 1, \ldots, n.$$

Finally, when wealth is positive, one can compute the weights allocated to the various risky assets as

$$w_{it} = \frac{q_{it}}{A_t}, \quad \text{for } i = 1, \ldots, n.$$

The sum of the weights is not necessarily equal to 1, and the balance $[1 - \sum_{i=1}^n w_{it}]$ is invested in cash. Thus, the third representation of a self-financing portfolio strategy is the weight vector process $\underline{w}$, where the value of the process on date t is the vector of weights $\underline{w}_t = (w_{1t}, \ldots, w_{nt})'$.

For the purpose of computing optimal portfolio strategies according to various criteria, it is useful to express the expected return and the volatility of the portfolio in terms of the portfolio composition. To do this, it suffices to substitute the dynamics of the risky assets (Equation (2.1)) back into Equation (2.2). This gives the following two equivalent expressions:

$$dA_t = [r_t A_t + \underline{q}'_t \underline{\mu}_t]dt + \underline{q}'_t \underline{\sigma}'_t d\underline{z}_t,$$

$$dA_t = A_t[r_t + \underline{w}'_t \underline{\mu}_t]dt + A_t \underline{w}'_t \underline{\sigma}'_t d\underline{z}_t. \tag{2.3}$$

Thus, the portfolio expected excess return and volatility have the familiar expressions, respectively, given by a linear function and by the square root of a quadratic function of the weights

$$\mu_{Pt} = \underline{w}'_t \underline{\mu}_t, \quad \sigma_{Pt} = \sqrt{\underline{w}'_t \Sigma_t \underline{w}_t}.$$

Ruling out negative wealth may be desirable for several reasons. First, negative wealth for an individual investor means bankruptcy, which is a situation that investors generally seek to avoid at all costs. The second reason is of a theoretical nature. It is known that in continuous-time models, the existence of a state-price deflator (or equivalently, of an EMM) does not alone imply the absence of arbitrage opportunities.[2] One recovers the implication by imposing a non-negative wealth constraint (see Dybvig and Huang (1988)). It is important to have this condition in mind when computing a utility-maximising payoff (see Section 3.2.2 of Chapter 3).

In the presence of consumption, the budget equation (2.1) has to be modified. In the literature on dynamic portfolio choice, consumption is traditionally represented as a continuous-time process, but for the sake of realism, we model it here as a discrete process: the consumption dates are denoted as $T_1 < \cdots < T_p$, and comprised between 0 and T. The consumption of date t_j is denoted as c_{T_j}, and

---

[2]This is because "doubling strategies" are possible (see Harrison and Kreps (1979); Duffie (2001)).

is assumed to be a $\mathcal{F}_{T_j}$-measurable random variable, non-negative with probability 1.

Because of the presence of a consumption stream, the investor's portfolio is no longer self-financing, and because of the discrete nature of consumption, it is not even continuous, as was the case before in Equation (2.1). We define A_t as the wealth of date t, after the consumption expenditure has been made: thus, A is a right-continuous process with left limits. The left limit at date t, denoted by A_{t-}, is the value of wealth just before the consumption payment. Of course, jumps in wealth occur only on the consumption dates; wealth is continuous between two of these dates. To write the new budget equation, let us introduce a family of p Heaviside functions $(J_{T_1}, \ldots, J_{T_p})$, each of them being an indicator function (which is also right-continuous)

$$J_{T_j,t} = \begin{cases} 0 & \text{if } t < T_j \\ 1 & \text{if } t \geq T_j \end{cases}.$$

With these notations, the budget constraint becomes

$$dA_t = \sum_{i=1}^{n} N_{it} dS_{it} + \left[A_t - \sum_{i=1}^{n} N_{it} S_{it} \right] r_t dt - \sum_{j=1}^{p} c_{T_j} dJ_{T_j,t}. \quad (2.4)$$

Heuristically, the differential element $dJ_{T_j,t}$ can be thought of as a quantity equal to 1 when t equals T_j, and 0 otherwise.[3]

A last extension consists in the introduction of income in the budget constraint. This is in fact formally equivalent to having negative consumption. In order to alleviate the notational burden, we assume that the income dates coincide with the consumption dates. This entails no loss of generality, as it suffices to introduce additional payments equal to zero to satisfy this condition.

As usual, we take the income payments $y_{T_1}, \ldots, y_{T_p}$ to be measurable with respect to the filtration $(\mathcal{F}_t)_t$. The most general form of

---

[3]The rigorous mathematical definition of $dJ_{T_j,t}$ is as a Dirac measure: this measure assigns a mass of 0 to time intervals that do not contain T_j, and a mass of 1 to any interval that contains this date.

the budget constraint reads

$$dA_t = \sum_{i=1}^{n} N_{it} dS_{it} + \left[A_t - \sum_{i=1}^{n} N_{it} S_{it} \right] r_t dt$$

$$+ \sum_{j=1}^{p} y_{T_j} dJ_{T_j,t} - \sum_{j=1}^{p} c_{T_j} dJ_{T_j,t}. \qquad (2.5)$$

Again, A_{t-} denotes the value of wealth just before the income or consumption payment, and A_t is the value of wealth just after the cash flow.

2.2. Defining Affordable Goals

A key concept in goals-based wealth management is that of *affordable* goals, which are intuitively defined as goals that an investor can secure with full certainty with some suitably designed hedging strategy given available wealth and future income. The notion of affordability will subsequently be used in the classification of goals within three distinct groups, namely *essential* goals, *important* goals and *aspirational* goals (see Section 2.4). In this section, we first provide a formal definition of this concept, which is relatively straightforward in the absence of income, but becomes more involved in the presence of income cash flows because of the possible competition between current wealth and future savings in the process of securing the target consumption or wealth goals. The general definition of affordability that we derive, however, is not very operational. For this reason, we also introduce a number of sufficient and necessary conditions for affordability which can be used as verification criteria in practice.

2.2.1. *Affordability of wealth-based goals*

A first distinction exists between wealth-based goals and consumption-based goals. A wealth-based goal is expressed as a minimum level of wealth that the investor wants to reach at a certain horizon, and a consumption-based goal is a target (possibly inflation-linked) payment that the investor wants to make.

The main difference between the two types is that the achievement of
a consumption-based goal impacts the investor's wealth, while that
of a wealth-based one has no effect on the budget constraint.

2.2.1.1.   *Wealth-based goal with single horizon*

The first type of goal that we consider is a simple wealth-based goal
expressed as follows: assume that the investor has a horizon T, and
would like his wealth at date T to be above a level G_T. Having
such a wealth-based goal is analogous to imposing a floor on terminal wealth. The payoff G_T can be a constant (e.g. a target nominal
amount), or it can be uncertain at date 0, in case the investor requires
a wealth level contingent on the economic conditions prevailing on
date T. For instance, the goal may be expressed as a target real, as
opposed to nominal, wealth level, the objective being to protect the
purchasing power against erosion due to inflation. In the language
of the literature on option pricing and hedging, the wealth-based
goal is represented by an $\mathcal{F}_T$-measurable and non-negative payoff
G_T. In what follows, we adopt the following formal definition for the
affordability of a wealth-based goal at horizon T.

**Definition 1 (Affordability of a Wealth-Based Goal with a
Single Horizon).** A wealth-based goal characterised by the horizon T and the non-negative minimum wealth level G_T is said to
be affordable if there exists a portfolio strategy $\underline{w}$ such that, starting from the investor's initial capital, the wealth satisfies the budget
constraint (2.3) and the inequality $A_T \geq G_T$ with probability 1. Such
a strategy is said to secure the goal.

The question of the affordability of the goal encompasses in fact
two independent questions:

Q1. Is the payoff G_T replicable with the available risky assets?
Q2. If the answer to Q1 is positive, is the investor's initial wealth
     sufficient to attain the payoff?

The answer to Q1 is related to the risk factors that impact goal
value. In somewhat informal terms, if the goal value depends on
"unspanned" risk factors, that is, risk factors that cannot be hedged
with available securities, the payoff will not be replicable. This is the
case, for instance, if the goal value is indexed on inflation, and the

investment universe only contains stocks and nominal bonds. Because no portfolio of these assets can exactly replicate realised inflation, the payoff is not replicable. In such a situation, the markets are dynamically incomplete in the sense of Duffie (2001). Since the goal value cannot be replicated exactly, one can at best form a strategy that approximates the value in the sense of a hedging criterion. Various criteria have been proposed in the literature, some of which will be reviewed in what follows (see Section 3.2.1 of Chapter 3). In order to avoid the technicalities associated with non-replicable payoffs, we assume in what follows that all wealth-based goals are *replicable*, in the sense that there exists an initial capital $\tilde{G}_0$, and a dynamic portfolio strategy $\underline{w}_G$, referred to as the goal-hedging portfolio (GHP), such that G_T is the value at date T of the solution to the stochastic differential equation:

$$\frac{d\tilde{G}_t}{\tilde{G}_t} = [r_t + \underline{w}'_{Gt}\underline{\mu}_t]dt + \underline{w}'_{Gt}\underline{\sigma}'_t d\underline{z}_t,$$

with the initial condition $\tilde{G}_0$. In other words, G_T is the value at date T of some portfolio invested in the available risky assets and cash. In the previous equation, $\tilde{G}_t$ represents the present value of the goal, which is also the value of the GHP. An assumption that guarantees the existence of the GHP is the dynamic completeness of the markets: Duffie (2001) shows that if the number of risky assets (n) equals the number of independent risk factors (d), then any payoff is attainable. This assumption is only sufficient, however, but not necessary to guarantee the affordability of G_T.

The question Q2 is irrelevant if the goal is not replicable. A non-replicable goal is by definition not affordable. On the other hand, if G_T is replicable, then there exists a unique no-arbitrage price for this payoff, and this price is $\tilde{G}_0$. Then, by absence of arbitrage opportunities, having $A_T \geq G_T$ with probability one implies that the initial values satisfy $A_0 \geq \tilde{G}_0$. Conversely, if $A_0 \geq \tilde{G}_0$, then investing A_0 in the GHP delivers the wealth $\frac{A_0}{\tilde{G}_0}G_T$ at date T, a payoff which is clearly greater than or equal to G_T in any state of the world. Thus, a simple test for Q2 is the comparison between the investor's initial capital and the present value of the goal. If $A_0 \geq \tilde{G}_0$, then the goal is affordable; if $A_0 < \tilde{G}_0$, it is not. The following proposition summarises this simple but important result.

Proposition 1 (Affordability Criterion of a Replicable Wealth-Based Goal with a Single Horizon). *Consider a wealth-based goal represented by the non-negative minimum wealth level G_T, and assume that this goal is replicable. It is affordable if, and only if, the initial wealth and the present value of the payoff G_T satisfy $A_0 \geq \tilde{G}_0$. If this condition is satisfied, then the goal is secured by investing A_0 in the GHP.*

Two comments are in order. First, it is not because a goal is affordable that it will be secured with any strategy. The success in achieving a goal depends of course on the initial wealth, but also on how wealth is invested: the notion of affordability corresponds to the existence of at least one strategy that attains the goal with probability 1, but not all strategies will have this property. Second, the non-affordability does not imply that the goal will *never* be attained: it can still be attained in some states of the world, but the probability of having $A_T \geq G_T$ will be less than 1.

2.2.1.2. *Wealth-based goal with multiple horizons*

It can happen that a wealth-based goal is not expressed as a minimum level of wealth at a given horizon T, but as a series of minimum wealth levels at different dates. Formally, a wealth-based goal is defined by a set of horizons $\mathcal{T}$ and a family of random variables $(G_t)_{t \in \mathcal{T}}$, such that G_t is $\mathcal{F}_t$-measurable and non-negative. Note that this definition extends that of a wealth-based goal with a single horizon: for such a goal, $\mathcal{T}$ has a single element. On the other hand, in Case Study 1 (see Section 4.1 of Chapter 4), the investor is concerned with achieving a fixed minimum level of real wealth at the end of each year over the next 35 years; in this particular example, $\mathcal{T}$ has 35 elements.

The definition of affordability in the case of multiple horizons is a natural extension of Definition 1.

Definition 2 (Affordability of a Wealth-Based Goal with Multiple Horizons). A wealth-based goal represented by the set of horizons $\mathcal{T}$ and the non-negative minimum wealth levels $(G_t)_{t \in \mathcal{T}}$ is said to be affordable if there exists a portfolio strategy $\underline{w}$ such that, starting from the investor's initial capital, the wealth satisfies the budget constraint (2.2) and the inequality $A_t \geq G_t$ with probability 1 for all $t \in \mathcal{T}$. Such a strategy is said to secure the goal.

It is clear that this definition is more general than Definition 1: a wealth-based goal with a single horizon is merely a special case of a goal with multiple horizons, with a set of horizons reduced to a single element.

The first case study (see Section 4.1 of Chapter 4) provides two examples of such goals. First, the investor wants to protect a minimum level of real wealth at the end of each year: G_t is then equal to the initial wealth multiplied by realised inflation. Second, the investor wants, at the end of each year, to have at least 85% of the maximum wealth attained at previous year ends. This second goal is referred to as the drawdown (DD) goal. It is mathematically expressed as

$$A_{T_j} \geq m_{DD} \times \overline{A}_{T_{j-1}}, \quad \text{for all } j = 2, \ldots, p,$$

where $\overline{A}_t$ is the maximum to date of wealth, given by

$$\overline{A}_{T_{j-1}} = \max\left[A_{T_1}, \ldots, A_{T_{j-1}}\right],$$

and m_{DD} is a parameter, for which typical values are 90% and 85%.[4]

We are now interested in finding an affordability criterion similar to that of Proposition 1, which is based on the comparison between initial wealth and the present value of the goal. This extension is not straightforward, as there is no clear notion of "present value" for a sequence of payoffs occurring at different dates, even if each payoff G_t itself has a well-defined present value. Moreover, the case of the max drawdown goal (in short, max DD goal) must be treated separately. Indeed, the definition of the minimum wealth levels and investment decisions are intertwined in this case, so that the present value of the payoffs G_t depends on portfolio weights. We thus make a distinction between two types of wealth-based goals:

- A goal where the minimum wealth levels G_t are exogenous, that is, they are not affected by investment decisions;
- A goal such as the max DD goal, where the minimum wealth levels G_t are endogenous, that is, they depend upon investment decisions.

---

[4]Note that in the academic literature on drawdown constraints, the running maximum is taken over the continuum of dates that precede the current date.

The easier case is that of the DD goal. It turns out that this goal is affordable whatever the initial wealth, provided the short-term rate remains non-negative. Indeed, under this condition, the locally risk-free asset has only non-negative returns, so that its drawdown along each path is zero.

Proposition 2 (Affordability of DD Goal). *For any choice of m_{DD} between 0 and 1 and any initial wealth, the DD goal associated with the threshold m_{DD} is affordable if the short-term interest rate remains non-negative. This goal is secured by investing the entire wealth in cash.*

We now turn to an exogenous goal. To get a feel for the expression of the minimum capital to invest in order to secure a goal with multiple horizons, consider an example with two dates $T_1 < T_2$, and take a strategy that secures the goal. The value of the strategy satisfies (with probability 1)

$$A_{T_2} \geq G_{T_2}.$$

By absence of arbitrage opportunities, this implies that wealth at date T_1 must satisfy

$$A_{T_1} \geq \mathbb{E}_{T_1}\left[\frac{M_{T_2}}{M_{T_1}}G_{T_2}\right].$$

This equation says that wealth at date T_1 must be at least as large as the present value of the minimum to reach on the next date. Hence, wealth must be at least as large as the minimum at date T_1 and the present value of the next date minimum. Mathematically, this inequality is written as

$$A_{T_1} \geq \max\left[G_{T_1}, \mathbb{E}_{T_1}\left[\frac{M_{T_2}}{M_{T_1}}G_{T_2}\right]\right].$$

Using again the absence of arbitrage opportunities, we obtain that the initial wealth must be such that

$$A_0 \geq \mathbb{E}\left[M_{T_1}\max\left[G_{T_1}, \mathbb{E}_{T_1}\left[\frac{M_{T_2}}{M_{T_1}}G_{T_2}\right]\right]\right].$$

The right-hand side of this equation is the price of an exchange option that pays the maximum of the first goal value and the present value of the second goal value at date T_1. Similarly, for a larger number of dates, the idea is that at each goal date, wealth must be greater than or equal to the minimum at this date, but also than the present value of the minimum to attain on the next date. When carried from the last date backwards, this principle leads to an expression of the minimum capital to invest as the price of a sequence of nested exchange options. The following proposition gives a necessary and sufficient affordability criterion for a wealth-based goal with multiple horizons. In order to ensure that all exchange option payoffs are attainable, we maintain the assumption of complete markets, an assumption that implies the uniqueness of the state-price deflator.[5]

Proposition 3 (Affordability Criterion of a Wealth-Based Goal with Multiple Horizons in Complete Markets). *Assume that markets are complete and consider a wealth-based goal represented by the exogenous and non-negative minimum wealth levels* $(G_{T_1}, \ldots, G_{T_p})$ *on dates* $T_1 < \cdots < T_p$. *Let* $T_0 = 0$ *and* $G_{T_0} = 0$, *and define the recursive sequence of payoffs* $(K_{T_j})_{j=0,\ldots,p}$ *and their prices*

$$K_{T_p} = G_{T_p};$$

$$\tilde{K}_{T_{p-j}, T_{p-j+1}} = \mathbb{E}_{T_{p-j}} \left[\frac{M_{T_{p-j+1}}}{M_{T_{p-j}}} K_{T_{p-j+1}} \right] \quad \text{for } j = 1, \ldots, p;$$

$$K_{T_{p-j}} = \max \left[G_{T_{p-j}}, \tilde{K}_{T_{p-j}, T_{p-j+1}} \right], \quad \text{for } j = 1, \ldots, p.$$

Then, the wealth-based goal is affordable if, and only if, the initial wealth satisfies $A_0 \geq K_0$. *If this condition is satisfied, then the goal is secured by investing* A_0 *in a roll-over of exchange options expiring on dates* $T_1, \ldots, T_p$ *with payoffs* $K_{T_1}, \ldots, K_{T_p}$.

Proof. See Appendix A.1.1. □

A first important result contained in Proposition 3 is the formula for the minimum capital to invest in order to secure the goal, which is

---

[5]We recall that the maximum of two replicable payoffs is not necessarily a replicable payoff (see the case of a European call option written on an underlying asset with stochastic volatility, when volatility risk is not spanned by the underlying itself).

equal to K_0. More generally, Appendix A.1.1 shows that if a strategy secures the goal, then the wealth at each date T_j satisfies $A_{T_j} \geq K_{T_j}$ for $j = 1, \ldots, p$. Taking the present value of both sides of the inequality, we obtain

$$A_t \geq \tilde{K}_{T_j, T_{j+1}}, \quad \text{for } T_j < t \leq T_{j+1} \text{ and } j = 0, \ldots, p - 1,$$

hence the minimum capital to invest at date t is $\tilde{K}_{j+1, T_j}$. This property justifies the following definition of the "present value" for a goal with multiple horizons.

Definition 3 (Present Value of Wealth-Based Goal with Multiple Horizons). Consider an exogenous wealth-based goal with multiple horizons and the option payoffs defined in Proposition 3. The present value of the goal is defined as

$$\tilde{G}_t = E_t \left[\frac{M_{T_{j+1}}}{M_t} K_{T_{j+1}} \right], \quad \text{for } T_j < t \leq T_{j+1} \text{ and } j = 0, \ldots, p - 1,$$

$$\tilde{G}_0 = K_0.$$

The present value of the goal at date t is thus defined as the minimum capital to invest on this date to secure the goal.[6] It should be noted that unlike for a goal with a single horizon, this present value is not always continuous. It is left-continuous, but jumps may occur on the goal horizons. In what follows, we denote the right limit of the present value at date T_j with $\tilde{G}_{T_j+}$. Moreover, the product $M_t \tilde{G}_t$ does not follow a martingale.

A second contribution from Proposition 3 is to show that one can construct a GHP by rolling over the exchange options paying $\tilde{G}_{T_j}$ at date T_j, starting from the initial capital $\tilde{G}_0$. The value of the GHP is thus

$$\text{GHP}_t = \left[\prod_{k=1}^{j} \frac{\tilde{G}_{T_k}}{\tilde{G}_{T_k+}} \right] \times \tilde{G}_t \quad \text{for } T_j < t \leq T_{j+1} \text{ and } j = 0, \ldots, p - 1,$$

$$\text{GHP}_0 = \tilde{G}_0 \tag{2.6}$$

---

[6]We assume here the absence of non-portfolio income, an ingredient which will be discussed in Section 2.2.4.

(It is continuous on the dates $T_1, \ldots, T_p$.) Because $\tilde{G}_{T_k} = K_{T_k}$ is the maximum of G_{T_k} and $\tilde{G}_{T_k+}$, the product within the brackets is greater than or equal to 1. Hence,

$$\text{GHP}_{T_j} \geq \tilde{G}_{T_j},$$

that is, the value of the GHP is greater than or equal to the present value of the goal. In particular, at horizon T_j, the value of the GHP satisfies

$$\text{GHP}_{T_j} \geq \tilde{G}_{T_j} = \max[G_{T_j}, \tilde{G}_{T_j+}].$$

This property means that the GHP actually protects a wealth level that is higher than the minimum G_{T_j}. This apparent "over-protection" is due to the presence of other goals after date T_j. This property marks a difference with respect to the case of the single horizon. With a single horizon, the value of the GHP coincides with the present value of the goal, while the two concepts are distinct in the presence of multiple horizons.

In order to compute the GHP in practice, it is of interest to have analytical expressions for the option prices. For two horizons, this is a tractable task, at least under convenient parameter assumptions. Indeed, K_{T_1} is the maximum of G_{T_1} and the price on date T_1 of the payoff G_{T_2}, so that K_0 is the price of an option which pays the maximum of two payoffs. If G_{T_1} and G_{T_2} are log-normally distributed, and the interest rate and risk premia are constant, then the exchange option can be priced analytically. When the number of horizon dates exceeds two, the pricing exercise becomes more complex. To see this, it suffices to note that with three horizons, K_{T_1} involves the price of an option whose payoff is the maximum of G_{T_2} and the price of another option. Overall, for more than two horizons, it proves impossible in general to derive an analytical expression for the minimum initial capital requirement, K_0, and for the associated replicating portfolio strategy. Furthermore, a Monte-Carlo pricing is difficult to implement because the conditional expectation within the definition of $K_{T_{p-j}}$ must itself be estimated by Monte-Carlo.

These technical issues can be avoided in some cases, where the maximum operators can be eliminated from the expressions of the payoffs K_{T_j}. This is possible for instance when the goal values satisfy a certain "monotony condition" in the sense that at each goal date, the present value of the next date minimum is less than or equal to the minimum at the current date. The following corollary provides a formal statement of this condition.

Corollary 1 (Affordability Criterion of a Wealth-Based Goal with Multiple Horizons in Complete Markets). *Let the assumptions of Proposition 3 be satisfied, and assume in addition that the goal values satisfy the following monotony condition:*

$$\mathbb{E}_{T_j} \left[\frac{M_{T_{j+1}}}{M_{T_j}} G_{T_{j+1}} \right] \leq G_{T_j}, \quad for \ j = 1, \ldots, p-1. \tag{2.7}$$

Then, the payoffs K_{T_j} defined in Proposition 3 are given by

$$K_{T_j} = G_{T_j}, \quad for \ j = 1, \ldots, p,$$

and the present value of the goal is

$$\tilde{G}_t = \mathbb{E}_t \left[\frac{M_{T_{j+1}}}{M_t} G_{T_{j+1}} \right], \quad for \ T_j < t \leq T_{j+1} \ and \ j = 0, \ldots, p-1,$$

$$\tilde{G}_0 = \mathbb{E}[M_{T_1} G_{T_1}].$$

Proof.   See Appendix A.1.2.   □

Under the assumptions of the corollary, the computation of the exchange option payoffs is greatly facilitated, because at each goal date, the minimum wealth to attain reduces to the explicitly imposed level, irrespective of the minimum levels to attain on the next dates. The minimum capital to invest in order to secure the goal is simply the present value of the first goal value, and a strategy that secures the goal is to roll-over zero-coupon bonds which pay the goal values at the goal dates.

A first example of a situation where condition (2.7) is satisfied is when each goal value is the present value of the next one (i.e. the inequality in Equation (2.7) is an equality). It is then equivalent to securing the goal values on the intermediate horizons and to securing only the last goal value. This problem has been studied by Deguest *et al.* (2014).

A second example of a situation where condition (2.7) holds is when all goal values are equal to each other ($G_{T_j} = G_0$, where G_0 is some constant), and for all index j equal to $1, \ldots, p-1$, the nominal zero-coupon rate of maturity $h_j = T_{j+1} - T_j$ prevailing at date T_j is non-negative. Indeed, we have

$$\mathbb{E}_{T_j}\left[\frac{M_{T_{j+1}}}{M_{T_j}}G_{T_{j+1}}\right] = G_0 \times \mathbb{E}_{T_j}\left[\frac{M_{T_{j+1}}}{M_{T_j}}\right],$$

and the conditional expectation in the right-hand side is equal to $\exp[-x^n_{T_j,h_j}]$, where $x^n_{T_j,h_j}$ is the nominal zero-coupon rate of maturity h_j. If this rate is non-negative, then condition (2.7) is satisfied.

A third situation where the assumptions of the corollary are satisfied is when all goal values are equal to a constant G_0 times realised inflation, and the *real* zero-coupon rate of maturity h_j on date T_j is non-negative. To see this, let Φ_t denote the price index on date t, so that Φ_{T_j}/Φ_0 is the realised inflation between dates 0 and T_j. We have

$$\mathbb{E}_{T_j}\left[\frac{M_{T_{j+1}}}{M_{T_j}}G_{T_{j+1}}\right] = G_0 \times \frac{\Phi_{T_j}}{\Phi_0} \times \mathbb{E}_{T_j}\left[\frac{M_{T_{j+1}}\Phi_{T_{j+1}}}{M_{T_j}\Phi_{T_j}}\right]$$

$$= G_0 \times \frac{\Phi_{T_j}}{\Phi_0} \times \exp\left[-x^r_{T_j,h_j}\right],$$

where $x^r_{T_j,h_j}$ is the real rate. Again, (2.7) is clearly verified if this rate is non-negative. This sequence of goal values will appear in the first example of application of our framework (see Section 4.1 of Chapter 4).

2.2.2. *Affordability of consumption-based goals*

A consumption-based goal is expressed as a consumption expense or a series of consumption expenses to be financed. As in Section 2.1.2, we represent a consumption-based goal by the discrete-time process $(c_{T_1}, \ldots, c_{T_p})$. Dybvig and Huang (1988) define a "financed consumption plan" as a plan that leaves the final wealth non-negative, the rationale being that the agent should not be allowed to end up at terminal date with a net positive amount of debt. In the following definition, we adopt an apparently stronger criterion, which is that wealth should remain non-negative at all dates. In fact, as shown in Appendix A.1.3, this criterion is equivalent to the definition of Dybvig and Huang (1988).

Definition 4 (Affordability of a Consumption-Based Goal).
A consumption-based goal represented by the consumption date $T_1, \ldots, T_p$ and the non-negative consumption stream $(c_{T_1}, \ldots, c_{T_p})$ is said to be affordable if there exists a portfolio strategy $\underline{w}$ such that, starting from the investor's initial capital, the wealth satisfies the budget constraint (2.4) and the inequality $A_t \geq 0$ for all date t in $[0, T]$ with probability 1. Such a strategy is said to secure the goal.

As shown in Appendix A.1.3, the condition "$A_t \geq 0$ for all t in $[0, T]$ with probability 1" in Definition 4 can be replaced by "$A_T \geq 0$ with probability 1".

As for a wealth-based goal, two main questions arise:

Q1. Are the payoffs $c_{T_1}, \ldots, c_{T_p}$ replicable with the available risky assets?

Q2. If the answer to Q1 is positive, is the investor's initial wealth sufficient to finance the consumption stream?

In what follows, we will assume that the answer to Q1 is positive, which amounts to assuming that there exists a set of p securities (e.g. inflation-linked pure discount bonds) maturing on the consumption dates with payoffs equal to the consumption payments. The price of the jth replicating security is

$$\mathbb{E}_t \left[\frac{M_{T_j}}{M_t} c_{T_j} \right].$$

By taking a buy-and-hold position in these replicating securities, one can synthesise a portfolio with payoffs that match all consumption expenses. This portfolio is the GHP, and its price is

$$\tilde{G}_t = \mathbb{E}_t \left[\sum_{\substack{j=1 \\ T_j > t}}^{p} \frac{M_{T_j}}{M_t} c_{T_j} \right].$$

By definition, $\tilde{G}_t$ is the price excluding the payment of date t and it is therefore right-continuous, so the initial price of the consumption stream is $\tilde{G}_0$. It is shown in Appendix A.1.3 that wealth satisfies

$$A_t = \mathbb{E}_t \left[\frac{M_T}{M_t} A_T \right] + \tilde{G}_t, \quad \text{for all } t \text{ in } [0, T].$$

Hence, if the goal is affordable, that is, if A_T is non-negative, we have $A_t \geq \tilde{G}_t$ for all t, and in particular, the initial wealth satisfies $A_0 \geq \tilde{G}_0$.

The reciprocal implication sounds even more obvious: if the initial wealth satisfies $A_0 \geq \tilde{G}_0$, then one can purchase at least one share of the GHP, so that the dividends of the portfolio will cover the consumption outflows. Although this result is intuitive, we write a mathematical proof in Appendix A.1.4 in order to have an explicit expression for the wealth generated by this strategy. This expression is shown to involve the "total return index" for the GHP, which is the value of the GHP with dividends re-invested in it. If $\hat{G}_t$ denotes the total return index, we have

$$\hat{G}_t = \tilde{G}_t \prod_{\substack{j=1 \\ T_j \leq t}}^{p} \left(1 + \frac{c_{T_j}}{\tilde{G}_{T_j}} \right),$$

and it is shown in the appendix that the wealth achieved with the aforementioned strategy is

$$A_t = \tilde{G}_t + \left(\frac{A_0}{\tilde{G}_0} - 1 \right) \hat{G}_t.$$

In particular, the terminal wealth is 0, so the goal is attained. The following proposition summarises this discussion in the form of an affordability criterion.

Proposition 4 (Affordability Criterion of a Replicable Consumption-Based Goal). *Consider a consumption-based goal represented by the non-negative payment stream $(c_{T_1}, \ldots, c_{T_p})$, and assume that each payment is replicable. The goal is affordable if, and only if, the initial wealth and the present value of the consumption stream satisfy $A_0 \geq \tilde{G}_0$. If this condition is satisfied, then the goal is secured by the strategy that invests A_0 in the portfolio with dividends matching the consumption needs.*

2.2.3.　*Joint affordability of multiple goals*

The previous section has introduced affordability criteria for wealth-based and consumption-based goals taken in isolation. But in real-world situations, investors have in general multiple goals, like in the case studies presented in Chapter 4, and we therefore extend our affordability criteria to the case of multiple goals.

2.2.3.1.　*Multiple wealth-based goals*

We consider the most general case, where the goals have multiple horizons (a goal with a single horizon fits into this category). The definition of the joint affordability of multiple goals involves no subtlety, although it is more demanding in terms of notations than the similar definitions for individual goals.

Definition 5 (Joint Affordability of Multiple Wealth-Based Goals). Assume that the investor has L wealth-based goals, that the lth goal is characterised by the set of horizons $\mathcal{T}_l = (T_1^l, \ldots, T_{p_l}^l)$ and the non-negative minimum wealth levels $(G_{T_1^l}^l, \ldots, G_{T_{p_l}^l}^l)$. The L goals are said to be jointly affordable if there exists a portfolio strategy $\underline{w}$ such that, starting from the investor's initial capital, the wealth satisfies the budget constraint (2.2) and the inequalities

$$A_{T_j} \geq G_{T_j^l}^l, \quad \text{for all } j = 1, \ldots, p_l, \text{ for all } l = 1, \ldots, L.$$

Such a strategy is said to secure the goals.

It is in fact straightforward to summarise the multiple goals in a single goal. Formally, let $\mathcal{T}$ denote the union of the sets of horizons, and for each t in $\mathcal{T}$ and each $l = 1, \ldots, L$, let G_t^l be zero if t is not an element of $\mathcal{T}_l$. Then, define the payoffs

$$G_t = \max(G_t^1, \ldots, G_t^L), \quad \text{for } t \in \mathcal{T}.$$

The joint affordability of the L goals is equivalent to the affordability of the single goal characterised by the set of horizons $\mathcal{T}$ and the minimum wealth levels $(G_t)_{t \in \mathcal{T}}$. In other words, the multiple goal case is not different from the case of a single wealth-based goal with multiple horizons.

If all goals are exogenous, this remark in particular enables the minimum capital required to afford the L goals as in Proposition 3 to be computed. It would be of interest to have an expression for the present value of the single goal as a function of those of the L goals. This, however, is not a straightforward task, given that the value of the single goal is the maximum of the L goal values. In particular, computing its present value requires the pricing of exchange options between the various goals, which will involve in the best case a pricing equation with unobservable parameters such as volatilities as inputs. An easier objective is to provide a lower bound for the present value. The following proposition shows that — very intuitively — initial wealth must be at least as large as the largest of the dollar amounts required to secure one goal at a time.

Proposition 5 (Necessary Affordability Condition of Multiple Wealth-Based Goals). *Consider L exogenous wealth-based goals, and let $\tilde{G}_0^l$ be the present value of the lth goal in the sense of Definition 3 and $\tilde{G}_0$ be the present value of the multiple goals. Then,*

$$\tilde{G}_0 \geq \max\left(\tilde{G}_0^1, \ldots, \tilde{G}_0^L\right).$$

Proof. See Appendix A.1.5. □

This proposition confirms the obvious property that multiple goals cannot be jointly secured if at least one of them is not affordable. The converse implication is not true. It is not because all goals are affordable separately (which implies that $A_0 \geq \max(\tilde{G}_0^1, \ldots, \tilde{G}_0^L)$) that they are jointly affordable (which requires the stronger condition $A_0 \geq \tilde{G}_0$).

2.2.3.2. *Multiple consumption-based goals*

The notations here are the same as in Section 2.2.3.1. There are L goals, each of them being described by its own set of consumption dates, $\mathcal{T}_l$, and its own set of consumption payments. The definition of joint affordability is again a straightforward extension of the definition of affordability for a single goal.

Definition 6 (Joint Affordability of Multiple Consumption-Based Goals). Assume that the investor has L consumption-based goals, the lth goal is characterised by the set of consumption dates $\mathcal{T}_l = (T_1^l, \ldots, T_{p_l}^l)$ and the consumption expenses $(c_{T_1}^l, \ldots, c_{T_{p_l}}^l)$.

The L goals are said to be jointly affordable if there exists a portfolio strategy $\underline{w}$ such that, starting from the investor's initial capital, the wealth satisfies the budget constraint (2.4) and the inequality $A_T \geq 0$ with probability 1. Such a strategy is said to secure the goals.

As for wealth-based goals, one can represent the L goals as a single goal, by merging the sets of consumption dates in a single set $\mathcal{T}$, and by letting c_t^l be zero if t is not an element of $\mathcal{T}_l$ for each $l = 1, \ldots, L$. Then, the total consumption of date t is

$$c_t = \sum_{l=1}^{L} c_t^l, \quad \text{for all } t \in \mathcal{T}.$$

Thus, the L goals have been replaced by a single goal, which is the sum of the individual goals. It is then equivalent to be able to afford the L goals or the single aggregate goal. Unlike in the case of multiple wealth-based goals, where one has to price an exchange option to find the minimum capital required, the minimum dollar amount to invest to secure the L consumption-based goals is simply the sum of the dollar amounts required for individual goals. A formal statement is given in the following proposition.

Proposition 6 (Affordability Criterion of Multiple Consumption-Based Goals). *Consider L consumption-based goals, and let $\tilde{G}_0^l$ be the present value of the lth stream. Then, the goals are jointly affordable if, and only if, the initial wealth satisfies*

$$A_0 \geq \sum_{l=1}^{L} \tilde{G}_0^l.$$

Proof. The verification is immediate from the definition of the aggregate goal, since the present value of the sum of the L consumption payments is the sum of the L present values. $\square$

2.2.3.3. *Wealth-based and consumption-based goals*

From what precedes, multiple wealth-based goals can be re-expressed as a single wealth-based goal, and a similar operation can be performed for consumption-based goals. The only difference relates to the aggregation operation: while consumption-based goals simply add up, achieving several wealth-based goals is equivalent to achieving the highest goal. Hence, the most general situation, where the investor has various goals of both types, can be described in terms of two goals only: a wealth-based goal and a consumption-based goal.

The definition of the joint affordability in this context raises no particular problem, except that one has to specify how to assess the achievement of the wealth-based goal on a particular date if a consumption payment takes place on this very date. Indeed, it may happen that the wealth before consumption is larger than the minimum wealth level, while the consumption expense causes portfolio value to fall below the minimum. In this book, we adopt the convention that it is pre-consumption wealth that is compared to the minimum.

Mathematically, the definition reads as follows.

Definition 7 (Joint Affordability of a Wealth-Based and a Consumption-Based Goal). Consider a wealth-based goal represented by the horizons $\mathcal{T}^W$ and the minimum wealth levels $(G_t)_{t \in \mathcal{T}^W}$, and a consumption-based goal characterised by the consumption dates $\mathcal{T}^C$ and the expenses $(c_t)_{t \in \mathcal{T}^C}$. The two goals are said to be jointly affordable if there exists a portfolio strategy $\underline{w}$ such that, starting from the investor's initial capital, the wealth satisfies the budget constraint (2.4) and the inequality

$$A_{t-} \geq G_t, \quad \text{for all } t \in \mathcal{T}^W,$$

$$A_T \geq 0.$$

Such a strategy is said to secure the goals.

This definition does not give an operational affordability criterion because it requires finding a strategy that secures the goal. Thus, it would be useful to have an expression for the minimum capital at date 0 to invest in order to secure both goals. This question is addressed in the following proposition, which involves a sequence of compound option payoffs and prices, as with Proposition 3.

Proposition 7 (Joint Affordability Criterion for a Wealth-Based and a Consumption-Based Goal). *Consider a wealth-based goal represented by the minimum wealth levels $G_{T_1}, \ldots, G_{T_p}$, and a consumption-based goal characterised by expenses $c_{T_1}, \ldots, c_{T_p}$.*

Define the recursive sequence of payoffs

$$K_{T_p} = G_{T_p};$$

$$K_{T_j} = \max(G_{T_j}, \tilde{K}_{T_j, T_{j+1}} + \tilde{c}_{T_j, T_{j+1}}), \quad \text{for } j = 0, \dots, p-1;$$

$$\tilde{K}_{T_j, T_{j+1}} = \mathbb{E}_{T_j} \left[\frac{M_{T_{j+1}}}{M_{T_j}} K_{T_{j+1}} \right];$$

$$\tilde{c}_{T_j, T_{j+1}} = \mathbb{E}_{T_j} \left[\frac{M_{T_{j+1}}}{M_{T_j}} c_{T_{j+1}} \right].$$

Then, the two goals are jointly affordable if, and only if, the initial wealth satisfies $A_0 \geq K_0$.

Proof. The proof of this result is similar to that of Proposition 3. □

This result has the merit of being general, but as with Proposition 3, it is hard to apply in practice due to the complex structure of the payoffs. Nevertheless, it is not difficult to find a sufficient condition of affordability: if A_0 is larger than the sum of the present values of the two goals, then the goals are jointly affordable.

2.2.4. *Non-portfolio income and affordability*

At this point, the various definitions of affordability are based on budget constraints which either assume a self-financing portfolio or a portfolio with consumption outflows. One significant additional source of complexity is related to the presence of income cash flows, since the definition of affordability needs to be extended to account for the fact that future consumption goals can be financed and secured either from current wealth or from future savings. It turns out that the general definition that was given before (Definition 4) still applies in the presence of income, subject to a modification to the budget constraint, which now incorporates the non-portfolio income stream.

For brevity, and with no real loss of generality, we will focus the discussion on consumption-based goals, which are arguably of the most critical practical relevance, for example, in the context of financing a retirement goal. Wealth-based goals could be handled in a similar way. In this context, the general definition of affordability can be written as follows.

Definition 8 (Affordability of a Consumption-Based Goal in the Presence of Income). A consumption-based goal is said to be affordable if there exists a portfolio strategy $\underline{w}$ such that, starting from the investor's initial capital, the wealth satisfies the budget constraint (2.5) and the inequality $A_t \geq 0$ for all t in $[0, T]$ with probability 1.

This definition, however, does not provide an empirically testable criterion of affordability. The main focus of the remainder of this section is to provide necessary and sufficient conditions of affordability which can be applied in the presence of income streams. The second focus of this section is to discuss the corresponding GHP strategies, with an explicit analysis of the competition between current wealth and future income in the composition of the GHP.

Before introducing the general results, and in an attempt to ease the intuition, we first look at simple examples with a limited number of dates.

2.2.4.1. *One income cash flow and one consumption cash flow*

Let us first consider a highly stylised example with a consumption goal of $G_2 = \$100$ in year 2, an income $y_1 = \$40$ in year 1, and a initial liquid wealth $A_0 = \$100$. In this situation, the key question is not to assess whether the goal is affordable or not; it is clearly affordable since current wealth alone, without future income, is already sufficient to secure the consumption goal. The outstanding question in this situation is rather to determine what the "best" way to secure the goal is. In this context, it is useful to introduce the intuitive definition of the *cheapest GHP* as the portfolio strategy that allows an investor to secure a given consumption goal with the lowest amount of initial wealth. Such a strategy should be preferred to other strategies that would also lead to 100% probability of achieving the goal but would require a higher amount of initial wealth, since it is the one that leaves the highest dollar amount available for investing in performance-seeking assets (see Chapter 3 for more details on the optimal use of the remaining wealth, if any, that is, left after all essential goals have been secured).

In the example, one safe strategy (call it strategy LIQ, or liquid wealth only) would consist in purchasing a pure discount bond which pays $100 on date 2, at a price that is strictly less than $100 provided that nominal rates are non-negative. This strategy secures the goal, but it does not use income at all, and as a result has a high opportunity cost in terms of usage of current wealth, especially if interest rates are low and the discount bond trades close to par.

Another goal-hedging strategy would be based on the recognition that the $40 received at date 1 can be used to finance a fraction of the goal. Since the 1-year rate prevailing at date 1 is not known at date 0, we do not know what exactly this fraction will be, but we know that income will generate at least $40 at date 2 (still to the extent that nominal rates are non-negative). In this context, there remain $60 to finance with current wealth, which can be done by purchasing a pure discount bond that pays $60 at date 2. We refer to this strategy as INC-ZER because it assumes a zero re-investment rate for future income. According to the aforementioned definition, it is less expensive than strategy LIQ since it requires the use of a lower amount of initial wealth (the present value of $60, as opposed to the present value of $100).

It turns out that an even cheaper portfolio strategy exists. To see this, consider a strategy (call it strategy INC-CMP — this name will be justified in Section 2.2.4.2) that invests in a bond option that will pay $(100 \times b_{1,2} - 40)^{+}$ at date 1, where $b_{1,2}$ is the price at date 1 of a pure discount bond with $1 face value and maturing at date 2. In this particular example, for most reasonable values, we have that $100 \times b_{1,2} > 40$ almost surely: the price at date 1 of a 1-year pure discount bond paying $100 will be more than $40. Hence, the option will pay off $100 \times b_{1,2} - 40$, an amount to which will be added $40 worth of yearly income, so that the net cash flow is $100 \times b_{1,2}$, which is exactly the minimum amount of money needed to generate, after being invested in the 1-year pure discount bond at date 1, $100 at date 2. The required amount of initial wealth for this strategy, that is, the price of the bond option paying $(100 \times b_{1,2} - 40)^{+}$, is strictly lower than the present value of $60, so strategy INC-CMP is cheaper than strategy INC-ZER. In Section 2.2.4.2, we will provide a general result showing that this strategy (suitably extended to a context with multiple income and consumption dates as a roll-over of compounded options) is actually the cheapest replicating strategy, in the sense that there is no strategy that can replicate the goals starting with a lower amount of initial wealth.

In fact, the last statement only holds in the absence of forward contracts. If we assume that forward contracts exist, a cheaper replicating strategy is available. This strategy (call it INC-FWD) can be described as follows. Enter at date 0 (at no upfront cost) in a forward contract that will set the 1-year rate in 1 year from now equal to the current 1-year forward rate denoted by $f_{1,1} = \frac{b_{0,1}}{b_{0,2}} - 1$, and invest the present value of (the positive part) of $100 - 40 \times (1 + f_{1,1})$ in the pure discount bond with maturity 2 years. It is obvious that strategy INC-FWD is cheaper than strategy INC-ZER, but it also turns out to be cheaper than strategy INC-CMP. Indeed, the cost of protection at date 0 with strategy INC-CMP is

$$\mathbb{E}[M_2 \times [100 - 40 \times (1 + f_{1,1})]^+] = [100 \times b_{0,2} - 40 \times b_{0,1}]^+,$$

where M_2 denotes the state-price deflator at date 2.

With strategy INC-CMP, the cost is the price of the call option which pays $(100 \times b_{1,2} - 40)^+$ on date 1, and this price is larger than the intrinsic value of the call, which is precisely the right-hand side of the previous equality.

In brief, this simple example has allowed us to obtain a first understanding of various strategies that can be used to secure a goal in the presence of income, with a key focus on the desire to use the lowest amount of initial wealth to reach the objective, thanks to the best possible use of future income. In Section 2.2.4.2, we extend the analysis to a set-up with two income cash flows and one consumption cash flow.

2.2.4.2. *Two income cash flows and one consumption cash flow*

We now consider an example with a consumption goal $G_3 = \$100$ in year 3, with $A_0 = \$100$ and income streams $y_1 = \$40$, $y_2 = \$10$ in years 1 and 2, respectively. The goal is again clearly affordable since it can be secured with current wealth only. To do this, the investor may simply invest the present value of $100 in a pure discount bond with maturity 3, which is a replicating strategy (strategy LIQ) that does not rely at all on future income, and as such is very expensive in terms of use of current wealth. Another strategy (strategy INC-ZER) consists at date 0 in investing the present value of $100 - (40 + 10) =$ $50 in a 3-year pure discount bond, at date 1 investing the present value of $100 - 10 - 50 = \$40$ in a 2-year pure discount bond, and at date 2 investing the present value of $100 - 40 - 50 = \$10$ in a 1-year pure discount bond. This strategy will clearly replicate the goal, and is less expensive than strategy LIQ since the present value of $50 is lower than the present value of $100.

A cheaper strategy involves a compound option, and is thus referred to as INC-CMP. At date 0, purchase the compound option which pays $(P_1 - 40)^+$ at date 1, where P_1 is the price at date 1 of the bond option which pays $(100 \times b_{2,3} - 10)^+$ at date 2. At date 1, use the compound option payoff, which will be equal to $(P_1 - 40)$ if the option expires in the money (this will be the case here for reasonable parameter values), to which will be added year 1 income to generate $P_1 - 40 + 40 = P_1$ to purchase the 1-year bond option. At date 2, use the bond option payoff, which will be equal to the quantity $(100 \times b_{2,3} - 10)$, almost surely positive for reasonable parameter values, to which will be added year 2 income to generate $100 \times b_{2,3} - 10 + 10 = 100 \times b_{2,3}$ which is exactly the lowest amount of money to use at date 2 to invest in a 1-year pure discount bond so as to secure the $100 consumption goal at date 3. As in the previous example, it can be shown that this is the cheapest replicating strategy in the absence of forward contracts.

The replicating strategy with forward contracts looks as follows: at date 0 enter (at no upfront cost) into forward contracts that will set the 2-year rate in 1 year from now and the 1-year rate in 2 years from now equal to the current corresponding forward rates and invest from current wealth the present value of $100 - 40 \times (1 + f_{1,1})(1 + f_{2,1}) - 10 \times (1 + f_{2,1})$ in a pure discount bond with maturity date 3 years. Here, we have the forward rates defined, respectively, by $f_{1,1} = \frac{b_{0,1}}{b_{0,2}} - 1$, $f_{2,1} = \frac{b_{0,2}}{b_{0,3}} - 1$. This strategy is obviously less expensive than strategy INC-ZER since $100 - 40 \times (1 + f_{1,1})(1 + f_{2,1}) - 10 \times (1 + f_{2,1}) < 50$, and it can be shown that it is also less expensive than strategy INC-CMP in situations when the forward contracts exist (see Section 2.2.4.6 for a justification).

2.2.4.3. *An example with five cash flows*

In the previous two examples, the income dates precede the consumption date. This corresponds to the retirement goal, which we will study in more detail in what follows (see Section 2.2.4.6). Let us now consider a schedule with alternating periods of income and consumption. There are five cash flow dates as follows:

- At date 1, income is \$50;
- At date 2, consumption is \$20 and at date 3, it is \$50;
- At date 4, income is \$20;
- At date 5, consumption is \$100.

A first obvious strategy (strategy LIQ) that secures the goal is to purchase a bond that will pay at each date the excess, if any, of consumption over income. This bond will have irregularly spaced cash flows: it will pay \$20 at date 2, \$50 at date 3, \$100 at date 5, and nothing at dates 1 and 4. Its price at date 0 is

$$C_1 = 20 \times b_{0,2} + 50 \times b_{0,3} + 100 \times b_{0,5}.$$

But this policy ignores the possibility of carrying forward the unspent fraction of income from one date to the other. For instance, a cash flow of \$20 at date 2 is not necessary if one has secured the \$50 received at date 1.

This remark leads to the definition of the following strategy, which assumes that excess income is invested at a zero rate. It is referred to as INC-ZER. Suppose that the \$50 of date 1 are invested in a 1-year zero-coupon at date 1, so that they become \$50 at date 2 in the worst case (the case where the -year rate at date 1 was zero). The \$50 will finance the \$20 of consumption, and there will be a surplus of \$30 left. Investing these \$30 in a new 1-year zero-coupon bond leads to an income of \$30 (at least) at date 3. These \$30 do not fully cover the consumption expenditure, which is \$50. To make up for the gap, the investor has to purchase at date 0 a 3-year zero-coupon that will pay \$20 at date 3. Similarly, if the investor secures the \$20 received at date 4 by investing them at the 1-year rate, he will be left with a deficit of \$80 at date 5: to compensate for this deficit, he needs to purchase at date 0 a zero-coupon that will pay \$80 at date 5. Thus, the cost of the protection as seen from date 0 is

$$C_2 = 20 \times b_{0,3} + 80 \times b_{0,5}.$$

We clearly have $C_1 > C_2$, so the strategy INC-ZER is less expensive than the one that uses liquid wealth only.

2.2.4.4.   The general case: Affordability conditions and the cheapest goal-hedging portfolio

The three examples discussed above allow us to emphasise that future income should be preferred to current wealth when it comes to securing goals. Indeed, doing so leaves the highest amount of current wealth available for investment in performance-seeking assets, which in turn is critically needed to achieve with a positive probability some non-affordable goals. Note that this discussion is based upon the implicit assumption that future income is obtained with certainty; if there is uncertainty about future income, an investor may prefer to use liquid wealth to secure the goals with probability 1.

We now provide a series of general results that extend the intuitions gained in the simple examples to a general setting with multiple income and consumption dates. We start with a necessary and sufficient affordability condition of a consumption-based goal in the presence of income, which corresponds to a generalised version of the strategy denoted by strategy INC-CMP in the analysis of the simple examples.

Proposition 8 (Affordability Criterion of a Consumption-Based Goal in the Presence of Income). *Assume that markets are complete, let wealth evolve according to the budget constraint (2.5), and consider a consumption-based goal with the same payment dates as the income dates. Let $T_0 = 0$ and $y_{T_0} = 0$, and define the recursive sequence of payoffs $(V_{T_j})_{j=0,\dots,p}$ and their prices:*

$$V_{T_p} = (c_{T_p} - y_{T_p})^+;$$

$$\tilde{V}_{T_{p-j},T_{p-j+1}} = \mathbb{E}_{T_{p-j}}\left[\frac{M_{T_{p-j+1}}}{M_{T_{p-j}}}V_{T_{p-j+1}}\right], \quad \text{for } j = 1,\dots,p;$$

$$V_{T_{p-j}} = (\tilde{V}_{T_{p-j},T_{p-j+1}} + c_{T_{p-j}} - y_{T_{p-j}})^+, \quad \text{for } j = 1,\dots,p.$$

Then, the wealth-based goal is affordable if, and only if, the initial wealth satisfies $A_0 \geq V_0$. If this condition is satisfied, then the goal is secured by investing A_0 in a roll-over of compound exchange options expiring on dates $T_1,\dots,T_p$ with payoffs $V_{T_1},\dots,V_{T_p}$.

Proof.   See Appendix A.1.6.   □

V_0 is the minimum capital that the investor must hold in liquid wealth at date 0 in order to secure the goal, which can also be interpreted as the price of the cheapest GHP in the sense defined in Section 2.2.4.1. Its backward recursive definition may look complex, but the mechanics is simple. The investor wants to ensure that wealth after the last date (T_p) is non-negative. If the income of this date covers consumption, this will be the case, whatever the wealth just before date T_p. If income is less than consumption, then the wealth before income and consumption, i.e. the quantity A_{T_p-}, must be greater than $(c_{T_p} - y_{T_p})$. It must also be non-negative, so A_{T_p-} must be greater than $V_{T_p} = (c_{T_p} - y_{T_p})^+$. Thus, the investor has an implicit wealth-based goal of horizon T_p. By absence of arbitrage opportunities, the wealth at date T_{p-1} must be greater than the present value of V_{T_p}, the minimum wealth to attain one step further. This condition means exactly that $A_{T_{p-1}}$ must be greater than $\tilde{V}_{T_{p-1},T_p}$. The reasoning is then the same as for date T_p: $A_{T_{p-1}-}$ must be greater than $(\tilde{V}_{T_{p-j},T_{p-j+1}} + c_{T_{p-j}} - y_{T_{p-j}})$ if this quantity is positive. Because it must also be non-negative, it must in fact be greater than $V_{T_{p-1}}$. A backward induction, which is formally written in Appendix A.1.6, shows that A_0 must be greater than V_0.

Appendix A.1.6 also shows that V_0 lies between the following two bounds:

$$(\tilde{G}_0 - \tilde{H}_0)^+ \leq V_0 \leq \tilde{G}_0.$$

In this equation, $\tilde{H}_0$ denotes the present value of all future income payments, i.e. the human capital, at date 0.

The upper bound $\tilde{G}_0$ has a very intuitive interpretation: due to the existence of future income, the minimum capital requirement is less than the price of the bond the cash flows of which match the consumption expenses. V_0 will approach this upper bound as the income payments shrink to zero. In general, an investor endowed with income uses this income rather than liquid wealth to finance consumption expenses. Liquid wealth will be used to purchase options that make up for the "funding gap", which at date T_j is formally defined as the payoff V_{T_j}, and can be loosely thought of as the excess of future consumption over future income.

The lower bound is the minimum initial liquid wealth that would be required if no non-negativity condition was imposed to liquid wealth. Indeed, the investor would be allowed to borrow against future income, and negative liquid wealth would be possible, as long as the sum of liquid wealth and the human capital stays non-negative. Definition 8 imposes a tighter condition because it precludes negative wealth, so the initial capital requirement is more severe. V_0 will approach the lower bound as the non-negativity constraint on liquid wealth is progressively relaxed. This corresponds to the case where the investor cannot rely on future income to finance consumption, because income is too low. More specifically, V_0 will be equal to the lower bound if income is systematically lower than consumption. This statement can in fact be extended. As shown in Appendix A.1.6, we have

$$V_0 = \tilde{G}_0 - \tilde{H}_0$$

provided that the present values of the goals and the income payments satisfy

$$\tilde{G}_{T_j-} \geq \tilde{H}_{T_j-}, \quad \text{for all } j = 1, \ldots, p.$$

(We recall that the left limit $\tilde{G}_{T_j-}$ is the present value of future consumption payments, with date T_j included, while $\tilde{G}_{T_j}$ is the present value excluding the payment of date T_j.)

2.2.4.5. *Examples of strategies securing the goal in the general case*

As appears from the analysis of the examples, an investor endowed with non-portfolio income has (at least) three possibilities to protect a consumption-based goal.

1. LIQ: Use liquid wealth only

This strategy consists in purchasing at date 0 a bond that pays the excess, if any, of consumption over income. The minimum capital required is

$$E_0 = \sum_{j=1}^{p} \mathbb{E}[M_{T_j}(-e_{T_j})^+],$$

where $e_{T_j} = y_{T_j} - c_{T_j}$ is the net income.

2. **INC-ZER: Use income assuming a zero re-investment rate for future excess income**
   In this strategy, at date T_1, the investor uses income to finance the largest possible fraction of consumption. The excess income, if any, is invested in a zero-coupon bond that matures on the next consumption date, T_2. If nominal rates are non-negative, then in the worst case, the rate of return on this investment is zero. On date T_2, the capitalised excess income of date T_1 and the new income are used to finance consumption, and the excess, if any, is invested in a zero coupon maturing on date T_3. This operation is repeated at dates $T_1, \ldots, T_{p-1}$. Mathematically, if c_{T_j} is the consumption of date T_j, y_{T_j} is the income and $u_{T_{j-1}}$ is the excess of date T_{j-1} invested at a zero rate (with the convention $u_{T_0} = 0$), the deficit to finance on date T_j is

$$(-e_{T_j} - u_{T_{j-1}})^+,$$

   so, the minimum capital requirement is

$$U_0 = \sum_{j=1}^{p} \mathbb{E}[M_{T_j}(-e_{T_j} - u_{T_{j-1}})^+].$$

   The recursion relationship between the quantities u_{T_j} is $u_{T_j} = (u_{T_{j-1}} + e_{T_j})^+$. Proposition 9 that follows formally shows that this strategy secures the goal.

3. **INC-CMP: Use income and a compound option**
   This is the strategy corresponding to Proposition 8. At date 0, the investor purchases a compound option of price V_0 maturing at date T_1. At this date, he uses the option payoff, V_{T_1}, plus income, to finance consumption. By definition of V_{T_1}, we have

$$V_{T_1} = \max(\tilde{V}_{T_1, T_2}, y_{T_1} - c_{T_1}),$$

   so, the investor can afford the option that pays V_{T_2} at date T_2, and moreover, this option can be purchased by using only the option payoff and the received income. This strategy is repeated at dates $T_2, \ldots, T_{p-1}$. The minimum capital requirement is V_0.

The following proposition formally states that strategy INC-ZER does secure the goal.

Proposition 9 (Sufficient   Affordability   Criterion   for Consumption-Based Goal with Income). *If $A_0 \geq U_0$ and nominal rates are non-negative, the strategy INC-ZER can be implemented and it secures the goal.*

Proof.   See Appendix A.1.7.   □

Because strategy INC-ZER secures the goal, Propositions 8 and 9 imply that U_0 is greater than or equal to V_0.[7] Moreover, it is clear (since the quantity $u_{T_{j-1}}$ defined above is non-negative) that U_0 is less than or equal to E_0. Eventually, the respective costs of protection associated with the three strategies are ordered as follows:

$$V_0 \leq U_0 \leq E_0.$$

This result provides two sufficient affordability conditions for the goal: it suffices to check that $A_0 \geq U_0$ or $A_0 \geq E_0$. These conditions have a practical interest because the price of the compound option, which is the cost of the cheapest protection, is difficult to compute. But it should be acknowledged that U_0 and E_0 have simpler forms, although U_0 also involves option pricing because $u_{T_{j-1}}$ is a nonlinear function of income and consumption.

2.2.4.6.   *Other examples in the case of the retirement goal*

A practically important situation is the case of retirement investment decisions. In this case, the investor is assumed to have a net positive saving in the first part of his life (accumulation phase), while consumption exceeds income in the second phase (decumulation phase). The retirement goal is formally defined as a goal for which there exists a date T_r such that consumption is less than income until T_r and greater afterwards

$$c_{T_j} \leq y_{T_j}, \quad \text{for } j = 1, \ldots, r,$$
$$y_{T_j} \leq c_{T_j}, \quad \text{for } j = r+1, \ldots, p.$$

---

[7]This property can also be checked directly from the definitions of U_0 and V_0, without using the conclusions of Proposition 8.

This goal is affordable if, and only if, there exists a strategy such that the wealth of date T_{r+1} (before consumption and income) satisfies

$$A_{T_{r+1}-} \geq \tilde{G}_{T_{r+1}-} - \tilde{H}_{T_{r+1}-}$$

where $\tilde{G}_{T_{r+1}-}$ and $\tilde{H}_{T_{r+1}-}$ are the respective present values at date T_{r+1} of the consumption expenses and the income payments, with date T_{r+1} included. The affordability condition simplifies to this condition because net consumption is non-negative after retirement. Hence, the retirement goal is equivalent to a wealth-based goal of horizon T_{r+1}: There is a minimum wealth at the retirement date. To finance the purchase of the bond that pays net consumption during the decumulation phase, the investor can implement another strategy in addition to those listed in Section 2.2.4.5.

4. **INC-ZER-RET: Use a modified version of strategy INC-ZER**

In the strategy INC-ZER above, it is assumed that unspent income is carried forward from one income/consumption date to the next one by being invested at a zero rate for one period. In the strategy INC-ZER-RET, on the other hand, the savings of the accumulation phase are assumed to be invested at a zero rate for a period equal to the time to retirement. In order to finance his consumption objectives, the investor must reach a wealth level equal to $[\tilde{G}_{T_{r+1}-} - \tilde{H}_{T_{r+1}-}]$ at least at date T_{r+1}. Thus, the deficit to finance at date T_{r+1} as seen from date 0 is

$$U_{\text{ret},T_{r+1},0} = \left[\tilde{G}_{T_{r+1}-} - \tilde{H}_{T_{r+1}-} - \sum_{k=1}^{r} e_{T_k}\right]^{+},$$

where $e_{T_k} = y_{T_k} - c_{T_k}$ is the net income of date T_k (it is non-negative because the investor consumes less than what he earns). To finance this deficit, the investor must purchase an option that pays off $U_{\text{ret},T_{r+1},0}$, which has a cost denoted as $U_{\text{ret},0,0} = U_{\text{ret},0}$, the present value of the payoff, at date 0. The strategy is repeated at dates $T_2, \ldots, T_r$. At date T_j, an income payment y_{T_j} is cashed in, and is aggregated to liquid wealth. The forecasted deficit is now

$$U_{\text{ret},T_{r+1},j} = \left[\tilde{G}_{T_{r+1}-} - \tilde{H}_{T_{r+1}-} - \sum_{k=j+1}^{r} e_{T_k} \right]^{+}.$$

The investor must purchase an option paying $U_{\text{ret},T_{r+1},j}$, which has a cost denoted as $U_{\text{ret},T_j,j}$.

To formally prove that the strategy INC-ZER-RET is feasible, one has to verify that the wealth of date T_j is sufficient to afford the desired option. This is the content of the following proposition.

Proposition 9 bis (Sufficient Affordability Condition for Retirement Goal) If $A_0 \geq U_{\text{ret},0}$ and nominal rates are non-negative, the previous strategy can be implemented and it secures the goal.

Proof.   See Appendix A.1.8.   □

The details of the proof in Appendix A.1.8 show that we have the following inequality:

$$U_{\text{ret},T_j,j} \leq U_{\text{ret},T_j,j-1} + e_{T_j}, \quad \text{for } j = 1, \ldots, r.$$

This means that the price of the option to purchase at date T_j (in the left-hand side of the inequality) is less than or equal to the sum of the price of the option that was purchased at the previous date, plus the net income. That is, the new option can be purchased simply by liquidating the position in the existing one and using the unspent fraction of income, if any. An interesting consequence is that if the fraction of liquid assets that is not used to protect the goal is invested in some performance portfolio, then there is no need to liquidate a fraction of this portfolio in order to finance the new option. This remark will have implications in one of the case studies that we present in what follows (see Section 4.3 of Chapter 4).

By Propositions 8 and 9 bis, we have

$$V_0 \leq U_{\text{ret},0}$$

It should be noted that $U_{\text{ret},0}$ is in general different from U_0. But it is potentially easier to compute in applications because it is a simple exchange option (between the minimum level of wealth to attain at the retirement age and the sum of net income), while U_0 involves compound options.

As noted in the discussion related to the introductory examples, forward contracts can also be employed to secure the goal, which leads to the definition of the following strategy:

5. INC-FWD: Use income and forward contracts if they are available

If forward contracts are available, another hedging strategy consists in locking up as of date 0 the re-investment rates for the income inflows. In other words, the income cash flow of date T_j will be invested at the rate $f_{T_j, T_{r+1} - T_j}$, which is the forward rate at date T_j for maturity $(T_{r+1} - T_j)$. The deficit that remains to be financed at date T_r is the excess, if any, of the wealth-based goal value over the cumulative value of income payments invested at the fixed forward rates:

$$
W_{T_{r+1}} = \left[\tilde{G}_{T_{r+1}-} - \tilde{H}_{T_{r+1}-} - \sum_{j=1}^{r} e_{T_j} (1 + f_{T_j, T_{r+1} - T_j})^{T_{r+1} - T_j} \right]^+ .
$$

Let W_0 be the price of this option at date 0. The investor can afford the option if, and only if, the available liquid wealth is such that $A_0 \geq W_0$. It is obvious that the strategy to purchase the option at date 0 and invest the income cash flows at the forward rates will secure the goal.

In terms of usage of initial liquid wealth, this strategy is cheaper than INC-ZER-RET: this is obvious, since it assumes that income is invested at forward rates, which are positive, while INC-ZER-RET assumes a zero re-investment rate.

Perhaps more surprisingly, the strategy INC-FWD can also be shown to be cheaper than the strategy INC-CMP under some conditions, in the sense that

$$
W_0 \leq V_0, \tag{2.8}
$$

a property that has already been mentioned in the context of the simple examples with two or three income/consumption payment dates, and can be extended to an arbitrary number of dates. As a consequence, the strategy INC-FWD is, at least when (2.8) holds, cheaper than any of the aforementioned policies that also secure the goal.

A situation where (2.8) is verified is when all cash flows before retirement are deterministic and the inequality

$$\tilde{G}_{T_{r+1}-} - \tilde{H}_{T_{r+1}-} \geq \sum_{j=1}^{r} e_{T_j}(1 + f_{T_j, T_{r+1}-T_j})^{T_{r+1}-T_j}$$

holds almost surely. Then, we have

$$W_0 = b_{0,T_{r+1}} \times \left[-e_{T_{r+1}} - \sum_{j=1}^{r} e_{T_j}(1 + f_{T_j, T_{r+1}-T_j})^{T_{r+1}-T_j} \right]^+$$

$$= [-b_{0,T_{r+1}} \times e_{T_{r+1}} - \sum_{j=1}^{r} e_{T_j} b_{0,T_j}]^+ = [\tilde{G}_0 - \tilde{H}_0]^+$$

which is the lower bound for V_0.

2.3. Taxes and Affordability

Taxes are a typical example of frictions in real-world financial markets. They usually apply to cash flows such as dividend and coupon payments, but also to the capital gains from selling financial securities. In this section, we make a general presentation of the taxation principles that we will apply in the case studies of Chapter 4, and we revisit the definition of affordable goals.

2.3.1. *Taxation principles*

As noted in the introduction to this section, taxes apply to dividend and coupon payments and to the capital gains achieved when selling a share of a security at a higher price than the purchase price. To compute the taxes on cash flows, we simply multiply the cash flow by a tax rate ζ, so the investor effectively receives a net payment equal to $(1 - \zeta)$ times the pre-tax dividend or coupon. A tax rate must be specified in applications.

The taxation of capital gains involves more degrees of freedom:

- Which tax rate should be used? In practice depending on whether the gains are treated as short-term gains (less than a year) versus long-term gains (more than a year), and trading in taxable versus non-taxable versus tax-deferred accounts, the effective tax rate will be different.
- How are taxable gains computed? The principle is to tax gains on sales operations: if an asset share is sold at a higher price than the price at which it was purchased, taxes are applied to the gain. To specify which shares of an asset are sold in the event of a partial liquidation of the position, the standard options are LIFO (last in first out), FIFO (first in first out) and HIFO (highest in first out).
- Is there an option to write off losses within the year or to have a compensation of gains and losses within the portfolio?

In the case studies, we will use for simplicity a unique tax rate for all operations, and we will take 20% as the base case value. Taxes will be computed on an annual basis, which means that the investor will pay taxes once a year, for all the gains that occurred within the fiscal year. Regarding the computation of taxable gains, we will use the LIFO option: to decrease exposure to an asset class, the investor liquidates the shares by starting from the most recently purchased ones. Appendix A.6.5 gives the mathematical expression for the annual tax payment.

Finally, we will allow for the write-off of losses within a given year up to the amount of capital gains earned for this particular year, and for compensation between the constituents within the portfolio: if losses are recorded for an asset, they decrease the amount of taxes to be paid at the end of the year, the final tax payment being floored at zero. But we will exclude any possibility of carrying forward losses to another year.

Because they represent cash withdrawals from the portfolio, taxes can be regarded as a form of consumption. But the analogy with a consumption goal is only imperfect because unlike the consumption goals, taxes are endogenous: the amount to pay depends on the investor's exposure to each asset class, and the taxes on capital gains crucially depend on rebalancing decisions.

2.3.2. *Affordable goals*

We now reconsider the notion of goal affordability in the presence of taxes. The general idea behind the definition is not substantially modified with respect to the situation without taxes: a wealth-based goal is affordable if the wealth is above the minimum levels and a consumption-based goal is affordable if the wealth after consumption is non-negative. The only modification with respect to the definitions given in Section 2.1.2 is the budget constraint, which has to incorporate the tax payments. Formally, we let $\Theta_{t_1}, \ldots, \Theta_{t_m}$ be the tax payments, which occur on dates $t_1, \ldots, t_m$. We recall that the differential element $dJ_{t_j,t}$ is equal to 1 when $t = t_j$, and 0 the rest of the time. In the absence of consumption outflows, the budget constraint reads

$$dA_t = A_t[r_t + \underline{w}_t'\underline{\mu}_t]dt + A_t\underline{w}_t'\underline{\sigma}_t'd\underline{z}_t - \sum_{k=1}^{m} \Theta_{t_k} dJ_{t_k,t}. \tag{2.9}$$

A wealth-based goal is said to be affordable if there exists at least a portfolio strategy $\underline{w}$ such that the minimum wealth levels are attained at all goal horizons, subject to the budget constraint (2.9). It should be noted that this definition is independent from a particular set of taxation rules, and in particular does not depend on the specification of the tax rate or the rules applied in the computation of taxable capital gains.

Similarly, a consumption-based goal is said to be affordable if there exists a strategy $\underline{w}$ such that the wealth generated by the following budget equation:

$$dA_t = A_t[r_t + \underline{w}_t'\underline{\mu}_t]dt + A_t\underline{w}_t'\underline{\sigma}_t'd\underline{z}_t - \sum_{j=1}^{p} c_{T_j} dJ_{jt} - \sum_{k=1}^{m} \Theta_{t_k} dJ_{t_k,t}$$

$$\tag{2.10}$$

remains non-negative. These definitions can be extended to situations with non-portfolio income without difficulty.

2.4. Hierarchical Classification of Goals

The distinction between wealth-based and consumption-based goals is useful from a technical standpoint to characterise the notion of

affordability, but it abstracts away from any concept of priority ranking among goals, which is of relevance in most practical applications
since investors typically have an explicit or sometimes implicit hierarchy ranking among the goals. In this context, Chhabra (2005) proposes another key distinction between *essential goals, important goals*
and *aspirational goals.*

Intuitively, essential goals are goals that the investor wants to
achieve with full probability at all costs. Among essential goals, one
can, for example, identify the long-term objective of protection from
anxiety or poverty, which is often implicit in investors' preferences,
and justifies home ownership or cash holdings. In addition to such
implicit safety goals, explicit minimum (nominal or inflation-linked)
wealth and/or consumption levels are also often included at various
dates until horizon. Lastly, short-term safety goals, such as protection
against drawdown risk, are also included in this category.

Important goals essentially relate to goals that are slightly lower
in terms of priority, but that are still of high relevance to investors.
They may include ensuring a high probability of maintaining one's
standard of living, or high probability of paying for children's education, etc. Since these goals are important but not essential, an
investor may decide not to invest the required amount of wealth to
secure them.

Finally, aspirational goals typically relate to generating a reasonable probability of a substantial wealth increase or even wealth mobility for consumption or bequest objectives. Among such aspirational
goals, one can precisely distinguish between ambitious performance
goals remaining within a given affluence class (e.g. capital growth
objectives over long-term horizons) versus the more dramatic (and
less likely) opportunity of affluence class mobility, that is, moving
upward substantially in the wealth spectrum of society.

In what follows, we introduce a formal definition for each type of
goal in relation to the concept of affordability.

2.4.1. *Essential, important and aspirational goals*

As explained before, a key input expected from the individual
investor in a goals-based wealth management framework is an
ordered list of goals, by which we mean a list of goals and the associated priority ranks. A first task is to classify these goals as affordable

and non-affordable. If there are several goals, it is necessary to use the definitions of joint affordability given in Section 2.2.3. If a set of goals is jointly affordable, then any smaller set of goals is also affordable. This leads to the definition of the maximal set of affordable goals, which we denote with $\mathcal{AF}$.

Definition 9 (Maximal Set of Affordable Goals). Let the investor's goals (wealth-based or consumption-based) be represented by the symbols $G^1, \ldots, G^{N_G}$, where N_G is the number of goals and the goals are ranked by order of decreasing priority. The maximal set of affordable goals, $\mathcal{AF}$, is defined as follows:

- If all goals are jointly affordable, then $\mathcal{AF} = \{G^1, \ldots, G^{N_G}\}$;
- Otherwise, $\mathcal{AF} = \{G^1, \ldots, G^i\}$, where i is such that the goals $G^1, \ldots, G^i$ are jointly affordable and $G^1, \ldots, G^{i+1}$ are not.

It should be emphasised that $\mathcal{AF}$ is not the set of goals which are individually affordable. This is obvious for consumption-based goals, which are additive: two goals may be separately affordable in the sense that the investor can afford to secure the more expensive of the two hedging portfolios which finance the related consumption expenditure, but may not be able to secure both of them simultaneously. Hence, $\mathcal{AF}$ is not the same as "the set of affordable goals".

Definition 9 serves as the basis for the formal distinction between the three classes of goals of Chhabra (2005). First, we define essential goals as goals that must be reached with a virtually 100% probability, which implies two requirements. First, they must be part of the maximal set of affordable goals. Second, the strategy chosen by the investor must secure each goal, that is, it must reach all of them with a 100% probability.[8] In contrast, important goals are also defined as being part of $\mathcal{AF}$, but differ from essential goals in the fact that they are not included as part of the set of goals to be secured. Finally, the goals that are not part of $\mathcal{AF}$ are said to be aspirational goals. The following definition summarises the distinction between the three types of goals.

---

[8]By a "100% probability", we mean 100% chances of success in the absence of gap risk or default risk on the safe assets. On the other hand, this assessment of the 100% probability of success should not be subject to model or parameter uncertainty.

Definition 10 (Essential, Important and Aspirational Goals). Consider the maximal set of affordable goals, $\mathcal{AF}$, defined in Definition 9.

- Essential goals are the elements of $\mathcal{AF}$ that the investor decides to secure (affordable and secured goals);
- *Important goals are the elements of* $\mathcal{AF}$ that the investor decides not to secure (affordable but non-secured goals);
- Aspirational goals are the goals which are not contained in $\mathcal{AF}$ (non-affordable, and therefore non-secured, goals).

The first step in the classification of goals is thus the identification of the maximal set of affordable goals. It is important to keep in mind that the affordability of a goal depends on the asset mix available to the investor. The introduction of a new asset which is not redundant with the existing ones may turn a non-replicable payoff into an attainable payoff. An example is given by inflation-linked bonds: the goal of respecting a certain inflation-adjusted minimum level of wealth is not affordable until an inflation-indexed bond is introduced in the asset mix because the floor value cannot be exactly replicated with other securities. Making this minimum wealth level attainable is the first step towards making the goal affordable: the next requirement is that investor's liquid wealth, and possibly future income, covers the price of the indexed bond.

A non-affordable goal can also become affordable if suitable contracts are offered to the investor. For instance, as explained in Section 2.2.4.6, one can secure a consumption objective upon retirement by entering forward contracts to lock up the re-investment rates of future income: when the consumption and income payments are known in advance, this turns out to be the cheapest hedging strategy, even cheaper than the strategy which consists in purchasing the compound option that makes up for the gap between income and consumption (see Proposition 8). As a consequence, the investor's liquid wealth may be less than the option price, while being sufficient to secure the goal with the forward contracts. In other words, the goal would not be affordable without the forward contracts, but becomes so if the contracts exist.

Another example is an insurance contract which pays the goal value. Such contracts may be available in the context of goals related to events whose occurrence is not certain, such as health contingencies. In the chapter on case studies, we will consider the goal of paying for nursing home fees (see Section 4.2 of Chapter 4). In this case, the expense is triggered by an exogenous event, known as a long-term care (LTC) event. An insurer may propose a contract whose benefits cover the expense. This contract completes the market if no option otherwise exists that would pay the goal value exactly when the LTC event occurs. Even if the option exists, the contract may be less expensive if the present value of the premiums is less than the option price. This present value depends on the pricing policy of the insurer among other factors, but it will hopefully always be less than the price of the bond that would super-replicate the goal value by paying the fees in all states of the world, whether the LTC event occurs or not. Thus, the goal may become affordable thanks to the insurance contract.

2.4.2. *Interpretation and implications of the classification of goals*

We now discuss some key implications of Definition 10. One first implication of the presence of an explicit hierarchy within and across types of goals is that cash flows related to lower priority goals that occur before cash flows related to higher priority goals should be paid only if the payment of these cash flows will not have too strong an impact on the subsequent goals. More precisely, the presence of a formal hierarchy of goals implies the following set of rules:

- An important or aspirational goal with consumption cash flows occurring at dates before the consumption dates for some essential goals will be satisfied if and only if the satisfaction of this goal will not turn any one of the essential goals into aspirational goals.
- An important goal with consumption cash flows occurring at dates before the consumption dates for some other more important goals will be satisfied if and only if the satisfaction of this goal will not turn any one of these more important goals into aspirational goals.
- An aspirational goal with consumption cash flows occurring at dates before the consumption dates essential goals will be satisfied if and only if the satisfaction of this goal will not turn any one of the essential goals into aspirational (hence, non-affordable) goals.

- An aspirational goal with consumption cash flows occurring at dates before the consumption dates for some other important goals will be satisfied if and only if the satisfaction of this goal will not decrease the probability of achieving any one of these other goals.

We now turn to a more detailed discussion of the interpretation of each type of goal.

2.4.2.1. *Essential goals*

An essential wealth-based goal should actually be regarded as a floor in the sense that it represents a minimum level of wealth that the strategy must respect with 100% probability. In case the initial wealth of the investor makes it impossible to ensure the achievement of the essential goals with full certainty, the investor must bring additional contributions, either now (immediate increase in the dollar budget) or later (under the form of higher saving rates). In case the investor proves to be unable or unwilling to increase these dollar budgets, then he should be willing to accept lower essential goal levels.

All the examples of essential goals given above fit into this definition. Indeed, the goal of home ownership can be seen as a wealth-based goal, where the investor wants his wealth to remain greater than or equal to the house value. This goal is affordable and secured for those investors who own their residence. The goal of having a minimum level of wealth available at all times, in order to finance minimal levels of short-term consumption needs in scenarios such that income is dramatically decreasing, can be secured by holding a roll-over position in cash, since the value of cash never decreases.

It should be noted that in the previous two examples, goals are in general not explicitly formulated by the investor, and are only implicit. Other essential goals are explicit, and can be secured with an investment in a GHP such as those described in Section 2.2. In the end, the qualification of a goal as an essential one depends both on the affordability of the goal and on the investor's decision to secure it.

2.4.2.2. *Important goals*

By Definition 10, important goals are part of $\mathcal{AF}$. Hence, the investor would be able to secure them together with the essential goals, but decides not to do so. The reason why an investor may decide not to secure otherwise affordable important goals is to avoid investing an exceedingly large share of his wealth in hedging portfolios so as to allow for a higher level of investment in performance-seeking assets, and as a result generate more upside potential and increase the probability of achieving aspirational goals. In this case, the goals, which are not formally secured, may not be achieved with probability 1.

Eventually, the only difference between an essential and an important goal is that the investor decides to secure the former but not the latter. But it is also possible to secure an affordable goal only partially. Then, the goal is split in two new goals, respectively, an essential one (corresponding to the fraction of the goal to secure) and an important one (corresponding to the unsecured fraction). For instance, if an annual expense of $100,000 is affordable given the investor's current liquid wealth and future income perspectives, one may decide to secure only $75,000 by purchasing the appropriate GHP. The remaining annual expense of $25,000 is then treated as an important goal. An example of partial protection of an affordable goal will be presented in the case study chapter of this book (see Section 4.2 of Chapter 4).

2.4.2.3.   *Aspirational goals*

Aspirational goals are defined as goals which are not in $\mathcal{AF}$. They consist of two categories of goals. First, there are non-affordable goals, i.e. goals whose value is not replicable with the available assets, or goals that would be replicable but are too expensive to be affordable. For instance, a consumption-based goal such that the present value of the expenditure exceeds investor's wealth is an aspirational goal. The second class of aspirational goals consists of the elements of $\mathcal{AF}$ which are not labelled as essential or important. Being elements of $\mathcal{AF}$, these goals are individually affordable, but they cannot be secured together with other goals with higher priority ranking (that is, goals of the essential or important types).

2.5.   Building Blocks in Goals-Based Wealth Management

The fund separation theorem, which is a fundamental cornerstone of dynamic asset pricing theory, suggests that risk and performance are two conflicting objectives that are best managed when managed separately within dedicated building blocks. In practical terms, it implies that all investors should allocate (in addition to long or short positions in the risk-free asset) some fraction of their wealth to a common well-diversified performance-seeking risky portfolio (Tobin, 1958) as well as to some dedicated hedging portfolios designed to help the investor obtain protection against unfavourable changes in risk factors that impact their income streams as well as their wealth and consumption goals (Merton, 1971, 1973). In this section, we describe in more detail the various building blocks that will be involved in the design of goals-based strategies.

These building blocks can be classified as follows:

1. GHPs, specific to each (group of) individual investor(s);
2. A well-diversified performance-seeking portfolio (PSP, which should theoretically be the maximum Sharpe ratio portfolio, MSR), common to all investors;
3. Wealth mobility portfolios (WMPs), specific to each (group of) individual investor(s).

The distinction between GHPs, PSP and WMPs is isomorphic to Chhabra's classification of the three main categories of risks that an individual investor faces (Chhabra, 2005), which he named *personal risks*, *market risks* and *aspirational risks*.

The *personal risk* bucket is a broad category that includes events specific to an individual or family, which can have a material financial impact on their wealth. Protecting an investor against personal risk means protecting the investor against the anxiety of a dramatic decrease in his lifestyle. As a result, an individual may be willing to accept a low real return on a portfolio designed to help hedge these risks, a portfolio which is not designed to generate upside potential but instead offer protection against downside risk relative to the particular goals identified by the investor. More formally, the personal risk bucket is defined as the risk bucket containing all GHPs. On the other hand, investors need to take on *market risks*, and collect the associated risk premia, in order to grow with their wealth segment and maintain their standard of living. The design of this performance portfolio should be entirely dedicated to the efficient extraction of market risks via diversification so as to eliminate, or at least reduce as much as possible, the presence of unrewarded specific risk, and therefore increase the risk-adjusted performance (Sharpe ratio in the mean–variance context). In other words, the market risk bucket contains all tradable risky assets that are held by an investor for performance purposes, in contrast to those held for hedging purposes. Note that this particular building block should in principle be identical for all investors, since it is meant to capture broad market risks as opposed to risks related to a particular investor's specific goals. Finally, the *aspirational risk* bucket contains, if any, all assets privately held by investors, which have a strong upside potential and are typically the driving force that allows investors to achieve wealth mobility objectives within or across affluence segments. Typical examples of assets held within the aspirational risk bucket are human capital, stock and stock option compensation packages, ownership stakes in privately held companies, etc.

In what follows, we discuss these portfolios in more detail.

2.5.1. *Essential goal-hedging portfolios and personal risk bucket*

We first focus on the building blocks dedicated to the protection of essential goals.

To each replicable goal is associated one suitably designed GHP. The general objective assigned to this portfolio is to secure the goal with certainty. Its nature depends on the goal. For a consumption-based goal, the GHP is a bond with coupon payments matching the consumption expenses, or equivalently, a portfolio of pure discount bonds (see Proposition 4). For a wealth-based goal with multiple horizons, the GHP is a roll-over of exchange options which expire on the goal dates (see Proposition 3). This result simplifies in some instances (see Corollary 1), e.g. if the goal actually has a single horizon: the GHP is a zero-coupon bond which pays the minimum wealth level at horizon.

The following list provides selected examples of GHPs:

- If the goal is to avoid ending up homeless in case of a major financial downturn, then the GHP is a residential home.
- If the goal is to avoid starvation in case of a major financial downturn, then the GHP consists of cash holdings.
- If the goal is a (minimum/target) nominal or inflation-adjusted wealth level at horizon, then the GHP is a (nominal or real)

pure discount bond with maturity date corresponding to the goal/investment horizon.

- If the goal is a (minimum/target) consumption level at all dates, then the GHP is a portfolio of pure discount bonds, or an annuity if the terminal date is the investor's uncertain date of death.
- If the goal is a (minimum/target) nominal or inflation-adjusted wealth level at the end of every year until horizon, then the GHP is a roll-over of 1-year (nominal or real) bonds.
- If the goal is to keep the portfolio drawdowns below a given level, then the GHP is cash (which actually is a super-replicating portfolio in this case, in the sense that its performance will strictly dominate the performance of the flat floor).

From a theoretical perspective, cash is not necessarily the asset suitable for protecting a minimum level of wealth at all times. If the objective is to secure a minimum level of wealth at a given horizon, the safe asset is a zero-coupon bond with maturity date matching the investment horizon. If the objective is to protect a minimum level of wealth at various horizons, the safe asset is a roll-over of exchange options, as shown by Proposition 3. On the other hand, cash may appear to investors as safe in the sense that its value never decreases, while the value of a zero-coupon bond may fluctuate in response to interest rate changes. Moreover, a zero-coupon may be subject to the default risk of the issuer, a risk that is not unrealistic, even for sovereign issuers. Finally, funds held in the form of numeraire are perfectly liquid, while selling or buying a zero-coupon is an operation that incurs transaction costs. Overall, the holding of a cash reserve can be justified to finance an essential goal that consists in preserving a minimum wealth level at all dates.

By definition, the initial value of the GHP is the minimum capital to invest in order to secure the goal, and a goal is affordable if, and only if, the investor's wealth covers this minimum amount. If the goal is not affordable, the GHP may still be included in the investor's strategy, since it may secure a lower level of consumption or wealth, which is then formally regarded as the affordable essential goal for the investor.

In closing, GHPs tend to be concentrated portfolios with potentially unattractive performance, and their raison d'être is to ensure the highest possible probability of achieving some essential goals.

By definition, the assets that are held to secure (implicit or explicit) essential goals form the "personal risk bucket" of the investor. In addition to home ownership and holdings of a reserve of cash, GHPs which correspond to explicit essential goals are typically financial assets such as bond portfolios. In the case studies of Chapter 4, the initial personal wealth designates the aggregate value of the non-tradable assets held to secure the implicit goals (residence and cash account). Hence, this wealth is already assigned to the protection of implicit goals, and cannot therefore be regarded as available to secure other goals.

2.5.2.   *Performance-seeking portfolios and market risk bucket*

Unlike GHPs, performance-seeking portfolios (PSPs) are well-balanced portfolios enjoying a high reward per unit of risk, which provide access to a fundamental source of performance.

2.5.2.1.   *Performance portfolios*

If the initial wealth is exactly sufficient to fully finance all GHPs, then the investor will not be able to achieve relative upside potential in the absence of additional contributions. Given the need to generate performance so as to reach important and aspirational goals with a non-zero probability, it is in general desirable for investors to allocate some fraction of their assets to a well-diversified PSP, in order to benefit from risk premia on risky assets across financial markets.

Diversification (as opposed to *hedging*) is the risk management technique that allows investors to efficiently extract long-term risk premia out of performance-seeking assets. Indeed, by holding well-diversified portfolios, investors may be able to eliminate or at least reduce (*diversify away*) unrewarded risk in their portfolios, which allows them to enjoy higher rewards per unit of risk, and therefore a higher average funding ratio at horizon for a given risk budget.

While the benefits of diversification are intuitively clear, there is no straightforward definition of what exactly a well-diversified portfolio is. The most common intuitive explanation of *naive* diversification is that it is the practice of not "putting all eggs in one basket". Having eggs (dollars) spread across many baskets is,

however, a rather loose prescription.[9] A fully unambiguous definition of *scientific* diversification has been provided by Modern Portfolio Theory: more precisely, the prescription is that the PSP should
be obtained as the result of a portfolio optimisation procedure aiming
to generate the highest risk–reward ratio.

Portfolio optimisation is a straightforward procedure, at least in
principle. In a mean–variance setting, for example, if there are no
restrictions on leverage or short sales, the prescription consists of
generating an MSR portfolio based on expected return, volatility, and
pairwise correlation parameters for all assets to be included in the
portfolio. Formally, and with the notation introduced in Section 2.1,
the MSR portfolio is defined as

$$\underline{w}_{\mathrm{MSR},t} = \frac{\Sigma_t^{-1}\underline{\mu}_t}{\underline{1}'\Sigma_t^{-1}\underline{\mu}_t}.$$

The vector $\underline{1}$ in the denominator is the vector of size $N \times 1$ filled with
1. The denominator is adjusted to ensure that the sum of weights of
the MSR equals 1.

Once a set of input parameters are given, the optimisation
procedure can be handled analytically in the absence of portfolio
constraints. More generally, it can be handled numerically in the
presence of minimum and maximum weight constraints. Introducing
weight constraints can actually be regarded as a way to reduce estimation risk (see for example Jagannathan and Ma, 2003), which is a
key issue in practice, especially for expected return parameters (see
Merton, 1980).

2.5.2.2. *Portfolio diversification across and within asset classes*

The standard alternative approach widely adopted in investment
practice consists instead of first grouping individual securities in various asset classes as well as sub-classes according to various dimensions, e.g. country, sector, and/or style within the equity universe,

---

[9]See Deguest *et al.* (2013) for a detailed introduction to factor risk parity strategies based on a formal analysis of what is the true meaning of "many" and
"baskets".

or country, maturity, and credit rating within the bond universe, and subsequently generating the optimal portfolio through a two-stage process. On the one hand, investable proxies are generated for MSR portfolios within each asset class in the investment universe. We call this step the *portfolio construction step*. While market cap indices are natural default choices as asset class benchmarks, academic and industry research has offered convincing empirical evidence that these indices tend to exhibit a poor risk-adjusted performance, because of the presence of an excessive amount of unrewarded risk due to their extreme concentration in the largest cap securities in a given universe, as well as the absence of a well-managed set of exposures with respect to rewarded risk factors. For example, cap-weighted indices have a natural large cap and growth bias, while academic research — such as the seminal work by Fama and French (1992) — has found that small cap and value were instead the positively rewarded biases. The combination of these empirical and theoretical developments has significantly weakened the case for market cap-weighted indices (Goltz and Le Sourd, 2011), and a consensus has emerged regarding the inadequacy of market cap-weighted indices as efficient investment benchmarks. In this context, a new paradigm known as smart beta equity investing has been proposed, the emergence of which blurs the traditional clear-cut split between active versus passive equity portfolio management (see, for example, Amenc *et al.*, 2012).

After efficient benchmarks have been designed for various asset classes or sub-classes, these building blocks can be assembled in a second step, the asset allocation step, to build a well-designed multi-class PSP.

2.5.2.3.   *From asset allocation to risk allocation*

An interesting new framework, known as *risk allocation*, is increasingly used at the asset (or factor) allocation stage. This trend is related to the recognition, supported by recent research (e.g. Ang *et al.*, 2009), that risk and allocation decisions could be best expressed in terms of rewarded risk factors, as opposed to standard asset class decompositions, which can be somewhat arbitrary. More generally, given that security and asset class returns can be explained by their exposure to pervasive systematic risk factors, looking through the asset class decomposition level to focus on the underlying factor decomposition level appears to be a perfectly legitimate approach, which is supported by standard asset pricing models such as the intertemporal CAPM (Merton, 1973) or the arbitrage pricing theory (Ross, 1976). If the whole focus of portfolio construction is ultimately to harvest risk premia that can be expected from holding an exposure to rewarded factors, it seems natural indeed to express the allocation decision in terms of such risk factors.

In this context, the term "risk allocation" is a new paradigm advocating that investment decisions should usefully be cast in terms of risk factor allocation decisions, as opposed to asset class allocation decisions. A second interpretation for what the *risk allocation paradigm* might mean is to precisely define it as a portfolio construction technique that can be used to estimate what an efficient allocation to underlying components (which could be asset classes or underlying risk factors) should be. The starting point for this novel approach to portfolio construction is the recognition that a heavily concentrated set of risk exposures can be hidden behind a seemingly well-diversified allocation. The risk allocation approach to portfolio construction, also known as the risk budgeting approach, focuses on risk, as opposed to dollar, allocation. In a nutshell, the goal of the risk allocation methodology is to ensure that the contribution of each constituent to the overall risk of the portfolio is equal to a target risk budget. In the specific case when the allocated risk budget is identical for all constituents of the portfolio, the strategy is known as *risk parity*, which stands in contrast to an equally-weighted strategy that would recommend an equal contribution in terms of dollar budgets (see Maillard *et al.*, 2010; Roncalli, 2013, for further details).[10]

---

[10] Orthogonalising the factors is useful to avoid the arbitrary attribution of overlapping correlated components in the definition of risk budgets allocated to each of these factors. Principal component analysis (PCA) can be used to extract uncorrelated versions of the factors starting from correlated asset or factor returns. Alternatively, to avoid the difficulties related to the lack of stability and interpretability of principal components, and to generate uncorrelated factors that are as close as possible to the original assets or factors, one can use the minimal linear torsion (MLT) approach recently introduced in Deguest *et al.* (2013).

2.5.2.4. *Definition of the market risk bucket*

The market bucket consists of assets that are held for performance purposes, as opposed to being held for the purpose of securing an essential goal. This corresponds to assets which can be traded in the market, regardless of their liquidity, and could be in the custody of a financial advisor representative, such as equity and bond indices, federal, municipal and corporate bonds, mutual funds, hedge funds, etc. Ideally, these assets should be held in the form of a well-diversified portfolio, that is, some proxy for the MSR portfolio constructed using one of the aforementioned approaches. Illiquid assets such as private equities or hedge funds are considered as part of the market risk bucket, since they tend to be relatively diversified attempts to harvest market risk premia, including alternative risk premia not easily accessible with traditional investment vehicles in a long-only format.

Given that it contains the most liquid assets, the market risk bucket is the place in which excess non-portfolio income is re-invested and from which funds are withdrawn to finance non-essential consumption plans (the essential goals being, by definition, financed with personal assets).

2.5.3. *Wealth mobility portfolios and aspirational risk bucket*

The third risk bucket contains wealth mobility portfolios, which are typically strongly concentrated positions in illiquid privately held assets, which are held for wealth mobility purposes and are not intended as proxies for efficient portfolios in the sense of portfolio theory.

2.5.3.1. *Wealth mobility portfolios*

In the absence of leverage constraints, if an investor wants to achieve an exceedingly high expected return needed to allow for wealth mobility with a positive probability, the efficient approach would involve a leveraged allocation to the mean–variance efficient PSP. In the presence of leverage constraints, however, the use of a dedicated portfolio with a concentrated exposure to high performance assets will be needed to deliver returns materially higher than those of a diversified portfolio of asset classes, returns that are needed to achieve a given ambitious goal with a positive probability. In the limit case of a required target expected return equal to the highest expected return of all assets, the performance portfolio will be 100% invested in that particular asset, and therefore will be poorly diversified and not particularly attractive in terms of Sharpe ratio.[11] These concentrated speculative portfolios are typically restricted to assets that are already held by investors through the human capital component of their wealth, as opposed to being regarded as portfolios to be optimally designed by financial advisors.

2.5.3.2. *Definition of the aspirational risk bucket*

The aspirational risk bucket consists of assets without an immediate publicly available price and traditionally not managed by a financial advisor representative. Examples include the human capital, a stock option compensation, a privately held business, an art collection, a piece of land, etc. Some of these assets may be held for wealth mobility purposes. Their presence reflects the desire, or at least the potential, to achieve ambitious wealth levels that are not attainable with a mere efficient harvesting of risk premia in the presence of leverage constraints, and which can only be achieved through investments that involve a large amount of idiosyncratic risk. More often than not, the individual investor does not expect a financial advisor to manage this pool of assets, which are held for reasons that extend beyond the standard desire to extract performance from financial markets.

Overall, the three risk buckets represent a collectively exhaustive and mutually exclusive partition of the investor's wealth. The investor's total wealth is split across three buckets. It should be noted that a correspondence exists between risk buckets and goals. Indeed, while all assets contribute to the achievement of all goals, assets in the personal risk bucket are by definition required to ensure the achievement of essential goals with probability 1. In the same vein, assets in

---

[11]If the target expected return is higher than the highest expected return of all assets, including privately held businesses, then no performance portfolio can be designed to allow the investor to achieve their exceedingly ambitious performance goals, that is unless their human capital portfolio, which itself tends to be a heavily concentrated portfolio in terms of risk exposure, allows them to do so.

the market risk bucket contribute significantly to the achievement of important goals, while speculative assets are required to ensure the achievement of aspirational goals such as wealth mobility goals. In statistical terms, one might think of assets in the market portfolio as focusing on the body of the distribution of the wealth (or wealth relative to goal values), while safe assets in the personal risk bucket focus on the left tail of the distribution and risky assets in the aspirational risk bucket focus on the right tail of the distribution.

Chapter 3

Efficient Allocation Across Risk Buckets

The analysis presented in Chapter 2 has allowed us to define the efficient composition of the risk buckets that every investor should have. The outstanding question that remains to be analysed is the design and implementation of an efficient allocation across risk buckets at different points in time.

From a general perspective, the definition of an allocation strategy is guided by the following two principles:

1. The strategy must secure all essential goals;
2. It should lead to the highest possible success probabilities for non-essential goals, i.e. important or aspirational goals.

The first principle is a clear prescription, keeping in mind that we require that the 100% success probability for essential goals be robust with respect to assumptions on the dynamics of asset prices and to parameter choices. In other words, if implementation frictions lead to the existence of shortfalls with respect to the goals, such shortfalls should in principle be non-existent, and in practice should be limited in size and probability.

The second principle, on the other hand, is a somewhat vague recommendation, stating that while the protection of non-essential goals is (by definition) not required, the chosen investment strategy should generate a reasonably high chance to reach them.

It turns out that the problem of finding optimal strategies in the presence of a goal has been extensively studied in the academic literature. In Section 3.2, we precisely present a series of theoretical optimality results drawn from the literature, and in Section 3.3, we introduce implementable heuristic proxies for theoretically optimal strategies.

3.1.   From Buy-and-Hold to Dynamic Allocation Strategies

The broad question that we face here is to define what to do with the excess of liquid wealth, if any, which is left available after all essential goals have been secured within the personal risk bucket.

In goals-based wealth management, one natural benchmark strategy consists in securing all essential goals, and investing the available liquid wealth (that is wealth in the market risk bucket, or equivalently the investor's total wealth minus the wealth held in the personal and aspirational risk buckets) in a performance portfolio allowing for the most efficient harvesting of market risk premia, that is, a proxy for the MSR portfolio.

We now describe in more detail this *buy-and-hold* strategy. Consider a wealth-based or consumption-based goal with no income coming from sources outside the portfolio. Once the GHP has been identified, the simplest way to secure the goal is to purchase the GHP at date 0 and to invest the remainder of liquid wealth in some PSP. This is a buy-and-hold strategy, which generates the following wealth at date t:

$$A_{\text{BH},t} = (A_0 - \text{GHP}_0)A_{\text{PSP},t} + \text{GHP}_t. \tag{3.1}$$

In this equation, $A_{\text{PSP},t}$ denotes the value of the PSP with an initial investment of \$1. Note that the value of the GHP at date 0 is equal to the present value of the goal on this date, and that the goal is clearly secured by this strategy.

The strategy described by Equation (3.1) can be interpreted as a constant proportion portfolio insurance (CPPI) with a multiplier equal to 1. To see this, it suffices to note that the weights are given by

$$\underline{w}_{\text{BH},t} = \left(1 - \frac{\text{GHP}_t}{A_{\text{BH},t}}\right)\underline{w}_{\text{PSP},t} + \frac{\text{GHP}_t}{A_{\text{BH},t}}\underline{w}_{\text{GHP},t},$$

where $\underline{w}_{\text{PSP},t}$ denotes the weight vector of the PSP and $\underline{w}_{\text{GHP},t}$ that of the GHP.

Clearly, the strategy defined in Equation (3.1) is not the only one that secures essential goals with probability 1. Also, it is not necessarily among them the one that leads to the highest probability of achieving important and aspirational goals. In fact, it is a specific example of a wider class of *dynamic* goals-based investing (GBI) strategies, in which the allocation to the market risk bucket versus the personal risk bucket is taken as a multiple — possibly different from 1 — of the current wealth in excess of the present value of the goal.

The weights of a generic strategy that secures the essential goal(s) with probability 1 can be written as

$$\underline{w}_t = f(A_t, \widetilde{G}_t)\underline{w}_{\text{PSP},t} + [1 - f(A_t, \widetilde{G}_t)]\underline{w}_{\text{GHP},t},$$

where $f(A_t, \widetilde{G}_t)$ is some function of current wealth and the present value of the goal. For the goal to be secured, the strategy must keep the ratio $A/\widetilde{G}$ above one at all times. Indeed, if the ratio falls below one, the goal becomes non-affordable, and thus becomes an aspirational one.

For the ratio to stay above one, it makes intuitive sense that the volatility of the ratio $A/\widetilde{G}$ must shrink to zero when the ratio approaches one from above. Otherwise, unexpected fluctuations may occur that would cause the ratio to fall below one. By Ito's lemma, the volatility vector of $A/\widetilde{G}$ is $\underline{\sigma}_t[\underline{w}_t - \underline{w}_{\text{GHP},t}]$. Because the volatility matrix, $\underline{\sigma}_t$, is by nature independent from wealth, the only way to have zero volatility when $A/\widetilde{G}$ gets close to 1 is to have the difference $[\underline{w}_t - \underline{w}_{\text{GHP},t}]$ shrink to zero. Thus, $f(A_t, \widetilde{G}_t)$ has to become zero as current wealth approaches the present value of the goal.

This argument suggests that a necessary and sufficient condition to ensure the protection of essential goals is that the investor's wealth be fully invested in the essential GHP in case the amount of available wealth is exactly equal to the minimum wealth required to secure the goal with the corresponding strategy. The simplest specification that satisfies this property is a linear function: $f(A_t, \widetilde{G}_t) = m(A_t - \widetilde{G}_t)$. The case $m = 1$ corresponds to the static buy-and-hold strategy introduced earlier. While more complex functional forms that satisfy the limit condition at zero can be considered, we argue in Section 3.2 that strategies in which the allocation to the market risk bucket is taken to be a multiple of the distance between current wealth and the present value of the essential goals are of particular relevance, not only because they represent the *simplest* form of GBI strategies and require no unobservable parameters as inputs, but also because they actually coincide with the formal solution to an expected maximisation problem with (implicit) goals for a leverage-constrained myopic investor.

Before turning to the formal analysis of the GBI strategies in the academic literature, it should be noted that in the presence of income, the buy-and-hold strategy has to be modified. Taking the example of the retirement goal discussed in Section 2.2.4 of Chapter 2, a strategy that secures the retirement goal of horizon T_r is the following:

- At date 0, purchase the option which pays $(\widetilde{G}_{T_r} - \sum_{s \leq T_r} y_s)^+$ on date T_r and invest the remainder of wealth in the PSP;
- At each income date (T_j), purchase the option which pays $(\widetilde{G}_{T_r} - \sum_{T_j < s \leq T_r} y_s)^+$ on date T_r and invest the remainder of wealth in the PSP.

Since a rebalancing takes place on each income date, this is not a buy-and-hold policy, but a roll-over of buy-and-hold strategies (in the sense that the portfolio is on buy-and-hold between dates T_j and T_{j+1}).

3.2. Review of the Related Literature

In addition to the aforementioned seminal work by Chhabra (2005), as well as recent papers on asset–liability management in private wealth management (see, for example, Reichenstein, 2006; Reichenstein and Jennings, 2003; Wilcox *et al.*, 2006; or Amenc *et al.*, 2009), the GBI approach presented in this book is related to two main strands of the literature. The first strand of papers, mostly published in mathematical finance or operations research journals, focuses on investment solutions that are meant to optimise the value of some ad-hoc criterion such as the minimisation of shortfall probability, or the minimisation of expected shortfall with respect to a given objective. It should be noted that these papers often solve these programs to find an optimal hedging strategy for an option in an incomplete market where there is no perfect hedging strategy. The second strand of the literature, mostly published in finance journals, focuses on the mainstream objective of expected utility maximisation while the presence of the goal is accounted for by the introduction of minimum performance constraints. In Sections 3.2.1 and 3.2.2, we present these two strands of the literature separately, and we then comment on their similarities.

3.2.1. *Goals-based allocation strategies*

In this section, we provide a broad overview of the papers that have considered wealth-based goals with a single horizon. The mathematical formulation of this goal is $A_T \geq G_T$, G_T being the minimum wealth level.

The first natural objective is to maximise the success probability, i.e. the probability of reaching the goal:

$$\max_{\underline{w}} \mathbb{P}(A_T \geq G_T) \quad \text{subject to the budget constraint (2.3).} \quad (3.2)$$

This problem is only interesting for non-affordable goals (which are aspirational in the sense of Definition 10), that is, goals that cannot be reached with probability 1. If a goal is affordable, there exists at least one strategy that yields a 100% success probability, so this strategy is a solution to Program (3.2).

Less straightforward is the case where the goal cannot be reached with 100% probability. Föllmer and Leukert (1999) solve for the optimal payoff, A_T^*, both in complete and incomplete markets. For simplicity, we focus on the complete case. The optimal payoff is that of a digital option, which involves the value of the *growth-optimal* portfolio, which is defined as the portfolio strategy that maximises the expected logarithmic return at horizon T:

$$\max_{\underline{w}} \mathbb{E}\left[\ln \frac{A_T}{A_0}\right] \quad \text{subject to the budget constraint (2.3).} \quad (3.3)$$

The solution is derived by Long (1990) and can be written as

$$\underline{w}_{go,t} = \Sigma_t^{-1} \underline{\mu}_t.$$

It can also be written as a function of the weights of the maximum Sharpe ratio (MSR) portfolio

$$\underline{w}_{go,t} = \frac{\lambda_{MSR,t}}{\sigma_{MSR,t}} \underline{w}_{MSR,t},$$

$\lambda_{\text{MSR},t}$ and $\sigma_{\text{MSR},t}$ being the Sharpe ratio and the volatility of the MSR (see Amenc *et al.* (2010) for a mathematical proof). Unlike the MSR portfolio, the growth-optimal portfolio policy is in general not fully invested in the risky assets, and involves cash. It is sometimes called "myopic" in the literature because the weights do not depend on the investment horizon.

The probability-maximising payoff can then be written as a function of the goal value and the payoff of the growth-optimal strategy

$$A_T^* = G_T \times \mathbb{I}_{\left\{\frac{A_{\text{go},T}}{G_T} \geq \frac{A_0}{KG_0}\right\}}. \tag{3.4}$$

The constant K in this equation is adjusted in such a way that the budget constraint $\mathbb{E}[M_T A_T^*] = A_0$ holds. The result given by Equation (3.4) is in fact a special case of the more general result given in Proposition 10, which provides the optimal payoff subject to a minimum wealth constraint. Taking the minimum equal to zero, one recovers the optimal payoff written in Equation (3.4).

Finding the optimal strategy requires computing the Greeks of the digital option. This can be carried out analytically only under restrictive assumptions on parameter values. For instance, having stochastic risk premia will imply that A_{go} has stochastic volatility, which prevents from obtaining a closed-form expression. A stochastic interest rate permits an analytical computation to the extent that the ratio $A_{\text{go},T}/G_T$ remains log-normal, which is satisfied for example if the short-term interest rate follows a Gaussian model (e.g. as in Vasicek (1977)), but not if it follows a square-root process (as in Cox, Ingersoll and Ross (1985)). Browne (1999) derives the hedging strategy under the assumption that the goal is constant, and that expected returns, volatilities and the short-term rate are deterministic functions of time, which ensures that $A_{\text{go},T}/G_T$ is log-normal and allows for the use of the Black and Scholes (1973) option pricing formula. The optimal strategy involves the MSR portfolio and cash. Since the risk-free asset coincides with the GHP when the goal is constant and the short-term rate is deterministic, it is equivalent to say that the optimal strategy is a dynamic combination of the MSR portfolio and the GHP. A remarkable property of these strategies is that the allocation to the former building block is decreasing in the ratio of current wealth to goal value. In other words, one allocates more to the "performance" block if wealth is far from the goal.

The payoff (3.4) has a clear drawback, which is that it can take the value zero with positive probability. It is because a zero payoff is not penalised by the objective function of Equation (3.2), and is tolerated as long as they it serves the purpose of increasing the success probability. Nevertheless, a zero terminal wealth means that the investor loses all money invested, which is hardly acceptable for most individuals. To address the bankruptcy issue, Browne (1999) maximises the success probability subject to the constraint that wealth remains above a floor, which represents the amount of wealth necessary to afford a minimum standard of living. The optimisation program reads

$$\max_{\underline{w}} \mathbb{P}(A_T \geq G_T) \quad \text{subject to the budget constraint (2.3)}$$

$$\text{and } A_T \geq F_T. \tag{3.5}$$

The payoff F_T can be thought of as an essential wealth-based goal. As for the goal G_T, we assume that F_T is replicable with a "floor-hedging portfolio" (FHP) $\underline{w}_{\text{FHP}}$, an assumption that is made because it ensures that there exists at least a strategy that satisfies the constraint $A_T \geq F_T$ almost surely.[1] We let $\widetilde{F}_t$ denote the present value of the payoff F_T, which is the wealth obtained by investing $\widetilde{F}_0$ in the FHP. Browne (1999) solves the optimisation program (3.5) when F_T is a fraction less than 100% of G_T. The following proposition slightly extends his result by providing the optimal payoff when F_T is simply assumed to be less than G_T. We go back to Browne's assumption that the floor and the goal are proportional in order to write the optimal strategy.

Proposition 10 (Probability-Maximising Strategy with a Floor). *Assume that:*

- *The market is complete;*
- $0 \leq F_T < G_T$ *almost surely;*
- $\widetilde{F}_0 \leq A_0 \leq \widetilde{G}_0;$

---

[1]Strictly speaking, replicability is a sufficient, but not necessary, condition for the existence of a strategy such that $A_T \geq F_T$ almost surely.

- *There exists a constant K such that $\mathbb{E}[M_T X^*] = A_0$, where X^* is the random variable*

$$X^* = F_T + (G_T - F_T) \times \mathbb{I}_{\left\{ A_{\text{go},T} \geq \frac{A_0}{K(\widetilde{G}_0 - \widetilde{F}_0)}(G_T - F_T) \right\}}.$$

Then X^* is the optimal payoff in (3.5).

Assume in addition that $F_T = \alpha G_T$ for some $0 \leq \alpha < 1$, so that $\underline{w}_{\text{FHP}} = \underline{w}_{\text{GHP}}$, and that the vectors $\underline{\lambda}_t$ and $\underline{\sigma}_t \underline{w}_{Gt}$ are deterministic functions of time. Then, the optimal vector of weights is

$$\underline{w}_t^* = \varphi_t \underline{w}_{\text{go},t} + (1 - \varphi_t) \underline{w}_{\text{GHP},t},$$

with

$$\varphi_t = \frac{1}{\kappa_{t,T}} \frac{\widetilde{G}_t - \widetilde{F}_t}{A_t^*} n \left[\mathcal{N}^{-1} \left(\frac{A_t^* - \widetilde{F}_t}{\widetilde{G}_t - \widetilde{F}_t} \right) \right],$$

$$\kappa_{t,T} = \sqrt{\int_t^T \| \underline{\lambda}_s - \underline{\sigma}_s \underline{w}_{\text{GHP},s} \|^2 ds},$$

and n and $\mathcal{N}$ being, respectively, the probability distribution and the cumulative distribution functions of the standard normal distribution.

Proof. See Appendix A.2.1. □

By Proposition 10, the probability-maximizing payoff is of the digital type, as in the absence of a floor constraint, but the outcome zero is replaced by the floor value. It is also shown in Appendix A.2.1 that the optimal allocation to the growth-optimal performance portfolio shrinks to zero in two situations: if current wealth approaches the goal present value ($\widetilde{G}_t$) or the floor present value ($\widetilde{F}_t$). In other words, whenever wealth approaches either the lower or the upper bound, the agent invests only in the "safe portfolio" to secure the wealth level he has reached and prevent it from exceeding the target value of dropping below the floor value.

Another way of penalising low wealth levels is to minimise some measure of shortfall size. Following this idea, Cvitanic (2000) minimises the expectation of the discounted shortfall:

$$\min_{\underline{w}} \mathbb{E}\left[\frac{(A_T - G_T)^+}{S_{0T}}\right].$$

The optimal payoff he obtains corresponds to a digital option, which pays either the goal value, or some fraction (comprised between 0 and 1) of the goal value. It is clear that by avoiding bankruptcy, such a payoff leads to lower shortfalls than the probability-maximising one. Föllmer and Leukert (2000) solve a related problem, which is to minimise the expectation of some loss function of the shortfall, a formulation that nests the expected shortfall minimisation as a special case. But again, an explicit computation of the optimal strategy is only possible in a simple Black–Scholes setting. In addition to these objectives, the literature on optimal option hedging also suggests a number of alternative criteria to be minimised. For instance, Föllmer and Schweizer (1990) minimise the expected squared difference between final wealth and the goal defined as an option payoff that has been sold to a counterparty. From a technical and mathematical perspective, this problem is easier to solve than the minimisation of expected shortfall. On the other hand, one conceptual problem with the "mean–variance" hedging criterion is that it equally penalises upside and downside deviations from the goal.

A related strand of the literature has considered another somewhat related problem, which is to minimise the expected time to reach a goal. While the expected time to success is not a standard risk management indicator, using it as an optimisation criterion reflects the idea that an investor seeks to secure a goal that was not initially affordable as soon as possible. In this case, the goal is represented by a process $(G_t)_{t\geq0}$, and the problem has an infinite horizon. Note that this goal is a wealth-based goal with multiple horizons.

Mathematically, the time to success is defined as the first hitting time of the goal process by the wealth process, and the objective to minimise is the expectation of this time

$$\min_{\underline{w}} \mathbb{E}[\tau] \quad \text{subject to the budget constraint (2.3)},$$

$$\tau = \inf\{t \geq 0 \,;\, A_t \geq G_t\}. \tag{3.6}$$

If $A_0 \geq G_0$, then the expected time to success is trivially zero, for any strategy. The interesting case is when $A_0 < G_0$. It has been solved by Heath and Sudderth (1984) in the case of constant risk and return parameters (i.e. constant volatilities and expected returns for risky assets and constant interest rate) and a constant goal. The optimal policy is shown to be the growth-optimal strategy that is a mixture of the MSR portfolio and cash.

It also turns out that the minimal expected time is decreasing in the Sharpe ratio of the MSR portfolio (which is a fixed-mix given the assumption of constant parameters). However, the extension of such results to more general economies, with possibly time-varying parameters, is a formidable challenge. Kardaras and Platen (2010) propose to solve a modified version of the problem, in which the hitting time is measured according to a "market clock", as opposed to the usual calendar time. The speed at which market time flows is proportional to the squared Sharpe ratio of the MSR portfolio: for instance, it flows faster when investment opportunities are good and the MSR Sharpe ratio is high. In this context, the growth-optimal portfolio is still shown to be optimal. Because the market clock is equivalent to the calendar clock when parameters are constant, this result encompasses that of Heath and Sudderth (1984). Another variant of the original problem which leads to a closed-form solution is studied in Aucamp (1977). Overall, Problem (3.6) is very hard to solve explicitly in its original form.

Nevertheless, a limit of the growth-optimal strategy is that it does not secure the goal once it has been reached. Even if the goal is quickly reached, there is no guarantee that the value of the growth-optimal portfolio will never fall below it thereafter. Instead, one might expect from a GBI strategy that it secures the goal after it has managed to reach it.

3.2.2. *Expected utility maximisation*

The second strand of literature takes as an objective the maximisation of expected utility in the presence of a goal. This can be done in various ways, depending on how the goal is incorporated in the optimisation program. Broadly speaking, the goal can be introduced either directly in the objective function or in additional constraints.

In this section, we briefly review the properties of utility-maximising strategies in the absence of a goal, and we then present a set of optimality results that account for the presence of the goal, which are of a highest degree of relevance in the context of goals-based wealth management.

3.2.2.1. *Utility maximisation in the absence of a goal*

A general formulation of the expected utility maximisation problem reads

$$\max_{\underline{w}} \mathbb{E}[U(A_T)], \quad \text{subject to the budget constraint (2.3).} \quad (3.7)$$

This version assumes that the portfolio is self-financing. Another form, which allows for intermediate consumption, reads

$$\max_{\underline{w}} \mathbb{E}[U(A_T)], \quad \text{subject to the budget constraint (2.4).} \quad (3.8)$$

It should be noted that this formulation differs from the one of Samuelson (1969), who seeks to maximise intertemporal utility derived from consumption. Indeed, we take consumption as an exogenous variable, rather than a control variable that can be optimised over. It turns out that the solution of Program (3.8) can be expressed as a simple function of the solution of Program (3.7) (see Proposition 14). Hence, we focus in what follows on Program (3.7).

The seminal contributions on utility maximisation in an intertemporal setting are by Samuelson (1969) and Merton (1971, 1973). Their papers solve the optimisation program via the dynamic programming approach, which produces a nonlinear partial differential equation (the Hamilton–Jacobi–Bellman equation). This equation can only be solved under specific assumptions of model parameters. A first important finding is that if all risk and return parameters (i.e. the short-term interest rate, the expected returns and the volatilities in (2.1)) are constant, and the utility function is of the Constant Relative Risk Aversion (CRRA) type, as in the equation

$$U(x) = \begin{cases} \frac{x^{1-\gamma}}{1-\gamma} & \text{for } x > 0 \\ -\infty & \text{for } x \leq 0 \end{cases},$$

then the optimal policy is a fixed-mix strategy. In detail, the optimal weights are given by

$$\underline{w}^* = \frac{1}{\gamma}\underline{w}_{go} = \frac{\lambda_{\text{MSR}}}{\gamma\sigma_{\text{MSR}}}\underline{w}_{\text{MSR}}. \qquad (3.9)$$

Since the weights do not sum up to 1 in general, cash is used to make the balance: the fraction of wealth invested in cash is $[1 - (\underline{w}^*)'\underline{1}]$.

Merton (1971) also solves the problem (3.7) for a broader class of utility functions, known as the "Hyperbolic Absolute Risk Aversion" (HARA) functions. Note that the CRRA class of utility functions has an interesting property, namely that marginal utility of wealth grows to infinity as wealth approaches zero, as can be seen from the expression of the first derivative of the utility function

$$U'(x) = x^{-\gamma}.$$

This property, which means an investor starting with low wealth will enjoy a large welfare improvement if given a small additional endowment, is important because it ensures that terminal wealth cannot be negative at the optimum. For some other utility functions, marginal utility stays bounded as wealth approaches zero. This is the case, for instance, with the CARA function, also a member of the HARA class, defined as

$$U(x) = \exp(-\alpha x).$$

With such utility functions, solving the utility maximisation Program (3.7) without a non-negativity constraint on wealth leads to an optimal wealth which can take on negative values (see Merton, 1992, Chapter 6). Given that terminal wealth at the final date is not admissible, since it would mean that the investor would exit with a non-repaid debt, the non-negativity constraint has to be imposed explicitly.

An alternative to the dynamic programming technique which allows to easily incorporate the non-negativity constraint on final wealth is the "convex duality", or "martingale" approach of Cox and Huang (1989). The first step in this approach consists in computing the optimal terminal wealth as a function of the state-price deflator. The second step is to find the replication strategy for this optimal payoff, which provides the optimal strategy. This approach is particularly simple in a complete market setting because this assumption guarantees the uniqueness of the state-price deflator and the attainability of any payoff (up to technical measurability and integrability requirements). On the other hand, solving for the optimal payoff in an incomplete market setting involves the computation of the "minimax state-price deflator", which is the optimal deflator chosen by the utility maximiser among the infinity of possible deflators (see He and Pearson, 1991, for more details), and as such depends on investor's horizon and risk aversion.

In a complete market setting, Cox and Huang (1989) show that the optimal terminal wealth has the form

$$A_T^* = [U'^{-1}(\nu M_T)]^+,$$

where U'^{-1} is the inverse of the marginal utility function, M is the unique state-price deflator and ν is a constant, which is implicitly given by the budget constraint $\mathbb{E}[M_T A_T^*] = A_0$. For utility functions with finite derivative at zero, the non-negativity constraint is not binding, meaning that the optimal terminal wealth may be zero, which complicates the pricing of the optimal payoff, hence the calculation of the optimal weights (Cox and Huang, 1989). For this reason, we follow a large body of the literature on optimal portfolio choice by assuming a CRRA function in what follows.

When risk and return parameters are not constant, the fixed-mix policy (3.9) is no longer optimal, and it is not even optimal to update the weights with time-varying parameter values. Indeed, as shown by Merton (1973), the optimal portfolio in this context involves a number of "intertemporal hedging demands" in addition to a dynamically revised MSR portfolio. For instance, if the uncertainty in investment opportunities can be summarised in the changes in R "state variables" $X_1, \ldots, X_R$, then the optimal strategy has the form

$$\underline{w}_t^* = \frac{\lambda_{\text{MSR},t}}{\gamma \sigma_{\text{MSR},t}} \underline{w}_{\text{MSR},t} + \sum_{r=1}^{R} a_{rt} \underline{w}_{\text{hed},r,t}, \tag{3.10}$$

where the portfolio $\underline{w}_{\text{hed},r,t}$ is the hedging portfolio against variable X_r, defined as the portfolio invested in risky assets that maximises the correlation with unexpected changes in X_r.[2] The coefficients a_{rt} are functions of a number of variables, including subjective parameters (risk aversion and investment horizon) as well as objective parameters (current values of state variables and parameters driving the evolution of the variables over time). One important effect of the presence of stochastic investment opportunities is that the optimal strategy depends on the investment horizon, a dimension which is absent in the case of constant parameters.

The task of computing the coefficients a_{rt} is sometimes difficult, especially when there are multiple risk factors. It is not the purpose of this section to present explicit derivations for the hedging demands. This subject has been the focus of a large body of literature. Selected references providing mathematical expressions for the hedging demands are[3]:

- Stochastic interest rate and constant risk premia (Brennan and Xia, 2002; Munk and Sorensen, 2004; Martellini and Milhau, 2012).
- Stochastic risk premia and constant interest rate (Kim and Omberg, 1996, and Wachter, 2002).
- Multiple stochastic state variables, including notably stochastic interest rate and risk premia (Munk, Sorensen and Vinther, 2004; Sangvinatsos and Wachter, 2005; Liu, 2007; Detemple and Rindisbacher, 2010; Martellini and Milhau, 2013; and Deguest, Martellini and Milhau, 2014).

For instance, in the presence of a stochastic interest rate, a demand arises for the zero-coupon bond that matures on the investor horizon date. This pure discount bond is the long-term safe asset for the investor, since it leads to a payoff with no variance at the investment horizon. In the presence of a stochastic equity risk premium, the optimal strategy (3.10) contains a hedging demand

---

[2]Nielsen and Vassalou (2006) show that the state variables which induce a hedging demand are those that impact the position of the intertemporal capital market line (ICML), namely its intercept (the nominal short-term rate) or its slope (the Sharpe ratio of the MSR portfolio). In particular, a state variable that affects volatilities without impacting the ICML does not give rise to a hedging demand.

[3]This short list is restricted to papers that provide closed-form solutions. A number of papers also compute optimal portfolios numerically.

against unexpected changes in equity premium risk. Its role is to hedge against unexpected changes in investment opportunities (see Merton, 1973). The hedging demand against unexpected changes in the equity risk premium is the portfolio of risky assets that has the highest squared correlation with changes in the equity risk premium. The design of that portfolio is a matter of empirical calibration. It is widely accepted that an increase (respectively, decrease) in realised returns of equities implies a corresponding decrease (respectively, increase) in their expected return. As a matter of fact, empirical research has found a strong negative correlation between expected returns on stocks and realised returns on stocks (see, e.g. Campbell and Viceira, 1999; Barberis, 2000; and Martellini and Milhau, 2013). As a result, the intertemporal hedging demand against changes in the equity risk premium mostly contains a long equity position that comes as an addition to the equity allocation already present in the MSR portfolio. The expression for this hedging demand is given in several papers (see, e.g. Kim and Omberg, 1996; Munk, Sorensen and Vinther, 2004; and Martellini and Milhau, 2013).

There are a few cases where hedging demands are in fact zero. First, this happens if investment opportunities are constant, since there is no need then to hedge. A second case is when the highest correlation that can be achieved with the state variable is zero, in which case there is a need to hedge but no ability to effectively hedge. A third case is when the risk aversion γ is equal to 1. Indeed, the CRRA function then coincides with the logarithmic function, so Program (3.7) is equivalent to maximising the expected logarithmic return (Program (3.3)). The solution to this problem is the growth-optimal portfolio scaled by $1/\gamma$: the reciprocal of risk aversion is also known as the risk tolerance.

3.2.2.2. *Optimal strategy in the presence of a wealth-based goal*

We now turn to expected utility maximisation in the presence of a wealth-based goal, focusing on goals with a single horizon to avoid the technicalities raised by the presence of multiple horizons.

Choice of Objective. Having a wealth-based goal G_T means that the investor is concerned with how terminal wealth compares to G_T. There are two main options to assess the value of wealth relative to the goal:

- The surplus, $A_T - G_T$;
- The funding ratio, A_T/G_T.

The idea is that an investor prefers large surpluses and high funding ratios, with as little uncertainty as possible. These preferences are captured by an increasing and concave utility function U. Thus, if Z denotes the quantity of interest (surplus or funding ratio), the portfolio choice problem consists in the determination of the strategy that maximises expected utility. This is mathematically written as

$$\max_{\underline{w}} \mathbb{E}[U(Z)], \quad \text{subject to the budget constraint (2.3).}$$

The choice of the variable of interest (surplus or funding ratio) is linked to the choice of the utility function. Indeed, if marginal utility grows to infinity near zero, then the random variable Z will be positive almost surely at the optimum. Thus, if Z has been chosen to be the surplus, the final surplus is positive with probability 1. By the absence of arbitrage opportunities, it follows that the initial wealth must be such that $A_0 > E[M_T G_T]$ for any state-price deflator. If this condition is not satisfied, then any strategy yields a positive probability that $A_T \leq G_T$, so that expected utility equals minus infinity. As a conclusion, the choice of a utility function with infinite derivative at 0 (such as the CRRA one) combined with the surplus as an objective does not allow for goals which are not affordable in the sense of Definition 1.

For these reasons, we take U to be the CRRA utility function, and Z to be the funding ratio. The fact that marginal utility grows to infinity at 0 ensures that the optimal terminal funding ratio is positive. In particular, the optimal terminal wealth is also positive, so the investor's problem reads

$$\max_{\underline{w}} \mathbb{E}\left[U\left(\frac{A_T}{G_T} \right) \right], \quad \text{subject to the budget constraint (2.3).} \quad (3.11)$$

To see the impact of the presence of a goal on the optimal investment strategy, it will be useful to compare the solution of this program to the solution of an otherwise identical program without the goal. In other words, our objective here is to find relationships between the solutions to Programs (3.7) and (3.11). For clarity, we denote by A^{*G} and $\underline{w}^{*G}$ the optimal wealth and the optimal portfolio weights in the program with the goal (Equation (3.11)), and by A^{*0} and $\underline{w}^{*0}$ the analogous quantities for the program without the goal (Equation (3.7)).

Optimal Strategy. If markets are incomplete, there are infinitely many state-price deflators and each expected utility maximisation program carries a specific deflator, known as the minimax state-price deflator (He and Pearson, 1991). In particular, (3.7) and (3.11) may lead to different minimax deflators, which would severely complicate the task of expressing the solution of (3.11) as a function of the solution of (3.7). We thus assume in what follows that markets are complete, which in turn ensures that the goal is replicable given a sufficient level of initial wealth.

Before we state the result comparing the solutions of both programs, we introduce an auxiliary stochastic process, which is the price $b_{t,T}$ of the zero-coupon bond that pays \$1 at date T. Its dynamics reads

$$\frac{db_{t,T}}{b_{t,T}} = [r_t + \sigma_{b,t,T}\lambda_{b,t,T}]dt + \underline{\sigma}'_{b,t,T}d\underline{z}_t.$$

Proposition 11 (Optimal Payoff and Strategy with Wealth-Based Goal). *Assume that markets are complete. Then, the optimal payoff in Program (3.11) is*

$$A_T^{*G} = \nu_1 A_T^{*0} G_T^{1-\frac{1}{\gamma}},$$

where

$$\nu_1 = \mathbb{E}\left[M_T^{1-\frac{1}{\gamma}}\right] / \mathbb{E}\left[(M_T G_T)^{1-\frac{1}{\gamma}}\right].$$

Moreover, if $\underline{\lambda}_t, \underline{\sigma}_{b,t,T}$ and $\underline{\sigma}_{Gt} = \underline{\sigma}_t \underline{w}_{Gt}$ are deterministic functions of time, the optimal strategy in (3.11) reads

$$\underline{w}_t^{*G} = \frac{\lambda_{\text{MSR},t}}{\gamma \sigma_{\text{MSR},t}} \underline{w}_{\text{MSR},t} + \left(1 - \frac{1}{\gamma}\right) \underline{w}_{Gt},$$

$$\underline{w}_t^{*G} = \underline{w}_t^{*0} + \left(1 - \frac{1}{\gamma}\right)[\underline{w}_{Gt} - \underline{w}_{bt}],$$

where $\underline{w}_{bt}$ is the portfolio that replicates the zero-coupon bond maturing at date T.

Proof.   See Appendix A.3.1.   □

The assumption of a deterministic $\underline{\lambda}_t$ is satisfied if the Sharpe ratios and the pairwise correlations of risky assets are constant in time, as can be seen by rewriting this vector as

$$\underline{\lambda}_t = \underline{U}_t \underline{\Omega}_t^{-1} \begin{pmatrix} \lambda_{1t} \\ \vdots \\ \lambda_{nt} \end{pmatrix},$$

where $\underline{\Omega}_t$ is the (instantaneous) correlation matrix of the assets and $\underline{U}_t$ is its Cholesky factor, i.e. the upper triangular matrix such that $\underline{\Omega}_t = \underline{U}_t' \underline{U}_t$. The condition on $\underline{\sigma}_{b,t,T}$ depends on the dynamics of the short-term rate. If this rate follows the Vasicek model (Vasicek, 1997), then $\underline{\sigma}_{b,t,T}$ is deterministic. More generally, this condition is also satisfied if the short-term rate is a combination of two mean-reverting processes with constant volatilities (see Brennan and Xia, 2002). Finally, the assumption of a deterministic $\underline{\sigma}_{Gt}$ is verified if the final goal value is proportional to realised inflation, the price index follows a Geometric Brownian motion and the short-term rate follows the Vasicek model (see Martellini and Milhau, 2012).

Under these conditions, the optimal strategy is a combination of the MSR portfolio and the GHP (plus cash, which is the third fund). The allocation to the MSR portfolio is decreasing in the risk aversion, and for an infinite risk aversion, it is optimal to invest only in the GHP, as the intuition suggests. This in turn yields a constant ratio A_T^{*G}/G_T, which was also expected: an infinitely risk averse investor seeks to minimise the dispersion of wealth relative to the goal, regardless of upside performance potential. This property is in fact very general, and extends beyond the present framework to general economies and utility functions (see Wachter, 2003). A similar fund separation result involving the MSR portfolio and the GHP as building blocks can be found in Martellini and Milhau (2012).

The presence of a stochastic risk premium for one of the risky assets, e.g. a stock index, does not modify the optimal terminal wealth as long as the uncertainty in this risk premium is spanned, thus allowing for the markets to remain complete. On the other hand, it gives rise to a dedicated "hedging demand" in the optimal strategy for Program (3.7). In detail, the optimal strategy for Program (3.7) is a combination of the MSR portfolio, the zero-coupon bond maturing at date T, the equity premium-hedging portfolio and cash: the references cited in Section 3.2.2.1 provide mathematical statements of this fund separation theorem. If a goal is introduced (as in Program (3.11)), the joint presence of the stochastic Sharpe ratio and the goal gives rise to interaction effects, so that the optimal strategy with the goal is not simply a combination of the optimal strategy without the goal, the GHP and the zero-coupon bond. On the other hand, it can still be shown that the optimal strategy is a combination of the same four funds as in Program (3.7), plus the GHP (see Martellini and Milhau (2013) for detailed expressions of optimal strategies with liabilities and a stochastic Sharpe ratio). However, the relationship between the solutions to Programs (3.7) and (3.11) is not as straightforward as in Proposition 11.

3.2.2.3. *Optimal strategy securing an affordable wealth-based goal*

Optimal Payoff and Strategy. Even if the goal is affordable, that is if $A_0 \geq \widetilde{G}_0$, the optimal strategy of Proposition 11 does not secure it with full probability, except if the investor has infinite risk aversion, which leads him to invest all available wealth in the GHP, and the goal is initially affordable. Indeed, there is always a positive probability for the terminal wealth A_T^{*G} to be less than G_T. To secure the goal, one may solve (3.11) subject to the additional constraint that $A_T \geq G_T$ almost surely. More generally, one may impose a floor on terminal wealth, as was done for the probability maximisation exercise. The constrained program is written as

$$\max_{\underline{w}} \mathbb{E}\left[U\left(\frac{A_T}{G_T} \right) \right], \quad \text{subject to (2.3) and } A_T \geq F_T. \quad (3.12)$$

As for the probability maximisation program in Equation (3.5), we assume that the floor is replicable, the FHP being denoted by $\underline{w}_{\text{FHP}}$. For Program (3.12) to have a solution, it must be the case that $A_0 \geq \widetilde{F}_0$, that is, the goal F_T must be affordable. Thus, in Program (3.12), F_T can be thought of as an essential goal, while G_T represents an important or aspirational goal.

Program (3.12) is a portfolio optimisation subject to a performance constraint. The solution is derived in various papers such as Tepla (2001), El Karoui, Jeanblanc and Lacoste (2005) and Deguest, Martellini and Milhau (2014), among others. Proposition 12 gives an important result from this literature, which is that the optimal payoff can be written as the sum of two payoffs: the payoff that would be optimal without the performance constraint, plus the payoff of an option that compensates for the possible gap between this unconstrained payoff and the minimum wealth to reach by the horizon. In order to make a distinction between the solution of Program (3.12) and the solution of the otherwise identical program without the constraint of securing the goal (Equation (3.11)), we denote with A_T^{*F} and $\underline{w}^{*F}$ the optimal payoff and weight vector in Program (3.12). The following proposition connects the solutions of Programs (3.11) and (3.12).

Proposition 12 (Optimal Payoff and Strategy Securing a Wealth-Based Goal). *Assume that markets are complete and that $A_0 \geq \widetilde{F}_0$. Then, the optimal payoff in Program (3.12) is*

$$A_T^{*F} = \nu_2 A_T^{*G} + [F_T - \nu_2 A_T^{*G}]^+, \qquad (3.13)$$

where A_T^{*G} is the optimal terminal wealth without the performance constraint (the solution to Program (3.11)), and ν_2 is the unique solution of the equation $\mathbb{E}[M_T A_T^{*F}] = A_0$ in the range $[0, 1]$ if $A_0 > \widetilde{F}_0$, and 0 if $A_0 = \widetilde{F}_0$.

Moreover, if $\underline{\sigma}_{Ft} = \sigma_t \underline{w}_{\mathrm{FHP},t}$ and $\underline{\sigma}_t^{*G} = \sigma_t \underline{w}_t^{*G}$ are deterministic functions of time, then the optimal strategy in the sense of Program (3.12) reads

$$\underline{w}_t^{*F} = \left[1 - \frac{p_{t,T}\widetilde{F}_t}{A_t^{*F}}\right] \underline{w}_t^{*G} + \frac{p_{t,T}\widetilde{F}_t}{A_t^{*F}} \underline{w}_{\mathrm{FHP},t},$$

where $\underline{w}_t^{*G}$ is the optimal weight vector for Program (3.11), and $p_{t,T}$ is the probability (under the probability measure that makes asset prices expressed in the numeraire $\widetilde{F}$ follow martingales) that the put option *in Equation (3.13) ends up in the money. It is given by*

$$p_{t,T} = \mathcal{N}(-d_{2t}),$$

with

$$d_{2t} = \frac{1}{\zeta_{t,T}} \left[\ln \frac{\nu_2 A_t^{*G}}{\widetilde{F}_t} - \frac{1}{2} \zeta_{t,T}^2 \right],$$

$$\zeta_{t,T} = \sqrt{\int_t^T \|\underline{\sigma}_{s^*G} - \underline{\sigma}_{Fs}\|^2 ds}.$$

Proof.   See Appendix A.3.2.   □

The introduction of the constraint to secure the goal in Program (3.12) implies that the optimal payoff is that of an exchange option between the goal value and the optimal "unconstrained" wealth, which is the wealth that would be optimal without the performance constraint. This payoff can be replicated by investing the amount $\nu_2 A_0$ in the optimal unconstrained strategy, and $(1 - \nu_2)A_0$ in a put option written on this strategy, with a stochastic strike price equal to G_T. Because the put option pays exactly the excess of the goal value over the unconstrained strategy, it can be called an "insurance put".

In terms of portfolio weights, the optimal strategy is a combination of the optimal "unconstrained" portfolio, which would be optimal for the same objective but without the performance constraint, and the FHP. As noted by Deguest, Martellini and Milhau (2014), it bears similarities to a CPPI strategy:

- The "risky" asset is the unconstrained strategy;
- The "safe" asset is the FHP, i.e. the portfolio that secures the floor;
- The floor is $p_{t,T}\widetilde{F}_t$;
- The (probability-adjusted) cushion is $[A_t^{*Gs} - p_{t,T}\widetilde{F}_t]$.

The amount invested in the unconstrained strategy is shown to be the product of a multiplier times the risk budget (known as the cushion in the context of CPPI strategies). It should be noted that while the objective is to have $A_T \geq F_T$ at the final date, the floor to respect at each date is the present value of the goal ($\widetilde{F}_t$) multiplied by a probability ($p_{t,T}$). Thus, the risk budget in the optimal strategy is the distance between current wealth and a probability-weighted floor which depends on the goal value and the likelihood of the risk budget being spent before the horizon. Since the probability is less than 100%, the risk budget of the optimal strategy is larger than current wealth minus the goal. As shown in Appendix A.3.2, the property of a vanishing risk budget when wealth approaches the goal value from above is preserved for these strategies despite the fact that the risk budget exceeds the distance to the floor: this is because the probability $p_{t,T}$ can be shown to converge to 1 when asset value converges to the floor.

Appendix A.3.2 also shows that when wealth grows to infinity, the risk budget $[A_t^{*F} - \widetilde{F}_t N(-d_{2t})]$ approaches A_t^{*F}. Hence, for a very large wealth, the investor acts as if there was no floor and follows the strategy that would be optimal if there was no floor.

3.2.2.4. *Cost of insurance for the optimal strategy securing a wealth-based goal*

As explained in Deguest, Martellini and Milhau (2014), the coefficient ν_2 in Proposition 12 has two equivalent interpretations. First, since it equals the ratio of optimal constrained wealth over optimal unconstrained wealth in those states of the world where the put option expires out of the money, it represents the access to the upside of the unconstrained strategy. Since ν_2 is less than 1, this access is less than 100%. In other words, when the insurance proves *ex-post* to be unnecessary, the final wealth is less than what would have been achieved without purchasing the put. This leads to the second interpretation: the price of the put is $(1 - \nu_2)A_0$, so the quantity $1 - \nu_2$ is the (relative) cost of insurance. This cost is always non-negative, and the following corollary shows that it is in fact positive, unless the optimal unconstrained strategy secures the floor with 100% probability (in which case insurance is unnecessary).

Corollary 2 (Cost of Insurance with a Floor). *The coefficient ν_2 of Proposition 12 satisfies*

$$1 - \frac{\widetilde{F}_0}{A_0} \le \nu_2 \le 1.$$

Moreover, if the optimal unconstrained wealth has a positive probability of underperforming the floor, i.e. if

$$\mathbb{P}(A_T^{*G} < F_T) > 0,$$

then, ν_2 is strictly less than 1, which means that the cost of insurance is strictly positive.

Proof. See Appendix A.3.2. □

The lower bound on ν_2 follows from the standard inequality $(1 - \nu_2)A_0 \leq \widetilde{F}_0$, which says that the put is less expensive than the zero-coupon bond with the same horizon. Hence, the optimal strategy makes insurance less expensive than a hedging strategy that would purchase the zero-coupon bond to secure the floor, and invest the remaining amount, that is $[A_0 - \widetilde{F}_0]$, in the unconstrained strategy. Deguest, Martellini and Milhau (2014) provide a detailed study of the cost of insurance by showing that it is increasing in the level of the goal and decreasing in the risk aversion parameter.

Corollary 2 has an important implication for the distinction between essential and important goals, because it explains why it is justified to decide not to secure an affordable goal in some contexts. The trade-off is between the protection of the goal and the loss of upside potential which arises from the purchase of the put. Thus, an investor may decide not to explicitly secure a goal, even if it is affordable, because the opportunity cost is deemed to be too large.

3.2.2.5. *Decreasing the cost of insurance by imposing a cap*

In addition to accounting for the presence of floors, the dynamic asset allocation strategies can also accommodate the presence of various forms of *caps* or *ceilings*. The idea of imposing a cap on wealth in order to reduce the cost of insurance against downside risk is discussed in detail in Martellini and Milhau (2012) and Deguest, Martellini and Milhau (2014). These strategies recognise that the investor has no utility beyond a *cap* target level of wealth, which represents the investor's goal (actually a cap) and can be a constant, deterministic or stochastic function of time. From a conceptual standpoint, it is not clear *a priori* why any investor should want to impose a strict limit on upside potential. The intuition is that by forgoing performance beyond a certain threshold, where they have relatively lower utility from higher wealth, investors benefit from a decrease in the cost of the downside protection. This is equivalent to adding a short position in a convex payoff to the long position in the unconstrained strategy and the insurance put, so as to generate a collar-like payoff, with a truncation of the wealth level distribution on the left-hand side (below the floor level) as well as on the right-hand side (above the cap level).

To set up the utility maximisation problem in formal terms, let C_T denote the terminal value of the cap, which is the maximum wealth that the investor is willing to accept. In addition to this maximum, the investor still imposes the floor F_T, and potentially includes a third goal, G_T, in the objective function. We recall that $\widetilde{F}_t$ and $\widetilde{G}_t$ denote the present values of the payoffs F_T and G_T, and we adopt the notation $\widetilde{C}_t$ for the present value of C_T. The cap-hedging portfolio (CHP) is denoted by $\underline{w}_{\mathrm{CHP}}$. The constraint to have $A_T \leq C_T$ with probability 1 implies that $A_0 \leq \widetilde{C}_0$, so that C_T can be thought of as a non-affordable or a "just affordable" (if $A_0 = \widetilde{C}_0$) goal. The optimisation program reads

$$\max_{\underline{w}} \mathbb{E}\left[U\left(\frac{A_T}{G_T}\right)\right], \quad \text{subject to the budget constraint (2.3) and}$$

$$F_T \leq A_T \leq C_T. \tag{3.14}$$

As shown in Martellini and Milhau (2012) and Deguest, Martellini and Milhau (2014), the optimal payoff consists of long positions in the optimal unconstrained strategy and the insurance put, plus a short position in a call option written on the unconstrained strategy. This combination gives a collar profile, which confines the terminal wealth between the bounds F_T and C_T. The following proposition gives a detailed expression.

Proposition 13 (Optimal Payoff and Strategy Securing a Wealth-Based Goal with a Cap on Wealth). *Assume that* $F_T \leq C_T$ *almost surely, that markets are complete and that* $\widetilde{F}_0 \leq A_0 < \widetilde{C}_0$.[4] *Then, the optimal payoff in the sense of Program (3.14) is*

$$A_T^{*C} = \nu_3 A_T^{*G} + [F_T - \nu_3 A_T^{*G}]^+ - [\nu_3 A_T^{*G} - C_T]^+, \tag{3.15}$$

where A_T^{*G} *is the optimal terminal wealth without the performance constraint (Program (3.11)), and* ν_3 *is the unique solution of the equation* $\mathbb{E}[M_T A_T^{*C}] = A_0$ *in the range* $[\nu_2, \infty[$ *if* $A_0 > \widetilde{F}_0$, *and* 0 *if* $A_0 = \widetilde{F}_0$.

---

[4]Observe that the second of these inequalities is strict.

Moreover, if $\underline{\sigma}_{Ft} = \sigma_t \underline{w}_{\text{FHP},t}$, $\underline{\sigma}_{Ct} = \sigma_t \underline{w}_{\text{CHP},t}$ *and* $\underline{\sigma}_t^{*G} = \sigma_t \underline{w}_t^{*G}$ *are deterministic functions of time, then the optimal strategy in Program* (3.14) *is*

$$\underline{w}_t^{*C} = \left[1 - \frac{p_{F,t,T}\widetilde{F}_t + p_{C,t,T}\widetilde{C}_t}{A_t^{*C}} \right] \underline{w}_t^{*G} + \frac{p_{F,t,T}\widetilde{F}_t}{A_t^{*C}}\underline{w}_{\text{FHP},t}$$

$$+ \frac{p_{C,t,T}\widetilde{C}_t}{A_t^{*C}}\underline{w}_{\text{CHP},t},$$

where $\underline{w}_t^{*G}$ *is the optimal weight vector for Program* (3.11), $p_{F,t,T}$ *is a risk-adjusted probability that the put option in Equation* (3.15) *ends up in the money and* $p_{C,t,T}$ *is a risk-adjusted probability that the call option in Equation* (3.15) *ends up in the money. These probabilities are given by*

$$p_{F,t,T} = N(-d_{F,2t}), \quad p_{C,t,T} = \mathcal{N}(d_{C,2t}),$$

with

$$d_{F,2t} = \frac{1}{\zeta_{t,T}}\left[\ln \frac{\nu_3 A_t^{*G}}{\widetilde{F}_t} - \frac{1}{2}\zeta_{t,T}^2 \right], \quad d_{C,2t} = \frac{1}{\chi_{t,T}}\left[\ln \frac{\nu_3 A_t^{*G}}{\widetilde{C}_t} - \frac{1}{2}\chi_{t,T}^2 \right],$$

$$\chi_{t,T} = \sqrt{\int_t^T \|\underline{\sigma}_s^{*G} - \underline{\sigma}_{Cs}\|^2 ds}.$$

Proof. See Appendix A.3.3. □

The optimal portfolio is now a combination of the portfolio that would be optimal in the absence of the floor and the cap, plus the FHP and the CHP. In order to better understand how the strategy allocates to these building blocks, it is interesting to analyse limit cases when current wealth approaches floor or cap levels. In the former case, the put option is deep in the money and the call option is deep out of the money, so the coefficients $d_{F,2t}$ and $d_{C,2t}$ go to minus infinity. Hence, the probabilities $p_{F,t,T}$ and $p_{C,t,T}$ approach, respectively, 100% and 0%, and the optimal weight vector, $\underline{w}_t^{*C}$, converges to the FHP. When wealth approaches the cap, the situation is symmetric: $p_{F,t,T}$ and $p_{C,t,T}$ approach, respectively, 0 and 1, so $\underline{w}_t^{*C}$ converges to the CHP. Hence, when a cap is imposed, there are two situations where the allocation to the unconstrained strategy vanishes, that is, either when wealth is close to the floor or when it is close to the cap.

The coefficient ν_3 represents the access to the upside of the unconstrained strategy when both options expire out of the money. By definition, ν_3 is greater than or equal to ν_2. The following corollary shows that the inequality is in fact strict provided the unconstrained wealth is not always lower than the cap.

Corollary 3 (Net Cost of Insurance with a Floor and a Cap). *Assume that the optimal unconstrained wealth has a positive probability of outperforming the cap, that is*

$$\mathbb{P}(\nu_2 A_T^{*G} > C_T) > 0.$$

Then, the coefficient ν_3 of Proposition 13 satisfies $\nu_3 > \nu_2$.

Proof. See Appendix A.3.3. □

Hence, by imposing a cap in addition to a floor, one captures a greater fraction of the performance of the unconstrained strategy. Equivalently, the net cost of insurance, i.e. the put option price minus the call option price, equal to $(1 - \nu_3)A_0$, is lower than the cost of insurance with a floor only.

3.2.2.6. *Optimal strategy in the presence of a consumption-based goal*

As explained above, we consider an exogenous stream of consumption, which is not optimised over. Thus, maximising the utility derived from intertemporal consumption, which is the standard objective in the literature on optimal consumption and portfolio choice, is not an appropriate program here. We choose instead to maximise the expected utility from bequest after all consumption expenses have been made. Mathematically, this corresponds to Program (3.8).

As for the wealth-based goal, we solve this program under the assumption of complete markets, in order to ensure the uniqueness of the state-price deflator, and thereby facilitate the comparison between the solutions of the program with a goal (Equation (3.8)) and the program without a goal (Equation (3.7)). We recall that the optimal wealth and weight vector for Program (3.7) are denoted by

A^{*0} and $\underline{w}^{*0}$, and we use the notations A^* and $\underline{w}^*$ for Program (3.8). We also recall that $\widetilde{G}_t$ denotes the present value of the goal, which is the price of the consumption stream and is uniquely defined if markets are complete. We let $\underline{w}_{\mathrm{GHP}}$ denote the GHP, which is a portfolio fully invested in the bond with coupons matching the consumption payments.

Proposition 14 (Optimal Wealth and Strategy with Consumption-Based Goal). *Assume that markets are complete and that $A_0 \geq \widetilde{G}_0$, where $\widetilde{G}_0$ is the initial price of the consumption stream. Then, the optimal wealth in Program (3.8) is*

$$A_t^* = \left(1 - \frac{\widetilde{G}_0}{A_0}\right) A_t^{*0} + \widetilde{G}_t,$$

and the optimal strategy is

$$\underline{w}_t^* = \left(1 - \frac{\widetilde{G}_t}{A_t^{*c}}\right) \underline{w}_t^{*0} + \frac{\widetilde{G}_t}{A_t^{*c}} \underline{w}_{\mathrm{GHP},t}.$$

Proof. See Appendix A.3.4. □

A first observation is that the optimal strategy secures the consumption-based goal, since the terminal wealth is $A_T^{*c} = \left(1 - \frac{\widetilde{G}_0}{A_0}\right) A_T^{*0}$, a quantity which is non-negative. This is a difference with respect to the wealth-based goal. Indeed, the optimal strategy for Program (3.7) does not secure the goal, unless the performance constraint is explicitly introduced (see Program (3.12)). Secondly, the optimal strategy with the consumption-based goal is reminiscent of an extended form of CPPI strategy, where the floor is the present value of future consumption streams, and the "safe asset" is the coupon-paying bond. When current wealth approaches the floor value, the investor invests a larger fraction of the portfolio in this bond.

3.2.3. *Comparison of the two strands of literature*

At this stage, it is interesting to compare the optimisation programs presented in the previous sections. We first comment on the choice of the objective function, and then highlight the similarities and the differences between the solutions of the programs.

3.2.3.1. Optimisation criteria

A first important difference between the frameworks lies in the choice of the objective function. Since the success probability is 100% for any strategy that secures the goal, a strategy that invests only in the GHP and the strategy that protects the goal by purchasing a put written on an unconstrained strategy (as in Proposition 12) are strictly equivalent in terms of this criterion. But they obviously have very different terminal payoffs. In other words, the success probability focuses on one very specific aspect of the distribution of wealth and is not rich enough to allow for a distinction between two distributions that are otherwise not equivalent. Hence, the choice of this criterion appears to be too restrictive. The expected shortfall is subject to the exact same criticism: both aforementioned strategies have zero expected shortfall, so they are still indistinguishable. More generally, the expected shortfall focuses only on what happens when the goal is missed, and leaves aside the right tail of the distribution of wealth.

On the other hand, the expected utility criterion incorporates the mean and the variance of the entire payoff distribution, as well as the higher-order moments. In the previous example, the "safe" strategy that invests only in the GHP and the strategy that involves an insurance put will lead to different levels of expected utility. A related observation is that as explained in Section 3.2.1, the success probability and the expected shortfall criteria do not lead to a uniquely defined optimal solution in the case of an affordable goal: the two strategies given as examples above are optimal. The non-uniqueness of the solution can be regarded as a drawback. The expected utility criterion leads to a unique optimal solution whether the goal is affordable or not. Hence, this criterion applies to both types of goals. Putting it differently, the certain achievement of essential goals should be taken as a constraint, and not as an objective, of the optimisation program.

3.2.3.2. Optimal payoffs

The mathematical derivation of optimal payoffs is in general possible both for heuristic risk management indicators and for expected utility maximisation. It is convenient to ask whether, beyond their formal optimality for a given criterion, these payoffs would be acceptable for an individual investor. The digital option payoffs display a clear disadvantage from this perspective, because they can be zero with positive probability. This drawback can be circumvented by imposing a floor on wealth in the probability maximisation, or by minimising the expected shortfall in order to penalise bankruptcy. But the optimal payoff remains of the digital type, which implies in particular that it is discontinuous. It is well known that the replication of such options raises difficulties in practice. In contrast, the utility-maximising payoffs considered in the previous propositions are all continuous and positive, and the positivity property is obtained because the marginal utility for the CRRA function grows to infinity at zero. This remark is important, because if a utility function does not verify this property, the optimal terminal wealth can be zero with positive probability. Overall, the utility-maximising payoffs appear to be more acceptable in practice.

Another difference between the two frameworks is that for a non-affordable goal, the probability-maximising and the shortfall-minimising payoffs never exceed the goal (Section 3.2.1), while the utility-maximising payoff can do so (Proposition 11). The property of being always less than or equal to the goal is not inconsistent with the fact of optimising a criterion: maximising the success probability or minimising the expected shortfall does not require the strategy to outperform the goal and large surpluses are not more valued than the small ones. In practice, individual investors are rarely concerned with a single goal. Beyond the explicitly formulated one, they may have in mind an implicit objective related to the upside of the strategy, with no well-defined threshold: an example is the bequest goal, which is to maximise the amount of money left to children upon death. Because expected utility depends positively on expected return, utility-maximising strategies leave room for outperformance beyond the goal unlike the probability-maximising and the shortfall-minimising strategies. It should be noted, however, that the upside potential of the utility-maximising strategy is reduced by the imposition of a minimal performance constraint: indeed, part of the initial capital must be devoted to the purchase of an insurance put, which leaves less money available to invest in performance-seeking assets (see Section 3.2.2.3).

3.2.3.3. *Optimal strategies: Building blocks*

The optimal strategies are the strategies that replicate the optimal payoffs. A first observation is that an analytical derivation is possible only under the assumption of deterministic Sharpe ratios and volatility vectors for goal processes. For the probability maximisation and the expected shortfall minimisation, these difficulties arise because of the option-like nature of the payoffs (digital options): stochastic Sharpe ratios or volatility vectors would imply stochastic volatilities for the underlying assets. Expected utility maximisation typically leads to more tractable payoffs. In the absence of minimum performance constraints, utility-maximising strategies can often be derived analytically even in the presence of stochastic investment opportunities[5]; on the other hand, the introduction of a minimum performance constraint leads to a call option payoff, and the assumption of deterministic parameter is again needed to arrive at an explicit expression for the optimal strategy (see Proposition 12).

Beyond this technical aspect, there are similarities between the dynamic strategies obtained in the two frameworks. In particular, they all involve the MSR portfolio and the GHP as building blocks. Intuitively, the presence of these blocks can be explained as follows. Investing in the MSR portfolio increases the expected return of the strategy: hence, it improves the chances to reach the goal, which has a positive impact on risk management indicators such as the shortfall probability or the expected shortfall. Because expected utility is increasing in expected return, the MSR portfolio also improves expected utility. Investing in the GHP serves the purpose of reducing the uncertainty over the value of wealth relative to the goal. The reduction in variance has a positive impact on the expected utility from the funding ratio. When the objective is to minimise a shortfall indicator, investing in the GHP ensures that the performance of the strategy does not deviate too much from that of the goal, which again leads to higher success indicators.

In order to make a more complete comparison between the sets of building blocks involved in the two families of strategies, one would need to have general fund separation theorems in both frameworks.

---

[5]Examples of mathematical expressions for optimal strategies with stochastic investment opportunities can be found in Kim and Omberg (1996), Munk *et al.* (2004), Sangvinatsos and Wachter (2005) and Liu (2007). Some of these expressions are "quasi-analytical" rather than completely analytical in the sense that they involve the solutions of univariate differential equations (Sangvinatsos and Wachter, 2005; Liu, 2007).

For expected utility, there exist general decomposition results (see e.g. Detemple and Rindisbacher, 2010), but for the shortfall indicators, the expressions for optimal strategies barely extend beyond the case of constant or deterministic investment opportunities.

3.2.3.4. *Optimal strategies: Investment rules*

In addition to the similarity of building blocks, there are also similarities in terms of the allocation rules to these blocks. To see this in detail, let us consider a specific case with two proportional wealth-based goals at the horizon T: F_T is an essential goal and is thus treated as a floor, and G_T is a non-affordable goal, hence an aspirational goal. F_T is equal to αG_T for some scalar α between 0 and 1, and the FHP coincides with the GHP since the essential and aspirational goals are perfectly correlated. As before, we take the notations $\widetilde{F}_t$ and $\widetilde{G}_t$ for the present values of the two goals. We also assume that all risk premia and volatility vectors are deterministic, which enables us to use the expressions of Section 3.2.1 for the optimal weight vectors.

By Proposition 10, the strategy that maximises the probability of reaching the goal G_T subject to the constraint of securing the floor F_T is

$$\underline{w}_t^{*\text{prob}} = \frac{\lambda_{\text{MSR},t}}{\sigma_{\text{MSR},t}} \varphi_t \underline{w}_{\text{MSR},t} + (1 - \varphi_t)\underline{w}_{\text{GHP},t},$$

with

$$\varphi_t = \frac{1}{\kappa_{t,T}} \frac{\widetilde{G}_t - \widetilde{F}_t}{A_t} n\left[\mathcal{N}^{-1}\left(\frac{A_t - \widetilde{F}_t}{\widetilde{G}_t - \widetilde{F}_t}\right)\right],$$

and $\kappa_{t,T}$ being a time-dependent coefficient, the expression of which does not matter here. By Propositions 11 and 12, the strategy that maximises the expected logarithmic utility of the ratio A_T/G_T while securing the floor is

$$\underline{w}_t^{*\text{EU}} = \frac{\lambda_{\text{MSR},t}}{\sigma_{\text{MSR},t}} \psi_t \underline{w}_{\text{MSR},t} + (1 - \psi_t)\underline{w}_{\text{GHP},t},$$

with

$$\psi_t = \frac{1}{\gamma}\left[1 - \frac{p_{t,T}\widetilde{F}_t}{A_t}\right].$$

In both cases, the allocation to each building block (MSR portfolio or GHP) depends on current wealth and the present value of the floor, and, as argued in Sections 3.2.1 and 3.2.2.3, the allocation to the MSR building block shrinks to zero as wealth approaches the floor. As a result, the optimal portfolio becomes fully invested in the GHP (and cash if the weights of the GHP do not add up to 1). In other words, both strategies have the same behaviour as wealth gets closer to the floor. A difference between the two portfolios is that the probability-maximising weights depend on the present value of the non-affordable goal, which is not the case for the utility-maximising ones. In fact, with the former strategy, wealth always remains below the non-affordable goal value, and the allocation to the MSR portfolio becomes zero as wealth approaches the goal from below. With the utility-maximising rule, wealth is not bounded from above, and for a very large wealth level, the allocation to the MSR component is $1/\gamma$, which is non-zero.

At this stage, it appears that the expected utility criterion is appropriate to find optimal strategies in the presence of both affordable and non-affordable goals, and is thus more general than probability maximisation or expected shortfall minimisation. Moreover, it yields more realistic payoffs than these two criteria, and it allows for the explicit derivation of optimal strategies in a broader class of models. Finally, the previous discussion shows that it leads to allocation recommendations that are similar to those of the probability criterion. For these reasons, we take expected utility maximisation as the reference criterion to construct allocation strategies in the GBI framework, and we now explain what exact proxy we recommend should be used in practice.

3.3.   Implementation Challenges

Once the PSP and GHP have been carefully designed, the next step is to determine what percentage of an investor's wealth should be allocated to each one of these building blocks. The theoretical optimality results given in Section 3.2 provide useful guidance with respect to the question of allocating to the PSP and the GHP. As explained in Section 3.2.3, we take expected utility maximisation as the starting point to build investment strategies. The purpose of this section is thus to describe the adaptation of utility-maximising investment policies to a realistic context.

3.3.1. *Strategies without performance constraints*

By an unconstrained strategy, we mean a strategy that does not target at securing any goal (although it can incidentally do so under some parametric assumptions). In this context, the strategy which maximises the expected utility from terminal wealth is a combination of the MSR portfolio, cash and a series of hedging demands dedicated to hedging changes in the opportunity set (see Section 3.2.2.1 and the references therein). If the objective is to maximise the expected utility from the terminal funding ratio (i.e. the ratio of wealth to the goal), then the optimal strategy is a combination of the MSR portfolio, the GHP, cash, and possibly additional hedging demands (see Section 3.2.2.2). The computation of these hedging demands requires the following inputs:

- The investor's risk aversion and horizon;
- The parameters of the models that describe the evolution of the risk factors in the opportunity set (interest rates, risk premia, volatilities, etc.).

For the second class of inputs, one has to specify a dynamic model for the stochastic variables of interest, and to calibrate the parameters to market data. Summarising changes in the opportunity set through a reduced number of factors is a parsimonious approach, but it inevitably generates model risk. In Section 3.4.1.2, we explain how the parameters required for implementing and simulating a GBI strategy can be estimated in coherence with available market information.

Investor's risk aversion is a non-observable attribute, but we argue that since investors' preferences have been thoroughly described in terms of the specific goals that needed to be achieved, there is no need to introduce another parameter to quantify attitude towards risk. For this reason, we assume a risk aversion parameter (denoted by γ in Section 3.2.2.1) equal to 1, which implies that all hedging demands are equal to zero. This has the advantage that the utility-maximising strategy is model-free, in the sense that it does not depend on the particular dynamics assumed for the state variable, since it avoids the computation of the hedging demands against changes in risk premia. For a unit risk aversion parameter, maximising expected utility is equivalent to maximising expected logarithmic return on wealth, hence the expression "logarithmic preferences". The strategy that maximises the expected utility from terminal wealth is the growth-optimal portfolio strategy

$$\underline{w}_t^* = \frac{\lambda_{\mathrm{MSR},t}}{\sigma_{\mathrm{MSR},t}} \underline{w}_{\mathrm{MSR},t}. \tag{3.16}$$

For some parameter values the ratio $\lambda_{\mathrm{MSR},t} / \sigma_{\mathrm{MSR},t}$ can be greater than 1, which implies that the investor should take a leverage exposure to the MSR portfolio financed with borrowing at the risk-free rate.

While it is theoretically optimal to hold the MSR portfolio, the introduction of a PSP that does not maximise the Sharpe ratio can be rationalised in the presence of leverage constraints. Indeed, the fund separation theorem saying that all investors endowed with mean–variance preferences should hold a combination of the MSR portfolio and the cash account breaks down if such constraints are imposed. In this setting, the portfolio selected by an investor is a combination of two mean–variance efficient portfolios that depend on the risk aversion (see the critical line method introduced by Markowitz, 1956). This justifies having a set of PSPs as opposed to a single portfolio intended as a proxy for the MSR portfolio. As a result, GBI strategies for a leverage-constrained investor endowed with logarithmic preferences will involve a dynamic allocation to GHPs and a performance-seeking portfolio, in addition to whatever wealth mobility portfolio the investor is already endowed with.

3.3.2.   *Strategies securing essential goals*

We now describe GBI strategies intended to secure one or more essential goal(s).

3.3.2.1.   *Wealth-based essential goal with a single horizon*

Consider first the case of a wealth-based goal with a single horizon, a goal which is represented by a (replicable) payoff F_T, defined as a minimum level of wealth to attain on date T. In the expected utility framework, the goal can be secured by imposing a minimal performance constraint, as is done in Program (3.12). Note that when the risk aversion is equal to 1, the solution of this program is independent from the deflator of the terminal wealth in the objective function. Indeed, the utility function is the logarithmic function, so for any goal G_T, the expected utility from the terminal funding ratio can be written as

$$\mathbb{E}\left[U\left(\frac{A_T}{G_T}\right)\right] = \mathbb{E}[\ln A_T] - \mathbb{E}[\ln G_T],$$

and the value of the second term in the right-hand side is independent from investment decisions. Hence, the utility-maximising policy is independent from the choice of G_T. Thus, we can assume without loss of generality that $G_T = 1$ in the design of the strategy.

We let $\widetilde{F}_t$ denote the present value of the goal to secure, and since the essential goal represents a floor, we refer to the goal-hedging portfolio (GHP) as the FHP. We also assume that the initial wealth is such that $A_0 \geq \widetilde{F}_0$, an assumption which is required for the goal to be affordable. Proposition 12 implies that the optimal strategy is to take a long position in the optimal unconstrained strategy and an insurance put. But with $\gamma = 1$, the optimal strategy is given by Equation (3.16). Hence, the optimal policy is given by the formula

$$\underline{w}_t^{*\text{Gs}} = \frac{\lambda_{\text{MSR},t}}{\sigma_{\text{MSR},t}}\psi_t\underline{w}_{\text{MSR},t} + (1 - \psi_t)\underline{w}_{\text{FHP},t}, \qquad (3.17)$$

where

$$\psi_t = 1 - \frac{p_{t,T}\widetilde{F}_t}{A_t},$$

and $p_{t,T}$ is the probability for the bucket invested in the MSR portfolio to underperform the floor (see Section 3.2.2.3). This probability is a function of model parameters, in particular of the risk premia and the goal volatility, with a detailed expression given in Proposition 12. This creates dependency with respect to the model and to unobservable parameters. In order to avoid this additional source of complexity, we suggest setting the probability equal to 100%, which implies more conservative (i.e. lower) risk budgets than if the actual probability was taken. A simplified version of the strategy is thus

$$\underline{w}_t = \frac{\lambda_{\mathrm{MSR},t}}{\sigma_{\mathrm{MSR},t}}\left(1 - \frac{\widetilde{F}_t}{A_t}\right)\underline{w}_{\mathrm{MSR},t} + \frac{\widetilde{F}_t}{A_t}\underline{w}_{\mathrm{FHP},t}. \qquad (3.18)$$

One can obtain a more general family of strategies by replacing the coefficient $\lambda_{\mathrm{MSR},t}/\sigma_{\mathrm{MSR},t}$ by a multiplier m, which controls the allocation to the MSR. Note that in implementation, the multiplier can be time-varying, in response to changes in the estimated values for the Sharpe ratios and volatilities.

We make two additional practical modifications to the optimal strategy (3.17). First, we consider a more general version, where the performance block is not necessarily the MSR portfolio, but some performance-seeking portfolio based on the principles listed in Section 2.5.2 of Chapter 2. Second, we take the weight of the FHP to be 1 minus the weight of the PSP. This ensures that the resulting portfolio contains no short or long cash holdings, in addition to cash that can be held in the personal risk bucket for hedging purposes.

We thus finally obtain the following strategy:

$$\underline{w}_t^{\mathrm{GBI,SH}} = m\left(1 - \frac{\widetilde{F}_t}{A_t}\right)\underline{w}_{\mathrm{PSP},t} + \left[1 - m\left(1 - \frac{\widetilde{F}_t}{A_t}\right)\right]\underline{w}_{\mathrm{FHP},t}. \qquad (3.19)$$

We refer to this strategy as the GBI strategy protecting the goal F_T. It can be regarded as an extension of the CPPI strategies studied by Black and Jones (1987) and Black and Perold (1992), the floor being the present value of the goal to secure and the safe asset being replaced here by the FHP. In implementation, a no short-sales constraint in the PSP and FHP blocks will be enforced. Indeed, for high multiplier values and large risk budgets, the allocation to the PSP prescribed by Equation (3.19) can be larger than 100%. The detailed expression of weights is given in Appendix A.6.3.

Strategy (3.19) can be regarded as the simplest form of strategy combining the PSP and the FHP in which the allocation to the FHP becomes 100% as wealth approaches the floor. The optimal strategy in Equation (3.14) has this property, too, but the dependence of weights with respect to current wealth and the floor is more complicated and nonlinear, due to the presence of the probabilities $p_{t,T}$. In contrast, the dollar amount invested in the FHP with Equation (3.19) is simply a linear function of the wealth and the floor. When the multiplier m is taken to be equal to 1, we recover as a special case the buy-and-hold strategy in which any excess of liquid wealth (that is excluding wealth in the aspirational risk bucket) remaining available after all essential goals have been secured through investments in dedicated hedging portfolios is invested in the well-diversified performance seeking portfolio.

At this stage, one can ask whether it would have been possible to further simplify the optimal strategy while securing the floor. Although it is not possible to give a general form for the weights of all portfolio strategies which secure a goal, there are many functional forms to achieve this property (see Section 3.2), and the utility-maximising rule allows us to identify one such strategy, but it involves a nonlinear function of the wealth and the floor. Strategy (3.19) removes this nonlinearity.

Another advantage of strategy (3.19) over the one in Equation (3.17) is that it involves only observable quantities, at least to the extent that the present value of the goal is observable. Indeed, the evaluation of the probabilities $p_{t,T}$ requires the knowledge of the full distributions of PSP and floor values. This estimation is unnecessary to implement strategy (3.19).

3.3.2.2. *Wealth-based goal with multiple horizons*

Consider now the case where the goal to secure is a wealth-based one with multiple horizons. Section 3.2.2 does not provide a utility-maximising strategy for this goal, but we construct a strategy combining the PSP and a safe asset according to the same principles as in the case of a single horizon. First, the safe asset must secure the goal. By Proposition 3, the FHP is a roll-over of exchange options, and the discussion in Section 2.2.1.2 of Chapter 2 shows that it actually super-replicates the floor: indeed the FHP value at each goal horizon is greater than the goal value. Second, the allocation to the PSP should vanish as wealth approaches a floor. The present value of the goal is a natural choice for the floor here for two reasons: first, it is the choice of floor already made in the case of the single horizon; second, the present value of a goal with multiple horizons is the minimum capital to invest in order to secure the goal. Having made this choice of floor, we define the risk budget as the distance between wealth and the floor, and the dollar amount allocated to the PSP is a multiple of the risk budget. Thus, the GBI strategy for a wealth-based goal with multiple horizons has exactly the same form as (3.19)

$$\underline{w}_t^{\text{GBI,MH}} = m\left(1 - \frac{\widetilde{F}_t}{A_t}\right)\underline{w}_{\text{PSP},t} + \left[1 - m\left(1 - \frac{\widetilde{F}_t}{A_t}\right)\right]\underline{w}_{\text{FHP},t}. \quad (3.20)$$

Again, short-sales constraints will be applied in this strategy.

Again, Strategy (3.20) has the form of a CPPI: the floor is $\widetilde{F}_t$, which coincides with the price of an exchange option between two horizons, and the safe asset is the FHP, which is a roll-over of exchange options. It should be noted that the risk budget, $RB_t = m(A_t - \widetilde{F}_t)$, is discontinuous on the dates $T_1, \ldots, T_p$: it is because wealth is continuous, but the goal present value is not (see Section 2.2.1.2 of Chapter 2).

Unlike the one in Equation (3.19), the strategy in Equation (3.20) is not entirely model-free because the risk budget involves the price of an exchange option. But under the monotony assumption of goal values made in Corollary 1, the option price coincides at each date with the present value of the next goal value, so an option pricing model is not necessary.

It makes intuitive sense that strategy (3.20) secures the wealth-based goal. Indeed, the allocation to the PSP shrinks to zero as wealth approaches the present value of the goal, so the portfolio becomes fully invested in the FHP, which super-replicates the goal. The following proposition formally shows that this intuition is correct and that the goal is indeed secured.

Proposition 15 (Protection of Essential Wealth-Based Goal by GBI Strategy). *Consider a wealth-based goal F_T with multiple horizons. Then, if the initial wealth satisfies $A_0 \geq \widetilde{F}_0$, where $\widetilde{F}_0$ is defined in Definition 3, the strategy in Equation (3.20) secures the goal, that is we have*

$$A_{T_j} \geq F_{T_j}, \quad \text{for } j = 1, \ldots, p.$$

Proof.   See Appendix A.4.1.   □

Proposition 15 gives a theoretical justification for the use of the GBI strategy (3.20). By varying the multiplier m, one obtains a class of risk-controlled strategies which secure the essential goal. But there is an important restriction to the result of Proposition 15: it holds under the assumption that the portfolio is rebalanced continuously. In real-world applications, trading is discrete, which may cause gap risk to arise: it is the risk for wealth to fall below the floor if the PSP severely underperforms the GHP between two rebalancing dates, and this risk becomes more important if the allocation to the PSP is large, hence if the multiplier is large.[6]

3.3.2.3. *Consumption-based essential goal*

In the case of a consumption-based goal, the utility-maximising strategy takes a simpler form than for a wealth-based goal because it involves no unobservable quantity such as the probability $p_{t,T}$. With $\gamma = 1$, Proposition 14 implies that it is given by

$$\underline{w}_t^{*c} = \frac{\lambda_{\text{MSR},t}}{\sigma_{\text{MSR},t}} \left(1 - \frac{\widetilde{G}_t}{A_t} \right) \underline{w}_{\text{MSR},t} + \frac{\widetilde{G}_t}{A_t} \underline{w}_{\text{GHP},t},$$

where $\underline{w}_{\text{GHP},t}$ is the portfolio fully invested in the bond with coupons matching the consumption expenses. Again, replacing the MSR by a more generic PSP, the ratio $\lambda_{\text{MSR},t}/\sigma_{\text{MSR},t}$ in front of the MSR weights by a generic multiplier m, and removing cash from the portfolio, we obtain the following implementable version of the optimal strategy:

$$\underline{w}_t^{\text{GBI},c} = m \left(1 - \frac{\widetilde{G}_t}{A_t} \right) \underline{w}_{\text{PSP},t} + \left[1 - m \left(1 - \frac{\widetilde{G}_t}{A_t} \right) \right] \underline{w}_{\text{GHP},t}.$$

$$(3.21)$$

As for the wealth-based goals, this strategy has the form of a CPPI, the floor being the present value of the forthcoming consumption expenses and the safe asset being the bond with coupons matching the expenses. This strategy does secure the goal, as shown by the following proposition. The proof is given in Appendix A.4.2.

---

[6]However, gap risk is limited to the case where $m > 1$. Indeed, one can show that strategy (3.20) implemented in discrete time with short-sales constraint on the PSP and the GHP is such that $A_t \geq \widetilde{F}_t$ for all t. In particular, it secures the goal.

Proposition 16 (Protection of Essential Consumption-Based Goal by GBI Strategy). *Consider a consumption-based goal represented by the payments* $(c_{T_1}, \ldots, c_{T_p})$. *Then, if the initial wealth satisfies* $A_0 \geq \widetilde{G}_0$, *where* $\widetilde{G}_0$ *is the present value of the payments, the strategy* (3.21) *secures the goal, that is we have*

$$A_t \geq 0, \quad \text{for all } t \text{ in } [0, T].$$

Appendix A.6.3 describes the short-sales constraints applied to the portfolio at the implementation stage.

3.3.2.4. *Multiple essential goals*

The utility-maximising strategies presented in Section 3.2 are obtained under the assumption that there is a single goal. Thus, an adaptation is needed to handle several essential goals. Consider first the case of two wealth-based goals. As explained in Section 2.2.3.1 of Chapter 2, two wealth-based goals can be reduced to a single goal by taking the maximum of the two minimum wealth levels. Thus, one option would be to convert the two goals to a single one and to compute the corresponding GBI strategy following Equation (3.20). While perfectly justified in theory, this approach raises practical difficulties, relating notably to the pricing of the exchange option between the two goals. In particular, the pricing exercise can only be carried out within the context of a particular model, which makes the strategy dependent on a number of unobservable parameters. We thus take a different approach, by taking as a floor the maximum of the two floor values, and as a safe asset the GHP which corresponds to the higher floor. This strategy relies on the simple intuition that the floor which is more likely to be breached is the higher one, so that it makes sense to favour the protection of this floor. The maximum is re-evaluated on each rebalancing date, so the strategy switches from one GHP to the other.

Mathematically, let $\widetilde{F}_{1t}$ and $\widetilde{F}_{2t}$ be the two floor values on date t, and denote the two GHPs by $\underline{w}_{\text{FHP1}}$ and $\underline{w}_{\text{FHP2}}$. The floor of the strategy is

$$\widetilde{F}_t = \max\left(\widetilde{F}_{1t}, \widetilde{F}_{2t}\right),$$

and the FHP can be written as

$$\underline{w}_{\text{FHP},t} = \mathbb{I}_{\{\widetilde{F}_{1t} > \widetilde{F}_{2t}\}} \underline{w}_{\text{FHP1},t} + \mathbb{I}_{\{\widetilde{F}_{1t} \leq \widetilde{F}_{2t}\}} \underline{w}_{\text{FHP2},t},$$

where $\mathbb{I}_{\{\tilde{F}_{1t} > \tilde{F}_{2t}\}}$ is the indicator function of the event that $\tilde{F}_{1t} > \tilde{F}_{2t}$: it is 1 if floor 1 is (strictly) greater and 0 otherwise. The GBI strategy has the form

$$\underline{w}_t^{\text{GBI,MG}} = m\left(1 - \frac{\tilde{F}_t}{A_t}\right)\underline{w}_{\text{PSP},t} + \left[1 - m\left(1 - \frac{\tilde{F}_t}{A_t}\right)\right]\underline{w}_{\text{FHP},t}.$$

(3.22)

Though it may seem heuristic, this investment policy can be justified to some extent by computing the portfolio that replicates the maximum of two floors at horizon T: Deguest, Martellini and Milhau (2014) perform this computation under the assumption that both floors follow Geometric Brownian motions, which leads to a closed-form expression for the price of the exchange option. The option price is not simply the maximum of the two floor values, but if one floor is much larger than the other, then the option price approaches the larger floor value. In this case, the portfolio that dynamically replicates the option also approaches the corresponding GHP. These two properties are also verified by the above floor value and FHP. Hence, $\tilde{F}_t$ and $\underline{w}_{\text{FHP},t}$ can be regarded as model-free proxies for the option price and dynamic replication strategy.

The specification (3.22) can clearly be extended beyond two wealth-based goals. It can be applied to consumption-based as well as wealth-based goals, and to an arbitrary number of goals, by taking the maximum over more than two floor values.

3.3.2.5. *Imposing a cap*

As discussed in Section 3.2.2.5, imposing a cap enables investors to capture a greater fraction of the performance of the unconstrained strategy. This suggests that the probability of reaching high wealth levels can be improved by imposing a maximum wealth level. When the risk aversion parameter is 1, Proposition 13 implies that the optimal strategy with a floor and a cap is

$$\underline{w}_t^{*C} = \frac{\lambda_{\text{MSR},t}}{\sigma_{\text{MSR},t}}\left[1 - \frac{p_{F,t,T}\tilde{F}_t + p_{C,t,T}\tilde{C}_t}{A_t}\right]\underline{w}_{\text{MSR},t} + \frac{p_{F,t,T}\tilde{F}_t}{A_t}\underline{w}_{\text{FHP},t}$$

$$+ \frac{p_{C,t,T}\tilde{C}_t}{A_t}\underline{w}_{\text{CHP},t},$$

the coefficients $p_{F,t,T}$ and $p_{C,t,T}$ being probabilities, the vector $\underline{w}_{\text{FHP},t}$ being the FHP and $\underline{w}_{\text{CHP},t}$ being the CHP.

It would not be appropriate to simplify this expression by taking both probabilities to be equal to 100%, because the strategy must respect the property that the allocation to the FHP (respectively, the CHP) approaches 1 when wealth approaches the floor (respectively, the cap), and that the allocation to the PSP vanishes in these two cases. In other words, one has to find coefficients $x_{\text{PSP},t}$, x_{Ft} and x_{Ct} such that the strategy

$$\underline{w}_t^{\text{GBI,cap}} = x_{\text{PSP},t}\underline{w}_{\text{PSP},t} + x_{Ft}\underline{w}_{\text{FHP},t} + x_{Ct}\underline{w}_{\text{CHP},t} \tag{3.23}$$

has the aforementioned properties. A simple functional form for $x_{\text{PSP},t}$ guaranteeing that the allocation to the PSP becomes zero when wealth approaches the floor or the cap is

$$x_{\text{PSP},t} = m \times \frac{RB_t}{A_t},$$

where the risk budget is computed as $RB_t = A_t - \widetilde{F}_t$ when wealth is below the threshold

$$\xi_t = \frac{\widetilde{F}_t + \widetilde{C}_t}{2},$$

and as $RB_t = \widetilde{C}_t - A_t$ when wealth is above ξ_t. To ensure that the portfolio coincides with the FHP when wealth approaches the floor, we take $x_{Ft} = 1 - x_{\text{PSP},t}$ when wealth is below ξ_t, and $x_{Ft} = 0$ otherwise. Symmetrically, we set $x_{Ct} = 1 - x_{\text{PSP},t}$ when wealth is above ξ_t, and $x_{Ct} = 0$ otherwise.

When wealth is below the threshold, the allocation to the PSP and the FHP are given by the same formulas as in the GBI strategy that protects a floor, regardless of the presence of the cap (Equation (3.19)). When wealth is above the threshold, the portfolio rule is also similar to a CPPI, but the risk budget is computed as cap minus wealth, as opposed to being equal to wealth minus floor.

Having recognised that imposing a cap may be useful in some contexts, it remains to fix its level. This choice is more arbitrary than for floors: a floor is a minimum wealth level to protect, which is an input from the individual investor, but the cap does not correspond to an observable parameter. An option consistent with the expected utility paradigm is to set the cap equal to a wealth level that achieves satiation of investor's preferences: thus, the cap value on a date t (i.e. the quantity denoted $\widetilde{C}_t$ above) can be the present value of the highest goal formulated by the investor.

3.3.2.6. *Impact of income*

As explained in Section 2.2.4 of Chapter 2, the presence of non-portfolio income decreases the minimum capital to invest in order to secure a goal. The general principle is that consumption expenses should be primarily financed with income, and that liquid wealth should be used only to finance the gap, if any, between consumption and income.

Let us consider the retirement problem already discussed in Section 2.2.4.6 of Chapter 2: the investor receives income during the first part of his life, and consumes more than what he earns during the second part (the retirement period). In order to secure the goal, he must be able to purchase on the retirement date a bond with cash flows equal to the consumption expenses. Thus, the consumption goal translates into a wealth-based goal with a horizon equal to the retirement date. If there were no income prior to retirement, the GHP to purchase at date 0 would be the bond itself. But in the presence of income, purchasing the bond at date 0 would consume an unnecessarily large fraction of liquid wealth and would leave little money available to invest in performance-seeking assets. The result would be a lower expected return on the liquid portfolio. The opportunity cost of this strategy can be measured as the difference between $\widetilde{G}_0$, which is the amount effectively dedicated to the goal protection, and V_0, which is the minimum capital required to secure the goal.

Minimising the cost of the protection is a valuable effort because it leads to the largest access to the upside of performance assets, i.e. assets that are not used for hedging purposes. But the cheapest strategy, which is introduced in Proposition 8, involves a series of compound options. Since these options are unlikely to exist, one may consider replicating them through a dynamic strategy, but this requires the calculation of their price and Greeks, which is a complex task given the nested nature of the payoffs. In the case of the retirement goal (which will be considered in Section 4.3 of Chapter 4), a possible way out is the strategy INC-ZER-RET described in Section 2.2.4.6 of Chapter 2. It consists in securing at date 0 the positive part of the difference between the minimum level of wealth to attain at the retirement date and the sum of the income payments that will be received by then, while leaving the rest of the money available for investing in performance assets. At each income date, an inflow is cashed in, and the allocation decision made at date 0 is repeated: the floor to secure is now the positive part of the difference between the minimum wealth at retirement and the sum of the forthcoming income payments. Using the same notations as in Section 3.2.2.6, we have that the wealth between dates T_j and T_{j+1} is

$$A_t = (A_{T_j} - W_{T_j,j})A_{\text{PSP},t} + W_{t,j}, \quad \text{for } T_j \leq t < T_{j+1}.$$

In this expression, $W_{t,j}$ is the price at date t of the option with maturity date T_r and payoff

$$W_{T_r,j} = \left[\widetilde{G}_{T_r} - \sum_{k=j+1}^{r} y_{T_k} \right]^+.$$

This simple option is in principle easier to price than a compounded one, which facilitates dynamic replication.

A more extreme approach is to choose to secure the goal by using liquid wealth only, without relying on future income. Although it is extremely conservative, as argued previously, it may be preferred to a strategy that partially relies on income to secure the goal in contexts where future income is too uncertain. Indeed, if future income cannot be guaranteed (e.g. because of the possibility of a job loss), the investor may prefer to secure the goal with liquid wealth only, and the framework introduced in this book can be used to provide an estimate for the implied opportunity cost in terms of the probability of achieving important and aspirational goals.

3.3.3. *Protecting essential goals in the presence of taxes*

An overview of the tax issue was given in Section 2.3 of Chapter 2. In this section, we discuss the important question of protecting an essential goal in the presence of taxes. Indeed, because they represent constrained payments, taxes can cause deviations from the objectives if they are not anticipated. As explained in Section 2.3 of Chapter 2, a distinction must be made between taxes from cash flows such as dividends and coupon payments and taxes from capital gains. Indeed, the former are easily predictable while the latter depend on rebalancing decisions that will take place in the future and are more difficult to forecast accurately.

3.3.3.1. *Taxes on cash flows*

A typical situation that will be encountered in the case studies of Chapter 4 is that of an investor with a consumption goal represented by the payments $c_{T_1}, \ldots, c_{T_p}$ on dates $T_1, \ldots, T_p$. In the absence of taxes, the GHP would be a bond with coupons equal to the target payments. If the coupons are taxed at the rate ζ, this GHP no longer secures the goal, as the investor will receive an after-tax payment of $(1-\zeta)c_{T_j}$ at date T_j. But it suffices to purchase $1/(1-\zeta)$ units of this bond to anticipate the taxes and fully secure the goal. This amounts to raising the price of the GHP, a simple adjustment that virtually cancels out the effect of taxes. Note that this technique applies both to constant and stochastic consumption expenses. But of course, it increases the initial capital requirement, so that depending on how high the tax rate is, a goal that would be affordable in the absence of taxes might become non-affordable when bond coupons are taxed.

3.3.3.2. *Taxes on capital gains*

Taxes on capital gains cannot be anticipated in the same way as taxes on cash flows because the amount of taxes due at the fiscal year end depends on the transactions performed within the entire year: on a given date, the amount of trading that will be performed in the future is not known, which makes it impossible to compute an expected value of the final payment.

A simple way to avoid taxes on capital gains is to avoid any rebalancing, i.e. to take only buy-and-hold positions in the assets subject to taxation. It should be noted that if the investor takes a buy-and-hold position in some building block which itself involves rebalancing in the taxable assets, he will pay taxes on these operations: indeed, the portfolio is buy-and-hold at the building block level, but not at the taxable asset class level. To take a concrete example, an investor may implement a GBI strategy like the one described by

Equation (3.21) in order to protect a consumption-based goal and take the multiplier m equal to 1. The portfolio is buy-and-hold in two building blocks, namely the PSP and the GHP, which is a bond with coupons equal to the consumption expenses. While being buy-and-hold at the building block level, the portfolio may involve rebalancing if the PSP is itself a rebalanced portfolio, e.g. a fixed-mix portfolio of the constituents, with weights chosen to maximise the long-term Sharpe ratio. The fixed-mix nature of the portfolio implies counter-cyclical rebalancing: constituents will be sold if they go up in order to maintain constant weights. This is likely to generate capital gains, hence taxes.

If a GBI strategy involves rebalancing between building blocks (the case where $m > 1$), there will be a second source of taxes. Due to the pro-cyclical nature of the strategy, the tax payments generated by the selling operations in the PSP should in principle be lower than those generated by the fixed-mix rebalancing within this block. Indeed, the idea of the strategy is to reduce the exposure to the PSP if the risk budget shrinks down, which will in general coincide with a market downturn: in this context, the PSP will have negative returns, which decreases the amount of taxes to pay. Nevertheless, the tax payment is still positive.

It is unclear how to design a GBI strategy that protects an essential goal despite the presence of taxes on capital gains, but one can propose an ad-hoc adjustment to the weights designed to limit the frequency and the size of deviations from the goal. The motivation is as follows. A GBI strategy of the form given in Equation (3.19) for a wealth-based goal, or Equation (3.21) for a consumption-based goal, aims at keeping wealth above a floor, which is the minimum capital required to secure the goal. If wealth becomes exactly equal to the floor, the portfolio gets entirely invested in the GHP, which guarantees success in reaching the goal. But in the presence of taxes, having wealth just equal to the goal present value is not enough to ensure a perfect protection: indeed, future taxes will decrease wealth, possibly below the goal present value. Thus, the idea is to raise the floor in order to acknowledge the presence of taxes. Ideally, one would want to increase the floor by an amount equal to the present value of the year-end tax payment, but this expected value depends on future rebalancing decisions, a complex dependency given the nonlinearity of the tax payment with respect to portfolio weights (see Appendix A.6.5 for detailed formulas). A more tractable option is to increase the floor by a tax provision equal to the amount of taxes generated by the transactions that have taken place since the beginning of the year. The risk budget is thus computed as

$$\text{RB}_t = A_t - \Theta_t - \widetilde{EG}_t^1,$$

where Θ_t is the tax provision.

In Chapter 4, we will test these various adjustments to GBI strategies to see their impact on the chances to reach essential or non-essential goals.

3.4. Inputs and Outputs of the Framework

The above framework proposes a classification of goals based on their funding status and the investor's preferences regarding their protection. It also leads to a number of strategies designed to secure essential goals and to achieve the non-essential ones with high probabilities. In Section 3.4.1, we review the inputs required for a proper implementation of the framework. Section 3.4.2 surveys the main expected outputs.

3.4.1. *Inputs*

We first summarise the inputs of the framework, which can be classified as subjective inputs (to be obtained from the individual investor) versus objective inputs (to be specified by the portfolio advisor).

3.4.1.1. *Subjective inputs: Investor's goals and risk allocation*

As explained in Section 2.3 of Chapter 2, the categorisation of goals is a combination of investors' views and a formal analysis of whether these goals are affordable. The discussion leading to the analysis of the affordability of the goals *a priori* set by the investor is a key ingredient in the process of designing an investment solution in wealth management because it results in a well-defined list of goals to be formally treated as essential.

It should also be noted that the classification of goals is subject to periodic revisions. Indeed, the funding status of a goal (i.e. its affordability or non-affordability) depends on its present value, thus on market conditions and notably on interest rates, and the investor's current wealth. Moreover, the investor's priorities may vary over time. For instance, a birth in the investor's family may give rise to a new goal, which is saving for financing education. Another example is the following: if wealth has increased substantially since the initial date, an investor may wish to secure a higher wealth level, that is, introduce a new higher level of essential or important goal.

The decision to turn a formerly important goal into an essential one is the result of a comparison between the benefits drawn from the action of securing the target wealth or consumption level, and the associated opportunity cost that it implies given that a lower amount of risk-taking eventually results in lower probabilities of reaching ambitious aspirational goal levels. Hence, every so often (say every year), the investor is expected to meet with the advisor and revise the *updated* list of goals, with an indication of which of the affordable goals, if any, should be treated as essential goals.

3.4.1.2. *Objective inputs: Parameter values*

Once goals have been identified, it is necessary to sort them as affordable versus non-affordable. The affordability criteria depend on the wealth-based or consumption-based nature of the goal (see the propositions given in Section 2.2). All of them require at some stage the computation of the present value of the goal (with a proper adjustment for income payments when the investor perceives non-portfolio income). It should be emphasised that these results are established in a very general context, with only minimal assumptions of uncertainty in the economy: no particular set of risk factors and no particular dynamics for interest rates, risk premia and volatilities have been assumed.

For a wealth-based goal with a unique horizon, the present value is simply the discounted minimum wealth level, and for a consumption-based goal, it is the sum of discounted cash flows. These values can be directly obtained from the current zero-coupon yield curve (nominal yield curve for fixed cash flows and real yield curve for inflation-linked cash flows). For instance, the present value of a consumption-based goal on date t will be computed as

$$\widetilde{G}_t = \sum_{T_j > t} \frac{c_t}{(1 + y_{t,T_j - t})^{T_j - t}},$$

where y_{t,T_j-t} is the zero-coupon rate of maturity $T_j - t$ prevailing at the date where the present value is computed.

Zero-coupon curves are available at high frequencies (such as daily) for large sovereign issuers. They are constructed from the observed prices of sovereign bonds. Because there exists in general no zero-coupon for each cash-flow maturity, the zero-coupon rates needed to discount the cash flows are not readily observable, but they can be recovered by bootstrapping or interpolation methods. For instance, the use of the Nelson–Siegel model for the yield curve represents a zero-coupon rate as the sum of three contributions from a level, a slope and a curvature factor (see Nelson and Siegel, 1987). In the end, discount rates are observable given knowledge of the current yield curve. Since the cash flows are specified by the investor, it follows that the present value of a consumption-based goal is observable, too.

Restricting the discussion to interest rate risk for the moment, we therefore conclude that the knowledge of the current yield curve is in general sufficient to qualify the affordability of a goal. On the other hand, a dynamic model for the yield curve is required to simulate the subsequent performance of a GBI strategy through Monte-Carlo generated scenarios. For instance, the equilibrium models such as those of Vasicek (1977) and Cox, Ingersoll and Ross (1985) lead to expressing each zero-coupon rate as a function of the maturity, the current value of a factor (here, the short-term interest rate), and a set of parameters that govern the dynamics of the factor. It is also possible to use a two- or three-factor model (see e.g. Duffee, 2002 for a general presentation of affine models with multiple factors). The increased number of factors implies a higher flexibility of the model, but a greater amount of estimation risk. Such models require the estimation of the factor values and of the parameters that describe the evolution of the factors.

On any particular date, one natural approach is to calibrate the model, required to perform Monte-Carlo simulation needed to estimate probabilities of achieving goals, by minimising the model pricing errors, that is, the distance between market prices and model-implied prices for a set of reference instruments. The calibration has to be performed on each date where the present value needs to be evaluated, which produces time-varying estimates for parameters, even though the model may assume that the true parameters are constant. This is similar to the extraction of implied volatilities from the Black–Scholes option pricing model, which itself assumes a constant volatility for the underlying.

An alternative approach consists of estimating, as opposed to calibrating, the parameters of the model. This can be done via various statistical techniques, which include likelihood maximisation, Kalman filtering or generalised methods of moments (see Duffee and Stanton, 2012, for a survey of these methods). By combining cross-section and time-series information, these techniques improve the statistical efficiency of parameter estimates. In the case studies presented in Chapter 4, given that we do not refer to any particular date at which a calibration exercise can be performed, we have chosen to derive the yield curve from a term structure model with parameters estimated over 50 years of data, so as to capture the long-term behaviour of interest rates. As a result, the parameters that we use in the simulation exercise are not intended to be consistent with a particular yield curve. But when the reported probabilities of reaching goals are tied to a specific point in time, the calibration procedure that is solely based on current market information should be preferred.

We emphasise again in closing that the simplified forms of GBI strategies analysed in this book are based on observable quantities, and their implementation is therefore not subject to model or parameter risk. The specification of a model, and the associated parameter values, is only needed to compute probabilities of achieving non-essential goals. In other words, the benefits of the framework, including the ability to secure essential goals with 100% probability while generating a substantial access to the upside potential of performance-seeking assets, is extremely robust with respect to model and parametric assumptions. What is more subject to model and parametric assumptions is the quantitative assessment of probabilities of reaching a given important or aspirational goal.

3.4.2. *Outputs*

The framework is meant to be used both as an engineering tool for generating meaningful portfolio advice as well as a tool for facilitating the dialogue with the investors, and provides a set of subjective outputs (probability of reaching goals and associated expected shortfall) as well as objective outputs (allocation recommendations at all points in time).

3.4.2.1. *Success indicators for goals*

For a given allocation strategy (e.g. a fixed-mix rebalancing towards the investor's current allocation), it is possible to obtain a set of success indicators for the various goals. The following list gives examples of indicators that are useful to report:

- The success probability for a goal is the probability of achieving this goal (at all horizons for a goal with multiple horizons).
- The expected maximum shortfall (abbreviated as expected shortfall) is computed as follows: first, we evaluate the shortfall with respect to the goal at each goal horizon; second, we take the maximum shortfall over all horizons; third, we compute the expectation of this maximum conditional on the event that at least one loss was recorded across horizons.
- The worst maximum shortfall is computed in the same way as the previous indicator, but the expectation in the final step is replaced by a maximum over all states of the world.

When the investor is also concerned with drawdown risk, i.e. the risk of experiencing losses above a certain threshold, it is useful to add two other indicators:

- The expected maximum drawdown is obtained in two steps: first, the maximum drawdown is computed along each path; second, the expectation is taken.
- The worst maximum drawdown is computed by taking the maximum over all possible paths in the second step.

Formal definitions of these indicators are given in Appendix A.6.4.

Because they are estimated by simulating future portfolio performance, the values of these indicators depend on the assumptions made regarding the future performance of the various assets and the evolution of the risk factors which impact goal values (including notably interest rate and inflation). As indicated above, the various risk and return parameters can be re-estimated on each date, in order to generate updated success indicators.

Another type of useful output of the framework is an *ex-ante* measure of the opportunity cost associated with a given essential goal. It can be measured as the additional required amount of initial wealth needed to be generated when the goal is secured the same probability of reaching an aspirational goal as when the goal is treated as important rather than essential, and is therefore not secured. One can in fact draw a distinction between two measures of opportunity cost, one related to the opportunity cost of the goal when it is optimally managed via a suitably defined GBI strategy, and one related to the higher additional cost involved when the goal is managed via some less efficient strategy, like the investor's current allocation. As a result, this analysis will not only allow the individual investor to assess the cost-and-benefit trade-off associated with setting various levels of essential goals; it will also allow him to measure the decrease in opportunity costs implied by the use of an efficient GBI strategy.

3.4.2.2. *Allocation recommendations*

Based on their funding status and investor's priorities, the framework enables to categorise goals as essential, important and aspirational. In order to be admissible, a strategy has to secure all essential goals, that is, it must yield a 100% probability of reaching them.

Besides, this 100% probability must be robust to the choice of the model and the parameter values. For instance, one might find that under the assumption of a sufficiently high equity risk premium and with a sufficiently long horizon, a stock index has a 100% probability of reaching a certain level. But the strategy of investing in the stock only is not a reliable one to secure the goal because the realised return may significantly differ from the assumed expected return. Thus, the 100% probability is model- and parameter-dependent. We require instead strategies which secure essential goals for any choice of model and parameter values. For instance, the GBI strategy in Equation (3.20) is suitable to protect a wealth-based goal because Proposition 15 shows that it secures the goal without referring to a particular model. Similarly, by Proposition 16, the GBI strategy in Equation (3.21) secures a consumption-based goal, and this property holds under any model. Hence, these strategies are admissible to secure essential goals.

3.5.　Mass Customisation Constraints

While providing each individual investor with a dedicated investment solution precisely tailored to meet their goals and constraints would

be desirable, and while the proposed goals-based wealth management framework is precisely designed to this end, such a high degree
of customisation would not be consistent with implementation constraints faced by financial advisors. In practice, it would be necessary
to group individual investors in clusters with somewhat similar characteristics, and the outstanding question is whether the benefits of
the framework are robust with respect to such mass-customisation
implementation constraints. To answer this question, it is important
to draw a distinction between the building blocks and the allocation
to the building blocks.

Turning first to the design of the building blocks, we note that
there is a high degree of scalability involved in this process. For
one thing, the composition of the market risk bucket, that is, the
part of the investor's portfolio that is invested in a well-diversified
performance-seeking set of investments, is in principle the same for all
investors. From Modern Portfolio Theory, we know indeed that *different* investors with *different* expected return targets should invest
in different proportions of the *same* two funds, namely the MSR portfolio and cash, with leverage used to achieve expected return targets
that exceed the expected return on the MSR portfolio.

In other words, the best implementation proxy for the
performance-seeking portfolio should in theory be offered to all
investors, so mass customisation would involve no welfare loss at
this level. In practice, however, the situation is somewhat different
because of the presence of frictions such as the presence of short-sale
constraints that justify more than one performance-seeking portfolio is needed to reach target expected return levels that extend
beyond the expected return of the MSR portfolio. In the same vein,
the presence of a home bias or any particular restriction on the
menu of asset classes, could justify that different investors hold different performance-seeking portfolios, but these constraints can be
accommodated by the means of a parsimonious approach involving
a limited number of performance building blocks.

On the other hand, essential goals are specific to each investor,
and the design of an essential GHP should therefore involve a high
degree of customisation. Indeed, the most efficient approach to interest rate risk management, known as cash-flow matching, involves
ensuring a perfect static match between the cash flows from the
asset portfolio and the cash flows required for consumption purposes. This technique, which provides the advantage of simplicity

and allows, in theory, for perfect risk management, has nevertheless at least two main limitations from a practical perspective. First of all, it will generally prove impossible to find fixed-income instruments with maturity dates matching exactly the dates of the pension payments. Moreover, most of those securities pay out coupons, thereby leading to the problem of reinvesting the coupons. To the extent that perfect matching is not possible, financial advisors will have to resort instead to a technique called *immunisation*. Broadly speaking, the key difference is that immunisation strategies aim at matching the factor exposures of the GHP to those of the goal value process, which is a weaker requirement than ensuring a match between cash-flow payments; in other words cash-flow matching obviously implies interest rate exposure matching, while the converse is not true.

The most basic form of implementation of the immunisation approach can be performed in terms of duration matching, but the interest rate risk management technique extends to more general contexts, including, for example, hedging larger changes in interest rates (through the introduction of a convexity adjustment) or hedging against changes in the shape of the yield curve (see, for example, Fabozzi, Martellini and Priaulet (2005) for interest rate risk management in the presence of non-parallel yield curve shifts). It should be noted that these approaches can be implemented in principle either via cash instruments, typically sovereign bonds, or via derivatives such as interest rates swaps or futures contracts, even though the former approach is likely to be the preferred option in wealth management.

In conclusion, regarding the design of hedging portfolios for essential goals, it appears from the previous discussion that financial advisors can implement GBI strategies in a robust way provided they have access to a series of bond portfolios (ideally with both a nominal and real versions available), with a limited number of target durations extending from the shortest to the longest durations, which can be used in most cases as reasonable proxies for GHPs. As a result, mass customisation can perfectly be applied with respect to the choice of the building blocks needed to implement GBI strategies. In an implementation stage, the appropriate granularity in terms of numbers and types of underlying building blocks can easily be assessed in terms of increases in probabilities of failing essential goals due to imperfect proxies for GHPs, with a key trade-off between increasing accuracy in implementing dedicated investment solutions and increasing costs of implementation.

On the other hand, turning from building blocks to allocation to building blocks, we note that it is in general impossible to offer a single strategy that would fit the needs of several investors, even if they were sufficiently similar in terms of their goals to be offered the same menu of goal-hedging building blocks. Indeed, the allocation to the various building blocks typically depends upon ingredients that are specific to each investor, including current wealth levels and distance with respect to wealth- or consumption-based goals.

An outstanding question remains to determine whether a limited number of portfolios can serve as *reasonable proxies* for customised policy portfolios for a multitude of individual investors who might share a number of common characteristics. In particular, it is possible to re-interpret current practices from financial advisors, who use a number of model portfolios (say portfolios with an equity allocation of 20%, 40%, 60%, 70%, 80%, with the rest in bonds or cash) within the context of goals-based wealth management. According to this interpretation, such model portfolios can be regarded as arguably crude proxies for the aggregate wealth allocated to the personal *and* market risk buckets for various kinds of investors who have different levels of attention to essential GHPs, including protection against losses (justifying cash) and/or protection for long-term consumption needs (justifying bonds).

More generally, however, the proper mass-scale implementation of GBI strategies requires a dedicated allocation to a limited number of building blocks, which implies that a critical factor of success is the presence of an information technology system that can effectively process and update the key inputs of the framework at each point in time for each investor.

The critical importance of information systems, as well as technological and transactional ability to implement in a cost-efficient way a large number of trades on behalf of individual investors, for the development of welfare-improving investment solutions has been emphasised by Robert Merton in his Nobel lecture on December 9, 1997: "Deep and widespread disaggregation [of financial services] has left households with the responsibility for making important and technically complex decisions involving risk $\cdots$ decisions that they had not had to make in the past, are not trained to make in the present, and are unlikely to efficiently execute even with attempts at education in the future. Financial engineering creativity, and the technological and transactional bases to implement that creativity, reliably and cost-effectively, are likely to become a central competitive element in the industry."

Chapter 4

Case Studies

In this chapter, we apply the framework to three different case studies that provide a fair representation of the variety of problems possibly encountered in wealth management.

The goal of these case studies is to show that the opportunity costs implied by the need to respect the essential goals are significantly lower when these constraints are optimally addressed through dynamic goals-based investing strategies, as opposed to being inefficiently addressed through excessive hedging and an unconditional decrease of the allocation to risky market and speculative assets. Intuitively, the pre-commitment to reduce the allocation to risky assets in times and market conditions that require such a reduction so as to avoid over-spending risk budgets related to essential goals allows investors to invest on average more in such risky assets compared to a simple static strategy that is calibrated so as to respect the same risk budget constraints.

These insights will be developed on a number of case studies, according to the typical classification of individual investors that involves two main dimensions: life stage and affluence.

One may typically identify three clusters in terms of life stage:

- LS1: Accumulation (age less than 55 years)
- LS2: Transition (age between 55 and 65 years)
- LS3: Decumulation (age higher than 65 years)

One may also identify three main clusters of affluence:

- A1: Mass affluent ($250,000 to $1m).
- A2: Affluent/high net worth (HNW) ($1–5m).
- A3: Ultra high net worth (UHNW) (>$5m).

Crossing these classes defines nine clusters, among which three coarser clusters can be formed:

- C1: Accumulation/transition < $5m (LS1/A1, LS1/A2, LS2/A1, LS2/A2).
- C2: Decumulation < $5m (LS3/A1, LS3/A2).
- C3: UHNW, whatever the life stage (LS1/A3, LS2/A3, LS3/A3).

In what follows, we present three case studies, each one related to one of the three clusters C1, C2, C3, so that our case study selection is as follows:

- **Case 1:** HNW/UHNW Transition — A HNW/UHNW individual with substantial assets in the transition phase. This is a proxy for cluster C1.
- **Case 2:** HNW Retiree — A HNW individual at the beginning of the decumulation/retirement phase. This is a proxy for cluster C2.
- **Case 3:** Affluent Accumulator — An affluent young individual in the middle of the accumulation phase. This is a proxy for cluster C3.

4.1. Case Study 1 (HNW/UHNW Transition)

In this first case study, the investor is an executive with a net worth of $4.5m, holding a substantial concentrated stock position. His highest priority goal is to maintain a minimum net worth of $3m at all times.

4.1.1. *Current allocation and goals*

4.1.1.1. *Description of risk buckets*

The detailed composition of the current risk and asset allocation (through the lens of Wealth Allocation Framework of Chhabra (2005)) is given in Table 4.1. The investor owns a house of value

Table 4.1.   Investor 1 — Current risk and asset allocation and goals.

(a) Risk and asset allocation.

	Value ($)	% of Total		Value ($)	% of Total		Value ($)	% of Total
Personal Bucket	900,000	20.0	Market Bucket	2,150,000	47.8	Aspirational Bucket	1,450,000	32.2
Residence	1,500,000	65.3	Equity	1,500,000	69.8	Concentrated Stock	1,250,000	86.2
Cash	100,000	4.3	US Fixed Income	600,000	27.9	Executive Stock Option	100,000	6.9
Adjustable Rate Mortgage	(700,000)	30.4	Cash	50,000	2.3	Investment Real Estate	100,000	6.9

(b) Goals.

Name	Goal	Time horizon (years)	Threshold
Goal 1 (wealth-based with multiple horizons)	Maintain minimum wealth (within liquid and aspirational)	1–35	$3m (inflation-adjusted)
Goal 2 (wealth-based with multiple horizons)	Avoid large drawdowns (within market)	1–35	15%
Goal 3 (wealth-based with single horizon)	Significantly increase wealth (within liquid and aspirational)	15	$7.2m (inflation-adjusted)

Notes: Panel (a) describes the current risk and asset allocation of Investor 1. Panel (b) describes his goals, which are ranked by order of decreasing priority.

$1.5m, and is repaying a mortgage loan with a face value of $700,000. The personal risk bucket also contains a position of $100,000 in cash. As explained in Section 2.5.1, personal assets play the role of a guarantee for a minimum standard of living. In other words, they serve as collateral against extreme adverse events: the investor does not want his family to end up homeless even in the event of huge losses within the other two buckets (market and aspirational) — hence the home ownership — and he wants to afford a minimum level of consumption — hence the cash reserve. Because of their special status, namely a guarantee for essential needs, the long positions in the house and the personal cash account will be considered as buy-and-hold strategies throughout the case study.

There is also cash in the market bucket (only for a small proportion, of 2.3%), but unlike the previous one, this position is liquid and tradable. The market bucket is otherwise dominated by equities, which represent 69.8% of the allocation, versus 27.9% for US fixed-income instruments. In the remainder of this case study, we will model equity as a broad US stock index, and the fixed-income class as a sovereign bond index (for brevity, we refer to the latter class simply as bonds). The last bucket consists of aspirational assets, that is, assets dedicated to wealth mobility. The dominant asset is a concentrated and illiquid stock position, which represents 86.2% of the current bucket value. Executive stock options and investment real estate account for the remaining 13.8% of aspirational wealth, with equal contributions. One important difference between the market and the aspirational assets lies in their respective liquidity. Indeed, while the equity and bond indices are liquid assets, the investment real estate is subject to significant transaction costs, and it may be difficult to find counterparties for the concentrated stock and the executive stock options. Thus, dynamic trading is conceivable only within the market bucket. On the other hand, the aspirational bucket is either left on buy-and-hold, or liquidated in one time at date 0 (we will study both situations in what follows).

In the absence of information on the fixed rate of the mortgage rate and the amortisation scheme, we abstract away from the presence of this loan within the balance sheet and the budget equations. This means that the annuities (which encompass interest payment and principal repayment) are covered by an exogenous and non-modelled source of income. As a consequence, we take the initial personal wealth to be equal to the sum of the values of the residence and the cash position, that is $A_{\text{per},0} = \$1.6\,\text{m}$.

Liquid wealth is the sum of market wealth and the amount invested in the liquid personal assets: with the current risk allocation, it is equal to market wealth, since none of the assets held within the personal portfolio are liquid. But when we introduce in the personal bucket an asset dedicated to the hedging of an essential goal (i.e. a goal-hedging portfolio), liquid wealth will be the sum of market wealth and the amount invested in the GHP.

For parsimony, we model the values of the residence and the investment property with a single stochastic process Y. Similarly, we use a single process for both the concentrated stock value and the

Table 4.2. Symbols for stochastic processes used in Case 1.

Symbol	Definition
t	Current date.
S_t	Equity index value.
B_t	Bond index value.
S_{0t}	Value of cash account.
Y_t	Real estate value (residence or investment real estate).
X_t	Illiquid stock value (concentrated stock price and executive stock option).
Φ_t	Price index.
$A_{per,t}$	Personal wealth.
$A_{mkt,t}$	Market wealth.
$A_{asp,t}$	Aspirational wealth.
$A_{liq,t}$	Liquid wealth.

Notes: This table contains the definitions of the mathematical symbols used in Case 1. All these symbols will be used again with the same meanings in Case Studies 2 and 3. Subscript t refers to the value of a process at date t.

executive stock option, which we gather under the name of "illiquid stock value".[1] This process is denoted by X, and we model it as a stochastic process with the same expected return as the stock index (12%), but with twice higher volatility (39.8% versus 19.9%).

Table 4.2 summarises our notations for the various stochastic processes (these notations will also apply to the other case studies). They are consistent with those of Section 2: wealth is still denoted by A_t, and we use sub-indices to make a distinction between personal, market and aspirational wealth. For notational clarity, we use different letters for asset prices, as opposed to denoting them with $S_{1t}, S_{2t}, \ldots$ The dynamics of the processes and the parameter values are given in Appendix A.5.

We report in Table 4.3 descriptive statistics on the simulated returns of the risky assets, because they are useful to interpret some of the results that follow. The average annual return, the volatility and the maximum drawdown are first evaluated in each of the 10,000

---

[1]Alternatively, one could derive the value of the stock option from an option pricing model (e.g. the Black–Scholes model).

Table 4.3.   Descriptive statistics on risky assets.

Process	Expected return	Volatility	Maximum drawdown
Stock	0.12	0.199	0.463
Bond	0.051	0.083	0.218
Real asset	0.063	0.141	0.402
Illiquid stock	0.12	0.398	0.861
Roll-over of 1-year indexed bonds	0.057	0.02	0.019
Price index	0.025	0.013	—

Notes: All statistics are first computed in each of the 10,000 simulated paths, and the 10,000 values thus obtained are averaged to produce the numbers shown in the table. Statistics are computed from monthly logarithmic returns, and expected returns and volatilities are expressed in annual terms. Expected returns are corrected for Jensen's inequality (i.e. one half of the variance is added to the mean logarithmic return). The equations governing the evolution of the processes and the associated parameter values are given in Appendix A.5.

scenarios, and the values are then averaged across scenarios to obtain the numbers in the table. The values are ordered as expected: the equity index and the illiquid stock have the highest expected returns (12%), but also the highest volatilities (19.9% and 39.8%) and the highest maximum drawdowns (46.3%, and a large 86.1% for the illiquid stock).

4.1.1.2. *Description of goals*

Goals are summarised in Table 4.1. The highest priority goal is Goal 1 (G1): it is a wealth-based goal that consists of ensuring that the sum of liquid and aspirational wealth never falls short of $3m. This level is adjusted for inflation, which means that the minimum value in year t is

$$G_t^1 = G_0^1 \times \frac{\Phi_t}{\Phi_0}, \quad t = 1, \ldots, 35.$$

(By convention, G_t^1 is zero if t is distinct from $1, \ldots, 35$.) In this equation, Φ denotes the price index and G_0^1 is the real-value of the goal, which is $3m. The ratio Φ_t/Φ_0 represents realised inflation between years 0 and t. In what follows, we shall normalise the current price index to 1, so we will omit the Φ_0 in the denominator. With the previous notation, G1 can be formally expressed as

$$A_{\text{liq},t} + A_{\text{asp},t} \geq G_t^1, \quad \text{for } t = 1, \ldots, 35.$$

Goal 2 (G2) is a wealth-based goal that applies to liquid wealth only: liquid wealth is the sum of market wealth and the capital invested in the GHP, and the objective is to protect at least 85% of the maximum liquid wealth ever attained. Denoting the maximum-to-date of wealth by $\overline{A}_{\text{liq},t}$, we can express this objective as

$$A_{\text{liq},t} \geq (1 - \delta)\overline{A}_{\text{liq},t}, \quad \text{for } t = 1, \ldots, 35,$$

with $\delta = 15\%$.

Finally, the third goal (G3) is to double the sum of current liquid and aspirational wealth in real terms within the next 15 years. Mathematically, this objective can be written as

$$A_{\text{liq},t} + A_{\text{asp},t} \geq G_t^3, \quad \text{for } t = 15,$$

$$G_t^3 = G_0^3 \times \frac{\Phi_t}{\Phi_0},$$

with $G_0^3 = \$7.2\text{m}$.

4.1.1.3. *Funding status of goals and goal-hedging portfolios*

For G1, a necessary and sufficient affordability criterion is given by Proposition 3. However, as explained in Section 2.2.1.2, the criterion takes a simple form if the 1-year real rate is non-negative at all dates. We explicitly impose this condition of non-negative 1-year real rates in our simulations.[2] Under these conditions, Corollary 1 shows that the present value of the goal, i.e. the minimum capital to invest in order to secure G1, is

$$\tilde{G}_0^1 = G_0^1 \times \exp[-x_{0,1}^r].$$

(We recall that $x_{t,1}^r$ denotes the 1-year real rate at date t.) By Proposition 3, a strategy that secures G1 consists in investing $\tilde{G}_0^1$ in a rollover of 1-year indexed bonds that pay G_0^1 plus realised inflation at

---

[2]We do this by imposing a floor on the nominal short-term rate in the simulations (see Appendix A.5 for details). If a lower floor, or no floor at all, is imposed, then negative 1-year real rates can occur, and the roll-over strategy does not reach G1 with probability 1.

the end of each year. The value of the GHP for G1 is the value of this roll-over. If $I_{s,t}$ is the price at date s of the indexed zero-coupon that pays Φ_t at date t, we have, by Equation (6)

$$\text{GHP}_{G1,s} = \exp\left[\sum_{u=1}^{t-1} x_{u,1}^r\right] \times G_0^1 \times I_{s,t},$$

$$\text{for } t - 1 < s \leq t \text{ and } t = 1, \ldots, 35,$$

$$\text{GHP}_{G1,0} = \tilde{G}_0^1. \tag{4.1}$$

Thus, G1 is affordable if, and only if, the investor is able to invest $\tilde{G}_0^1$ in the roll-over strategy. Given our parameter values, the constraint of a non-negative real rate is binding at date 0 in the simulations, so $\tilde{G}_0^1$ is simply the face value of the goal, namely \$3m. Thus, the minimum capital requirement to secure G1 is \$3m.

For the G3, the minimum capital to invest is given by Proposition 1: it is the price of an inflation-indexed zero-coupon bond that pays \$7.2m plus inflation in 15 years. Our parameter values imply that the price is \$4,810,724.

Table 4.4 summarises the investor's balance sheet. The asset side consists of market and aspirational assets and the liability side contains the goals. It appears that G1 cannot be secured with current market wealth only, but would be affordable if aspirational assets could be liquidated: indeed, current market wealth is less than the face value of G1, but the sum of market and aspirational wealth levels is greater. So, G1 is part of the maximum set of affordable goals. In what follows, we treat it as an essential goal, i.e. as a goal that the investor would like to secure, and we refer to it as essential goal 1 (EG1).

In contrast, G3 cannot be funded with current assets: even if aspirational assets can be liquidated, the indexed zero-coupon bond that secures this goal is not affordable. Hence, G3 cannot be treated as an essential or important goal, and will therefore be categorised as an aspirational goal (AG). The last line of Panel (ii) is the translation of Proposition 5 in the context of the case study: the minimum capital needed to secure two wealth-based goals is greater than or equal to the maximum of the two minimum capital requirements.

Finally, the drawdown-based goal (G2) is affordable regardless of the initial wealth, as a consequence of Proposition 3: it suffices to liquidate the current market bucket and to re-invest it in

Table 4.4. Investor 1 — Funding status of exogenous goals.

(i) Values of assets (in $).

Market wealth	2,150,000
Aspirational wealth	1,450,000
Total	**3,600,000**

(ii) Minimum capital required to secure one or more exogenous goal(s) (in $).

Goal 1	3,000,000
Goal 3	4,810,724
G1 and G3	**≥4,810,724**

Notes: The assets of Investor 1 consist of liquid market assets and less liquid aspirational assets. Panel (ii) shows the minimum capital required to secure the two exogenous goals, defined as the goals with levels independent from investment decisions made by the individual: G1 is to maintain a minimum level of wealth of $3m plus inflation over the next 35 years, and G3 is to double the sum of market wealth and aspirational wealth at the 15-year horizon. Goals are ranked by order of decreasing priority.

cash only, which guarantees that market wealth keeps growing. The categorisation of this goal as essential, important or aspirational, depends on whether it is jointly affordable with EG1. If it is, then it is part of the maximum set of affordable goals, and can thus be treated as essential or important, depending on whether or not the investor wants to secure it. Otherwise, it has to be considered an aspirational goal. The question is thus whether G2 can be secured along with EG1. The results that follow show that there do exist strategies that secure both goals: for instance, the GHP for EG1 or the cash account (see Section 4.1.2.4), and a dynamic GBI strategy that aims to protect the maximum of two floors (see Section 4.1.3.3). These results confirm that G2 is jointly affordable with EG1. As a consequence, there are two possible statuses for this goal: essential or important. We will treat it as essential, that is, as a goal that the investor would like to secure: it will be referred to as EG2.

As a conclusion:

• If aspirational assets are illiquid (i.e. cannot be liquidated at the initial date), G1 cannot be secured and must therefore be regarded as an aspirational goal;

- If aspirational assets are liquid, G1 is affordable and is treated as an essential goal;
- G3 cannot be secured, whether aspirational assets are liquid or not, and will be treated as an aspirational goal;
- G2 is affordable, and moreover it can be secured together with EG1. Therefore, it will be treated as an essential goal.

In what follows, we look in detail at the success indicators for various strategies.

4.1.2. Static strategies

Static strategies are defined as strategies with weights that do not depend on current wealth, as opposed to GBI strategies, which will be tested in what follows.

4.1.2.1. Current strategy and impact of liquidity of aspirational assets

The "current strategy" is defined as a fixed-mix strategy that would maintain the same weights of equity, bond and cash as today, with an annual rebalancing frequency. For this strategy as well as for the subsequent ones, we compute a number of "success indicators" which quantify the degree of achievement of goals. The values of these indicators are shown in Figure 4.1. It appears that the current strategy has a probability of 40% of missing EG1. Since this goal is said to be "essential", this is a serious concern for the investor. Moreover, the expected shortfall for this goal is relatively large, around 20%, and in the worst case, the gap between wealth and the goal value can be as high as 80% of the goal value. One might argue that the investment strategy cannot be blamed in itself for this poor result, because current market wealth is too low to secure EG1 (see Table 4.1). This argument is admissible, because by absence of arbitrage, it is impossible to reach a goal with certainty if wealth is too low, whichever strategy is taken. To see whether an increase in market wealth would lead to better success chances, we recalculate the success indicators by assuming that aspirational assets are liquidated at the initial date, and that the proceeds are re-invested in the market assets, with the same breakdown of weights as in the current market bucket. Figure 4.1 shows that although EG1 can now be secured, the shortfall

Figure 4.1. Investor 1 — Success indicators with current strategy and illiquid aspirational assets.

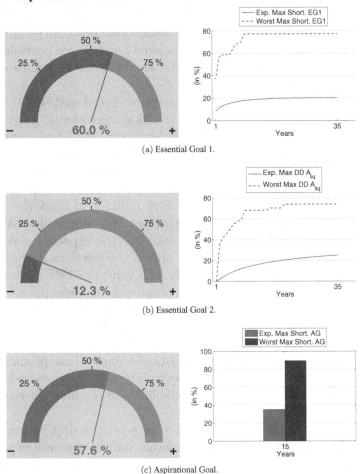

(a) Essential Goal 1.

(b) Essential Goal 2.

(c) Aspirational Goal.

Notes: The half circles represent the success probabilities for each goal: it is estimated as the percentage of scenarios in which the goal was reached. For wealth-based goals (EG1 and AG), the expected maximum shortfall on date t is the expectation of the value of the maximum relative loss recorded by date t, conditional on the event of a loss. The worst maximum shortfall is defined as the worst relative loss recorded by date t across all dates and paths. For the drawdown goal (EG2), the expected maximum drawdown on date t is the expected value of the maximum drawdown recorded by date t, and the worst maximum drawdown is the worst drawdown recorded by date t across all dates and scenarios. The "current strategy" is a fixed-mix policy with annual rebalancing towards the current market allocation. Aspirational assets are regarded as illiquid.

probability for EG1 is 21.4%, which is lower than in the illiquid case, but still far from 0: so, the investor has a significant probability of not having the desired minimum wealth level. That EG1 is not secured with the current asset allocation comes as no surprise, since the investor has no inflation-indexed bonds in his portfolio, but the numbers reported here show that shortfall risk is quantitatively important.

The success indicators for the drawdown-based goal (EG2) are by construction independent from the initial market wealth: indeed, the maximum drawdown of a fixed-mix strategy (and, more generally, for any strategy whose weights do not depend on wealth) is independent of the initial investment. Thus, the success indicators are the same whether aspirational assets are liquid or not. As appears from Figure 4.1, the current strategy is very unlikely to meet the objective of a 15% maximum drawdown, and high levels of maximum drawdown are to be expected: for instance, the expected maximum drawdown after 35 years is 25.2%, and in the worst case, the maximum drawdown takes the extremely high value of 73.9%. These high drawdown levels are due to the high proportion of stocks (69.8%): this asset class has the highest maximum drawdown among the market assets, and its weight is never revised, regardless of market conditions. Finally, Figures 4.1 and 4.2 show that the current strategy has more than 50% of chance to reach AG. Although these probabilities may seem attractive as far as a secondary goal is concerned, they do not compensate for the low probabilities of reaching the essential goals.

We next investigate the existence of a relationship between the probability of reaching high wealth levels and the presence of aspirational assets. Indeed, the expected returns on the aspirational assets may make them attractive for wealth mobility, although the aspirational bucket is not meant to be a well-diversified portfolio in the sense of Modern Portfolio Theory. First, Figure 4.3 shows the distribution of market plus aspirational wealth, expressed in real terms, (i.e. divided by the price index) after 15 years. It should be emphasised that the total wealth on date 0 is the same in both cases, so the total wealth levels after 15 years can be compared with each other. The presence of aspirational assets clearly spreads the distribution: the minimum (0.76m of today's dollars) is slightly lower than when the aspirational bucket is liquidated ($1.20m), but

Figure 4.2.   Investor 1 — Success indicators with current strategy and liquid aspirational assets.

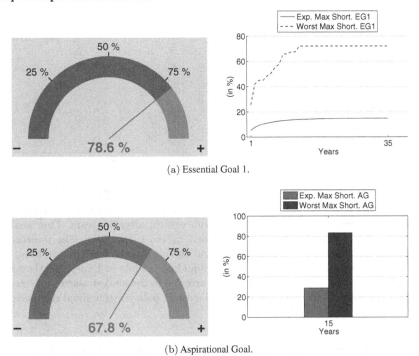

(a) Essential Goal 1.

(b) Aspirational Goal.

Notes: The definition of success indicators is given in the caption of Figure 4.1. The "current strategy" is a fixed-mix policy with annual rebalancing towards the current market allocation. Aspirational assets are liquidated at date 0, and the proceeds are re-invested in the market assets, with the same weights as in the initial market bucket. By construction, the success indicators for EG2 are the same as in the illiquid case (Figure 4.1), so they are not reported here.

the maximum of the distribution is much higher ($504.75m versus $93.01m). The larger span of the distribution in the illiquid case is of course due to the high volatility of the illiquid stock (39.8%). On the other hand, the median of the distribution slightly increases when aspirational assets are sold out (from $8.27m to $9.38m), which means that wealth levels around this median are more likely to be reached if aspirational wealth is re-invested in the market assets. As a conclusion, the presence of aspirational assets increases the uncertainty over future wealth levels, but it helps to attain "very ambitious" wealth levels, which otherwise would be out of reach (here,

Figure 4.3.   **Investor 1 — Impact of liquidity of aspirational assets on distribution of total wealth.**

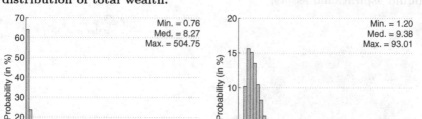

(a) Illiquid aspirational assets   (b) Liquid aspirational assets

Notes: This figure shows the distribution of total wealth, which is defined as the sum of market wealth and aspirational wealth, after 15 years. This wealth is expressed in real terms, i.e. it is divided by the price index. The indicators reported are the minimum, the median and the maximum of the distribution. In Panel (a), aspirational assets cannot be liquidated, while in Panel (b), they are liquidated at date 0, with the proceeds re-invested in the market assets. The strategy is the "current strategy", which is a fixed-mix policy with annual rebalancing towards the current market allocation.

the wealth levels comprised between \$93.01m and \$504.75m).[3] Figure 4.4 provides further evidence of the link between the performance of aspirational assets and the success chances for AG: it compares the success probability for this goal when the expected return of the illiquid stock equals that of the equity index (that is, $\mu_X = 12\%$), and when it is twice as high ($\mu_X = 24\%$). The second situation can model a private business with a very high expected return. The impact has the expected direction and it is substantial: the probability shifts from 57.6% to 81.9%.

---

[3]In unreported results, we have computed the success probabilities for a "very ambitious" aspirational goal, which would be to multiply the sum of market wealth and aspirational wealth by 10 in real terms at the 15-year horizon (the investor's AG is to multiply wealth by 2 only). This probability is 1.1% if one gives up aspirational assets, and 4.8% if they are kept in the portfolio.

Figure 4.4. Investor 1 — Impact of illiquid stock performance on probability of reaching aspirational goal.

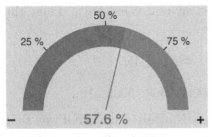

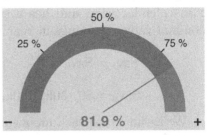

(i) Base case performance (12%/year)   (ii) Higher performance (24%/year)

Notes: This figure shows the probability of reaching the aspirational goal for two values of the expected return on the illiquid stock (parameter μ_X): 12% (the base case value, which is a reminder of Figure 4.1), and 24%. The strategy is the "current strategy", which is a fixed-mix policy with annual rebalancing towards the current market allocation.

In summary, if aspirational assets are not liquidated and the current market allocation is kept as it is today (in the form of a fixed-mix policy), the investor has substantial probabilities of being short each of the two essential goals. The probability of reaching EG1 increases if the aspirational bucket is liquidated, but remains low in view of the essential nature of this goal. These low success probabilities for essential goals are not compensated by the rather good success probabilities for AG.

Because EG1 cannot be secured with the current market wealth alone, we focus in what follows on the situation where aspirational assets are liquidated at the initial date, and we consider the illiquid case as a robustness check. Thus, unless otherwise stated, the investor's initial liquid wealth is

$$A_{\text{liq},0} = A_{\text{mkt},0} + A_{\text{asp},0} = \$3.6\text{m}.$$

4.1.2.2. *Impact of savings*

Intuition suggests that the probability of success for the various goals can be improved by saving money. To give a quantitative assessment of this effect, we introduce a non-portfolio income stream in the dynamics of market wealth. This stream occurs at the end of each calendar year, and has a constant real value Sav_0. Thus, the nominal value of savings in year t is

$$\text{Sav}_t = \text{Sav}_0 \times \frac{\Phi_t}{\Phi_0}, \quad \text{for } t = 1, \ldots, 35,$$

$$\text{Sav}_0 = \$0, \ 50\text{k}, \ 100\text{k}, \ 200\text{k}, \ 250\text{k}, \ 500\text{k}, \ 1\text{m}.$$

We assume that each money inflow is invested in such a way that the weights in stocks, bonds and cash remain the same immediately after the payment as before (see Appendix A.6 for formal expressions).

Figure 4.5 displays success indicators for the various goals. The expected shortfall is the expectation of the maximum shortfall recorded across goal horizons, conditional on the event of a shortfall; and the expected maximum drawdown is the expectation of the maximum drawdown recorded over 35 years. Of course, the numbers obtained for zero annual savings are identical to those reported in

Figure 4.5. Investor 1 — Impact of annual savings on success indicators.

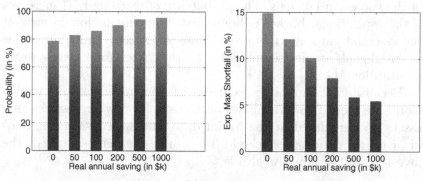

(a) Essential Goal 1.

Notes: Investor 1 saves an amount of money equal to $0, 50k, 100k, 200k, 500k or 1m plus inflation at the end of each year, and these savings are re-invested in the market assets. Aspirational assets are liquidated at date 0, and the proceeds are re-invested in stocks, bonds and cash. The strategy implemented here is the "current strategy", which is a fixed-mix policy with annual rebalancing towards the current allocation. The left column shows the success probabilities for investor's goals as a function of annual savings, and the right column shows the expected maximum shortfall for goals EG1 and AG, and the expected maximum drawdown (see the caption of Figure 4.1 for the definition of the success indicators).

Figure 4.5. (*Continued*)

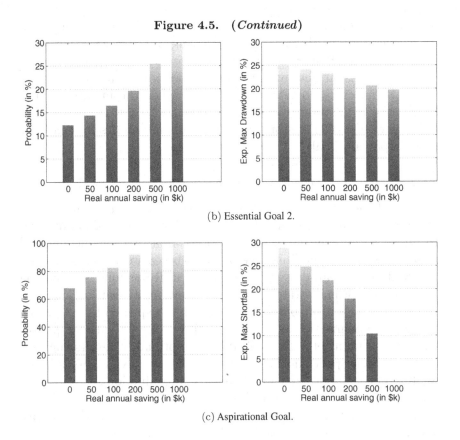

(b) Essential Goal 2.

(c) Aspirational Goal.

Figure 4.2. Unsurprisingly, higher savings imply higher chances to reach each goal, and lower average deviations from the targets. For instance, when savings grow from 0k to $200k, the success probability for EG1 grows from 78.6% to 90%, and the expected shortfall decreases from 14.9% to 7.94%. Nevertheless, the shortfall risk does not completely disappear, even for a level of savings of $1m per year, a huge level compared to the investor's current wealth, which is $4.5m including the personal risk bucket.

For the drawdown-based goal (EG2), the situation is worse, because the probability of keeping the drawdown below 15% remains capped at 29.6%, a value attained only with the unrealistic level of $1m of savings per year. The expected maximum drawdown is still 19.7% in this case. Hence, the drawdown of the portfolio is not under

control. It is only for the aspirational goal that the success probability reaches 100% with $1m of annual savings, but this does not make
up for the high chances of missing the essential goals.

As a conclusion, the current strategy does not reach essential goals
with a satisfactory confidence level, even when the investor infuses
substantial amounts of money into his market portfolio every year.
In other words, the investor cannot rely only on savings to secure the
most important goals.

4.1.2.3.   *Using diversification: MSR strategy*

In view of the impossibility of securing essential goals with the current strategy, one can think of using scientific diversification in order
to improve the chances of success. This approach can be justified
to some extent by the literature on goals-based wealth management
(see Section 4.3.2 au-dessus). Indeed, the MSR portfolio is a building
block of the optimal strategies for many optimality criteria: maximisation of success probability, minimisation of expected time to reach
the goal, maximisation of expected utility with or without performance constraint, etc. This collection of optimality results suggests
that the MSR portfolio has merits in the context of goals-based
wealth management, and motivates the introduction of a strategy
that invests only in this portfolio.

Constructing an MSR portfolio requires the knowledge of risk
and return parameters. The introduction of parameter uncertainty
is beyond the scope of this book, so we assume that these quantities
are perfectly known to the investor. However, this assumption does
not sound realistic for aspirational assets, which have low liquidity
and for which it may be difficult or impossible to find enough historical data to perform a reliable estimation. Thus, we only consider
an MSR portfolio of the equity and bond indices, and we leave the
aspirational bucket outside the optimisation. The parameter values
given in Appendix A.5 imply that the percentage weights of the MSR
portfolio in the equity and bond indices are

$$\underline{w}_{\mathrm{MSR}} = \begin{pmatrix} 0.8042 \\ 0.1958 \end{pmatrix}.$$

This allocation is different from the current allocation to stocks
and bonds. Indeed, after removing the leverage effect in the market

bucket, the stock weight is $0.698/(0.698 + 0.279) = 0.714$. We thus consider a fixed-mix strategy that maintains constant weights within the market bucket. We do monthly rebalancing: this is a relatively high frequency, but this choice prevents the weights from drifting too far away from the target. A first observation from Figure 4.6 is that the benefits of diversification are not sufficient to reach EG1 with certainty. The success probability (74.5%) is even slightly lower than with the current strategy (78.6%, in Figure 4.2). This arises because the MSR portfolio contains a lower fraction of bonds than the current market bucket (19.6% versus 27.9%): indeed, bonds, even though they are fixed-income securities, are better proxies than stocks for the roll-over of 1-year indexed bonds that secures EG1. The success probability for EG2 is also lower than with the current strategy (5.9% versus 12.2% in Figure 4.1): again, this is an effect of the higher stock weight in the MSR portfolio (the equity index has higher maximum drawdown than the bond index). This higher stock allocation also accounts for the higher probability of reaching AG.

Overall, scientific diversification implemented through a maximum Sharpe ratio portfolio does not enable the investor to secure essential goals such as protecting a minimum level of real wealth and avoiding large drawdowns. It should be noted that this result has nothing to do with imperfect parameter estimation, which is one of the main concerns raised by the implementation of mean–variance efficient strategies. The reason for the lack of success in reaching essential goals is simply that the construction process of the well-diversified portfolio does not explicitly aim at avoiding losses.

4.1.2.4. *Using hedging: Safe strategies*

In order to make sure that EG1 is attained with probability 1, we consider a strategy that fully invests in the roll-over of 1-year indexed bonds. Because aspirational assets are liquidated at date 0, the initial wealth ($3.6m) exceeds the goal face value ($3m). Section 4.1.1.2 shows that in this context, the roll-over policy secures EG1. In other words, the portfolio is not well diversified in the sense of mean–variance theory (because it is invested in a single asset and does not target any risk–return trade-off), but it is safe with respect to EG1: hence, it can be called a hedging portfolio. The success indicators reported in Figure 4.7 show that not only is EG1 secured, as

Figure 4.6. Investor 1 — Success indicators with maximum Sharpe ratio portfolio.

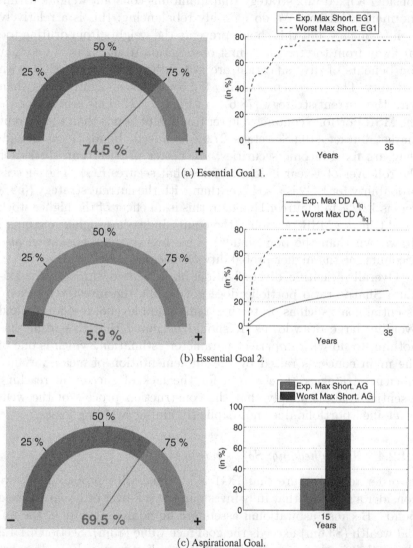

(a) Essential Goal 1.

(b) Essential Goal 2.

(c) Aspirational Goal.

Notes: Aspirational assets are liquidated at date 0, and the proceeds are re-invested in stocks and bonds. The strategy implemented here is a fixed-mix policy with monthly rebalancing towards the maximum Sharpe ratio allocation. The left column shows the success probabilities for the goals, and the right column displays the expected maximum shortfall for goals EG1 and AG, and the expected maximum drawdown (see the caption of Figure 4.1 for the definition of the success indicators).

Figure 4.7. Investor 1 — Success indicators with strategy safe for EG1.

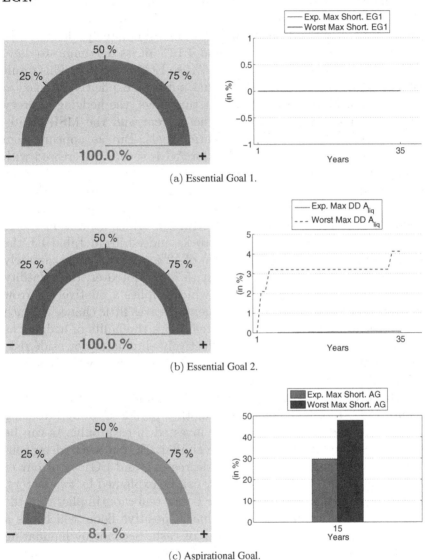

(a) Essential Goal 1.

(b) Essential Goal 2.

(c) Aspirational Goal.

Notes: Aspirational assets and existing positions in stocks and bonds are liquidated at date 0. The safe strategy is a roll-over of 1-year inflation-indexed bonds (see description in Section 4.1.1.2). The left column shows the success probabilities for the goals, and the right column displays the expected maximum shortfall for goals EG1 and AG, and the expected maximum drawdown (see the caption of Figure 4.1 for the definition of the success indicators).

was expected, but EG2 is reached with certainty, too. That is not to say that the roll-over has no drawdown risk at all, but it turns out that the worst maximum drawdown after 35 years is only 4.12%: this means that over the 35 years and across all simulated paths, the roll-over strategy never loses more than 4.12% of its maximum-to-date. This value lies comfortably below 15%, so EG2 is secured. This result is interesting because the roll-over has not been explicitly designed to ensure the achievement of EG2. At this stage, the hedging strategy represents an improvement over the current and the MSR strategies, in that it secures both essential goals. But as appears from Figure 4.7, the success probability for AG is severely decreased with respect to the other two strategies: it falls to 8.1% only, while the current and the MSR strategies displayed probabilities of 67.8% and 69.5%, respectively. The reason for this sharp decrease is that the roll-over is a rather conservative strategy, which invests in assets with lower expected returns than stocks: indeed, from Table 4.3, the equity index has an expected return of 12% per year, approximately twice as high as that of the roll-over (5.7%). Moreover, the volatility is low (only 2% for the roll-over), which implies a relatively narrow distribution for wealth, and consequently, leaves little chance to reach high wealth levels. This analysis exemplifies the limits of hedging as a risk management technique: it effectively eliminates downside risk, but does so at an exceedingly high opportunity cost, which compromises the ability to reach ambitious goals.

The previous strategy favours EG1 *ex-ante*, and turns out to secure EG2, too. One could take another perspective, by favouring EG2. This leads to a safe strategy invested in cash only. As can be seen on Figure 4.8, the results are similar. EG2 is secured by construction (the value of cash never decreases), and EG1 turns out to be secured, too. The latter property can be explained by two factors. First, the condition of non-negative 1-year real rates implies that the short-term rate cannot be lower than a positive floor, which has a positive impact on the performance of cash. Second, by liquidating the aspirational assets, one starts with an initial wealth of $3.6m, well above the face value of EG1, which is $3m: the difference of $600,000 provides a safety margin to absorb large positive inflation shocks. As a result, investing in cash secures EG1. But the upside potential of this second safe strategy is not much better than that of

Figure 4.8. Investor 1 — Success indicators with strategy safe for EG2.

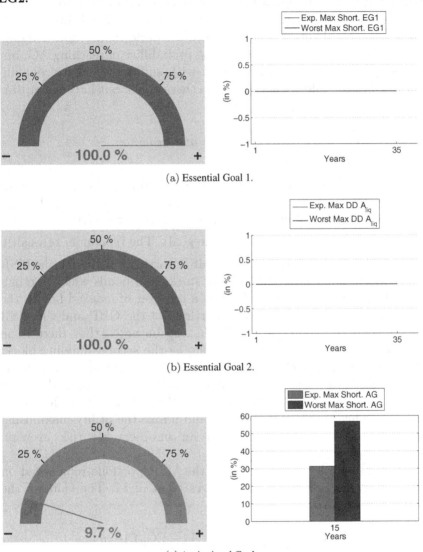

(a) Essential Goal 1.

(b) Essential Goal 2.

(c) Aspirational Goal.

Notes: Aspirational assets and existing positions in stocks and bonds are liquidated at date 0. The safe strategy is invested in cash only. The left column shows the success probabilities for the goals, and the right column displays the expected maximum shortfall for goals EG1 and AG, and the expected maximum drawdown (see the caption of Figure 4.1 for the definition of the success indicators).

the first one: the probability of reaching AG is only 9.7%, and the expected shortfall with respect to this goal is also close to 30%.

As a conclusion, the comparison between the MSR and the safe strategies highlights a trade-off between performance and hedging: the MSR strategy has an interesting probability of reaching AG, but does not attain the essential goals with sufficiently high probabilities, while the safe strategies secure these goals, but have low upside potential.

4.1.2.5. Combining diversification and hedging: Buy-and-hold strategy

Given the aforementioned trade-off, it is natural to seek to combine the respective advantages of the MSR portfolio and the GHP. Indeed, EG1 can be secured by purchasing one share of the GHP, which has a cost $\widetilde{\mathrm{EG}}_0^1$ (the present value of the goal). The remainder of wealth, $[A_0 - \widetilde{\mathrm{EG}}_0^1]$, is then invested in the MSR portfolio. Although the MSR portfolio is a fixed-mix portfolio of stocks and bonds which is rebalanced every month and the GHP is a roll-over of indexed bonds, the mixture strategy regarded as a portfolio of the GHP and the MSR portfolio is buy-and-hold. It should also be noted that there is no obligation to take the MSR portfolio as the second building block: for instance, this block could be fully invested in stocks, or it could be the result of an expected utility maximisation performed without the goal. The reason why we choose the MSR portfolio is that this building block has theoretical grounds, and unlike the utility-maximising policies, it does not depend on an unobservable risk aversion parameter.

Let $A_{\mathrm{MSR},t}$ denote the value of the MSR portfolio rebalanced on a monthly basis with an initial investment of \$1. The value of the buy-and-hold strategy is thus

$$A_{\mathrm{liq},t} = \mathrm{GHP}_{\mathrm{EG1},t} + (A_0 - \widetilde{\mathrm{EG}}_0^1)A_{\mathrm{MSR},t}.$$

Of course, for this quantity to be greater than $\mathrm{GHP}_{\mathrm{EG1},t}$, it is necessary to have $A_0 \geq \widetilde{\mathrm{EG}}_0^1$. This condition is satisfied since we have assumed that aspirational assets are liquidated at date 0. However, the amount of money invested in the MSR building block strategy is low, since the price of one share of the GHP represents a significant

Table 4.5. Investor 1 — Initial risk allocation with buy-and-hold strategy securing EG1.

	Value ($)	% of Total		Value ($)	% of Total		Value ($)	% of Total
Personal Bucket	3,900,000	86.7	Market Bucket	600,000	13.3	Aspirational Bucket	0	0
Residence	1,500,000	28.3	Equity	482,534	80.4			
Cash	100,000	1.9	US Fixed Income	117,466	19.6			
GHP EG1	300,000	56.6						
Adjustable Rate Mortgage	700,000	13.2						

Notes: This table shows the weights at date 0 of the buy-and-hold strategy that secures EG. The personal risk bucket contains assets that are used to finance the investor's implicit or explicit essential goals: the residence secures the goal of not being homeless, the cash reserve secures the goal of being able to afford a minimum standard of living, and the GHP is a roll-over of 1-year indexed bonds that secures EG1. The aspirational bucket contains in principle illiquid and concentrated positions held for wealth mobility purposes. It is empty here, as these positions are liquidated at date 0. The market bucket contains all other assets (equities and bonds here). The table displays the weights of the various assets within each bucket, as well as the relative weights of the buckets.

proportion of initial wealth. We have

$$A_{\text{liq},0} = \$3.6\text{m}, \quad \widetilde{\text{EG}}_0^1 = \$3\text{m},$$

so that only \$600,000 are invested in the MSR portfolio. In this context, we expect the buy-and-hold strategy to be closer to the safe strategy than to the MSR one, and hence to be a conservative policy.

The initial weights of the buy-and-hold strategy are shown in Table 4.5, and can be compared with those of the current strategy, in Table 4.1. For both strategies, the personal risk bucket contains the residence and the cash reserve, which serve to fund the implicit goals. But while the current allocation does not involve any asset dedicated to the protection of EG1, the buy-and-hold strategy assigns a positive weight to the GHP: since the role of this asset is to secure an essential goal, it is included in the personal bucket. It even turns out to be the dominant asset in this bucket, since it represents 56.6% of personal wealth. The conservative nature of the buy-and-hold strategy is reflected in the fact that the safety assets that constitute the personal bucket account for 86.7% of total wealth, while the market bucket represents only 13.3%.

Figure 4.9 confirms that the strategy resembles the safe strategy more than the MSR one. First, EG1 is secured, as it should be, due to the buy-and-hold position in the GHP. Second, drawdown risk is slightly higher than with the safe strategy (see Figure 4.7 for a comparison): the expected maximum drawdown over the 35 years is 5.57%, versus 1.91% for the roll-over. Moreover, some of the drawdowns exceed the 15% threshold, so that the success probability for EG2 falls from 100% to 93.4%: this is still a large probability. Finally, the success probability for AG is 27.4%, which is between the values obtained with the GHP (8.1%) and the MSR portfolio (69.5%).

Overall, the buy-and-hold strategy secures EG1, and gives success probabilities for EG2 and AG that lie between those of the separate building blocks. But EG2 is not fully secured although it is essential: there remains a 6.6% failure probability. Moreover, the probability of reaching AG seems low compared to what can be achieved with the MSR portfolio. This observation leads to the idea to test alternative strategies that still secure EG1 and improve the success indicators for the other two goals.

4.1.3. *Goals-based investing strategies*

In this section, we turn to the implementation of GBI strategies as described in Section 4.3.3.2.

4.1.3.1. *Goals-based investing strategy securing EG1*

The GBI strategy that we implement here is an adaptation of the one described in Equation (3.20). The difference between this equation and the strategy that we actually test is that we impose short-sales constraints and we take into account the possibility of floor violations caused by gap risk. The strategy has the same form as a CPPI, with the GHP playing the role of the safe asset and the MSR that of the performance asset. As follows from the discussion in Section 3.3.2.1, the floor is the present value of the goal, that is

$$\widetilde{\text{EG}}_s^1 = \text{EG}_0^1 \times I_{s,t}, \quad \text{for } t-1 < s \leq t \quad \text{and} \quad t = 1, \ldots, 35,$$

$$\widetilde{\text{EG}}_0^1 = \text{EG}_0^1 \times I_{0,1},$$

Figure 4.9. Investor 1 — Success indicators with buy-and-hold strategy securing EG1.

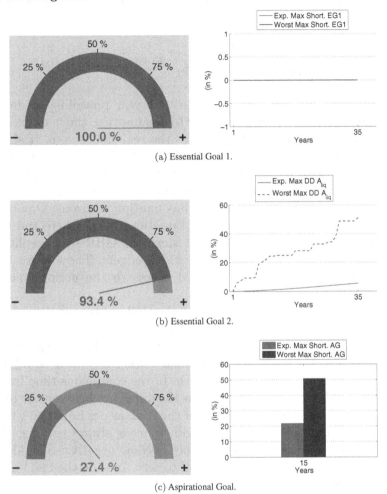

(a) Essential Goal 1.

(b) Essential Goal 2.

(c) Aspirational Goal.

Notes: Aspirational assets and existing positions in stocks and bonds are liquidated at date 0, and the proceeds are re-invested in a buy-and-hold strategy that secures EG1. This strategy invests an amount $\widetilde{\mathrm{EG}}_0^1$ in a roll-over of 1-year indexed bonds ($\widetilde{\mathrm{EG}}_0^1$ being the price at time 0 of the indexed zero-coupon that pays \$3m plus realised inflation after 1 year), and the remainder of wealth in the MSR portfolio. The MSR building block is rebalanced on a monthly basis. The left column shows the success probabilities for the goals, and the right column displays the expected maximum shortfall for goals EG1 and AG, and the expected maximum drawdown (see the caption of Figure 4.1 for the definition of the success indicators).

$I_{s,t}$ being the price of the indexed bond that pays Φ_t at the end of year t. This floor is discontinuous at the end of each year. Indeed, we have

$$\frac{\widetilde{EG}^1_{t+}}{\widetilde{EG}^1_t} = \frac{EG^1_0 \times I_{t,t+1}}{EG^1_0 \times \Phi_t} = \exp[-y^r_{t,1}],$$

where $y^r_{t,1}$ is the real rate of maturity 1 year prevailing at date t. Because real rates are non-negative by assumption, the floor exhibits a negative jump on this date, unless the real rate is zero. It should be noted that the floor is distinct from the GHP value, which is a difference with respect to a standard CPPI, where the safe asset replicates the goal value. The discrepancy between the two values comes from the fact that the goal has multiple horizons. One could envision an alternative version of Equation (3.20) where the floor is taken to be the GHP value, but since the GHP super-replicates the floor, this would lead to lower risk budgets. These lower budgets would likely result in reduced access to the performance of the MSR.

The next step in the definition of the GBI strategy is the calculation of the risk budget. From the definition of the goal, the reference wealth to take into account here is the sum of liquid and aspirational wealth levels. Because the aspirational bucket has been liquidated, this sum coincides with liquid wealth. In the continuous-time framework, the risk budget is computed as the difference between the reference wealth and the present value of the goal, as per Equation (3.20). With continuous rebalancing, this difference is always non-negative, but with discrete rebalancing, it may become negative. Should this happen, we set the risk budget equal to zero. In sum, the risk budget is computed as

$$RB_t = \max[0, A_{\text{liq},t} - \widetilde{EG}^1_t].$$

A second modification is the imposition of a no-short sale constraint in the GHP. Indeed, by Equation (3.20), the dollar amount invested in the MSR is $m \times RB_t$, which may exceed the liquid wealth if the risk budget and/or the multiplier is large. As a consequence, the investor would have a short position in the GHP. In order to avoid this, we cap the amount invested in the MSR to the value of liquid wealth, so that this amount is given by

$$q_{\text{MSR},t} = \max[A_{\text{liq},t}, m \times \text{RB}_t].$$

Appendix A.6.3.1 provides a detailed expression for the amounts invested by the strategy in the various assets.

The fact that the GHP value differs from the floor has a noteworthy implication when it comes to the GBI strategy with a multiplier of 1: if the two values are equal, the GBI with a unit multiplier would collapse to the buy-and-hold strategy tested in Section 4.1.2.5. But because they are distinct, the GBI strategy still involves rebalancing.

We implement the GBI strategy with a monthly rebalancing period, and we take a base case value of 5 for the multiplier. A justification for this particular value is that, on the one hand, m must be sufficiently high to guarantee decent access to the upside potential of the MSR portfolio; but on the other hand, a too high value will increase gap risk.

Table 4.6 shows the initial allocation implied by the GBI strategy, with assets sorted in personal and market buckets. The composition of the market bucket is the MSR allocation to stocks and bonds, and is therefore the same as for the buy-and-hold strategy. But a striking difference with respect to the latter strategy is that the personal bucket, which consists of all assets held for safety motives, accounts for 33.3% of total wealth, which is much lower than the fraction of 86.7% obtained with the buy-and-hold strategy. In view of this number, we expect the GBI strategy to be less conservative.

To check whether this is the case, we look at the success indicators in Figure 4.10. First of all, the success probability for EG1 is 100%. This result is not surprising in view of Proposition 15, which shows that the goal is secured if the portfolio is rebalanced continuously. But floor violations could have been observed due to the discrete (monthly) rebalancing: the number here shows that this is not the case, although we will see later that gap risk arises for larger multiplier values. In contrast, the success probability for EG2 is very disappointing: there is only a 8.7% probability of maintaining the drawdown below 15%, and the expected maximum drawdown after 35 years is as high as 27.4%. This result stresses the need to add a specific control for drawdown risk in addition to the risk control for EG1. Finally, the strategy yields a 62.7% probability of reaching AG,

Table 4.6. **Investor 1 — Initial risk allocation with GBI strategy securing EG1.**

	Value ($)	% of Total		Value ($)	% of Total		Value ($)	% of Total
Personal Bucket	1,500,000	33.3	Market Bucket	3,000,000	66.7	Aspirational Bucket	0	0
Residence	1,500,000	51.7	Equity	2,412,671	80.4			
Cash	100,000	3.4	US Fixed Income	587,329	19.6			
				587,329	19.6			
GHP EG1	600,000	20.7						
Adjustable Rate Mortgage	(700,000)	24.1						

Notes: This table shows the risk allocation at date 0 when the investor follows a GBI strategy of the form described by Equation (3.20) to secure EG1, with a multiplier equal to 5. The personal risk bucket contains assets that are used to finance the investor's implicit goals and the explicitly formulated essential goal: the residence secures the goal of not being homeless, the cash reserve secures the goal of being able to afford a minimum standard of living, and the GHP is a roll-over of 1-year indexed bonds that secures EG1. The aspirational bucket contains in principle illiquid and concentrated positions held for wealth mobility purposes. It is empty here as these positions are liquidated at date 0. The market bucket contains all other assets (equities and bonds here). The table displays the weights of the various assets within each bucket, as well as the relative weights of the buckets.

which represents a substantial improvement over the buy-and-hold portfolio implemented in Section 4.1.2.5.

4.1.3.2. *Impacts of multiplier, trading frequency and stock performance*

In this section, we study the impacts on the GBI strategy of the multiplier and the trading frequency.

Table 4.7 shows the allocation to personal assets as a function of the multiplier. It reports both the composition of the personal bucket, and the weight of this bucket within the investor's portfolio. The aspirational bucket is not shown in the figure because it is always empty, and the market bucket is not shown either, because its composition is independent from the multiplier (it is the MSR allocation to stocks and bonds) and its weight is simply one minus the weight of the personal bucket. It should be noted that the dollar amounts

Figure 4.10. Investor 1 — Success indicators with GBI strategy securing EG.

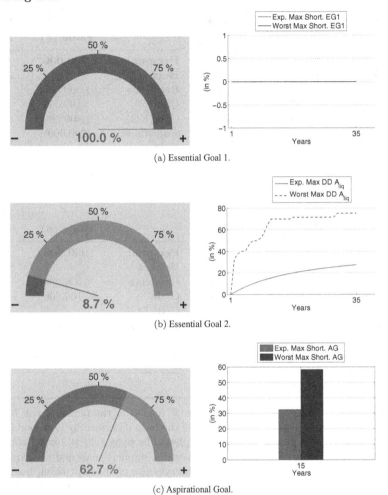

(a) Essential Goal 1.

(b) Essential Goal 2.

(c) Aspirational Goal.

Notes: Aspirational assets and existing positions in stocks and bonds are liquidated at date 0, and the proceeds are re-invested in a dynamic GBI strategy of the form described by Equation (3.20). The performance building block is the MSR and the safe block is the GHP, which is a roll-over of 1-year indexed bonds. The floor is the present value of the minimum wealth level to achieve at the end of the current year (and is therefore discontinuous). The portfolio is rebalanced on a monthly basis, with a multiplier $m = 5$. The left column shows the success probabilities for the goals, and the right column displays the expected maximum shortfall for goals EG1 and AG, and the expected maximum drawdown (see the caption of Figure 4.1 for the definition of the success indicators).

Table 4.7. Investor 1 — Impact of multiplier on initial allocation to personal assets.

	Value ($)	% of Total		Value ($)	% of Total
Personal Bucket	3,900,000	86.7	Personal Bucket	2,700,000	60.0
Residence	1,500,000	28.3	Residence	1,500,000	36.6
Cash	100,000	1.9	Cash	100,000	2.4
GHP EG1	3,000,000	56.6	GHP EG1	1,800,000	43.9
Adjustable Rate Mortgage	(700,000)	13.2	Adjustable Rate Mortgage	(700,000)	17.1
	(i) $m = 1$.			(ii) $m = 3$.	

	Value ($)	% of Total		Value ($)	% of Total
Personal Bucket	1,500,000	33.3	Personal Bucket	900,000	20.0
Residence	1,500,000	51.7	Residence	1,500,000	65.2
Cash	100,000	3.4	Cash	100,000	4.3
GHP EG1	600,000	20.7	GHP EG1	0	0
Adjustable Rate Mortgage	(700,000)	24.1	Adjustable Rate Mortgage	(700,000)	30.4
	(iii) $m = 5$.			(iv) $m = 7$.	

Notes: This table shows the composition at date 0 of the personal risk bucket when the investor follows a GBI strategy of the form described by Equation (3.20) to secure EG1, as a function of the multiplier. The personal risk bucket contains the assets that are used to finance the investor's implicit goals and the explicitly formulated essential goal: the residence secures the goal of not being homeless, the cash reserve secures the goal of being able to afford a minimum standard of living, and the GHP is a roll-over of 1-year indexed bonds that secures EG1.

invested in the residence and the cash reserve are constant (and equal to the values given in Table 4.1), but the weights of these two assets within the personal bucket vary with m because the allocation to the GHP depends on m.

This table simply describes the mechanics of the GBI allocation formula. The allocation to the personal bucket is decreasing in m, shifting from 86.7% for a multiplier of 1 to 20.0% for a multiplier of 7. This evolution reflects the growing allocation to the performance assets (stock and bond indices) contained in the market bucket as m increases. The weight of the GHP also turns out to be decreasing in m. This is because the amount invested in the GHP is by definition a decreasing function of the multiplier. Indeed, we have (see Appendix A.6.3 for details)

$$q_{\text{GHP},t} = \max[0, A_{\text{liq},t} - m \times \text{RB}_t].$$

As a result, the residence and the cash account represent increasing fractions of the personal bucket. For a very large m, the allocation to the GHP shrinks to zero because of the lower bound set to zero in $q_{\text{GHP},t}$. So, the personal bucket is entirely invested in the residence and the cash account, and its weight is the same as with the current allocation, that is 20.0% (see Table 4.1). It turns out that this limit is reached for a multiplier of 7.

We next perform a robustness check of the success indicators of the GBI strategy with respect to the multiplier and the trading frequency. The first purpose of this study is to check that EG1 is still secured. Indeed, a lower rebalancing frequency may increase gap risk, and conversely, it is expected that increasing the multiplier will lead to violations of the floor.

Figure 4.11 presents the results of the comparative static analysis with respect to these two parameters. In the static analysis with respect to frequency, m is kept equal to its base case value, namely 5, and throughout the analysis with respect to m, monthly rebalancing is assumed. We first let m vary from 0 to 10. When the multiplier is zero, the GBI strategy is fully invested in the GHP. It appears that EG1 is secured for any value of the multiplier between 0 and 6 (included), but gap risk starts to materialise as of a value of 7. Nevertheless, deviations from the goal remain extremely small, with an expected shortfall of less than 1%, even for m as large as 10.

On the other hand, decreasing the trading frequency from monthly to quarterly, semi-annual or annual, has more impact on the shortfall: with one rebalancing per year, the shortfall probability is almost equal to what was obtained with monthly trading and a multiplier of 9, but the expected shortfall exceeds 4%, while it was less than 0.7% in the other case. Hence, as far as the achievement of EG1 is concerned, decreasing the trading frequency appears to be more detrimental than increasing m.

Figure 4.11.   Investor 1 — Impacts of multiplier and trading frequency on success indicators with GBI strategy securing EG1.

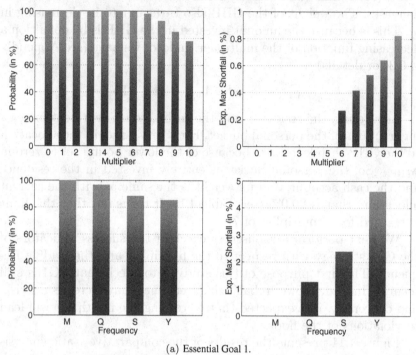

(a) Essential Goal 1.

Notes: Aspirational assets and existing positions in stocks and bonds are liquidated at date 0, and the proceeds are re-invested in a dynamic GBI strategy of the form described by Equation (3.20). The performance building block is the MSR and the safe block is the GHP, which is a roll-over of 1-year indexed bonds. The floor is the present value of the minimum wealth to achieve at the end of the current year. The base case multiplier is 5, and the base case rebalancing period is one month. We let the multiplier vary from 0 (portfolio fully invested in the GHP) to 10 and the rebalancing period can be one month, one quarter, one semester and one year. The left column shows the probabilities of reaching the goals, and the right column displays the expected maximum shortfall for goals EG1 and AG, and the expected maximum drawdown (see the caption of Figure 4.1 for the definition of the success indicators).

When it comes to EG2, it appears that the trading frequency has very little impact on the success indicators: the success probability remains close to 8%, which is very low, and the expected maximum drawdown is above 25%, much higher than the maximum tolerated level of 15%. The impact of m is weak as well, at least in the range

Figure 4.11. (*Continued*)

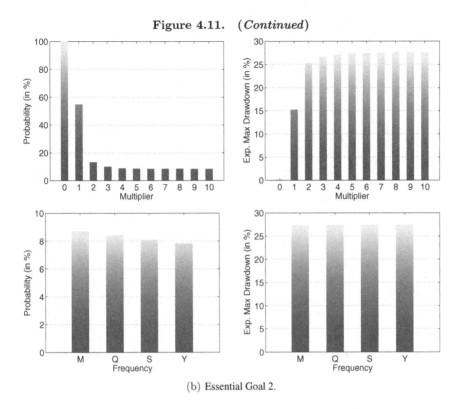

(b) Essential Goal 2.

[2, 10]. Only the values of 0 and 1 stand out, with lower shortfall probabilities and drawdown levels. Indeed, these strategies are rather conservative, with a low allocation to MSR portfolio, which even falls to zero when the multiplier is zero.

But these better scores for EG2 come at the cost of modest probabilities of reaching AG, especially for a zero multiplier, as we already know from Figure 4.7. It is only for a multiplier of 2 that the success probability exceeds 50%, reaching a maximum of about 62% when m is 5. The fact that the probability reaches a cap can be explained as follows. With high values of m, and given the initial risk budget, the portfolio is fully invested in the PSP at date 0, but one day the PSP value may suddenly fall below the goal present value (see Figure 4.6). On that date — the same for all values of m greater than or equal to 5 — the portfolio is invested in the GHP only, and remains so until wealth is back above the present value of the goal: this can happen since, by Equation (4.1), the GHP super-replicates, rather than

Figure 4.11. (*Continued*)

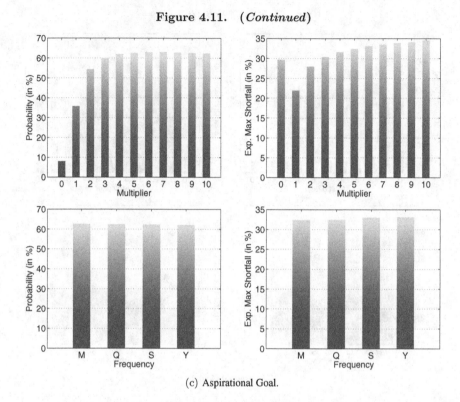

(c) Aspirational Goal.

replicates, the goal. Thus, all portfolios have the same composition until the GHP value exceeds the present value of the goal, which explains the closeness of the shortfall probabilities. The graph of the expected shortfalls highlights the usual trade-off between return and risk: a higher multiplier increases the probability of reaching the goal, but it also creates volatility, which increases the size of potential deviations. The rebalancing frequency has no visible impact on the success indicators for this goal.

Apart from the choice of a higher multiplier, another way of improving the probability of reaching high wealth levels is to invest in a stock index with a higher expected return. This can be achieved, for instance, by switching from a cap-weighted index to a smart-weighted index, which exhibits better performance (see Section 2.5.2.2 for a brief presentation). We model this change by raising the expected return of the stock index by 25%, that is, from its base case value of 12% to 15%. Figure 4.12 shows that gap risk is still negligible

Figure 4.12. Investor 1 — Impact of expected returns from stocks on the success probabilities with GBI strategy securing EG1.

 (i) Base case performance (12%/year).    (ii) Higher performance (15%/year).

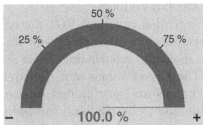 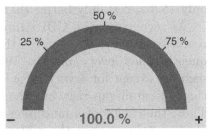

(a) Essential Goal 1.

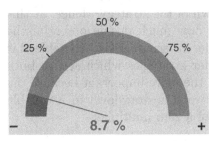 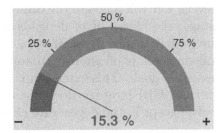

(b) Essential Goal 2.

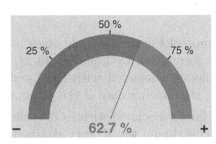 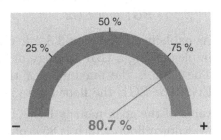

(c) Aspirational Goal.

Notes: Aspirational assets and existing positions in stocks and bonds are liquidated at date 0, and the proceeds are re-invested in a dynamic GBI strategy of the form given in Equation (3.20). The performance building block is the MSR portfolio and the safe building block is the GHP, which is a roll-over of 1-year indexed bonds. The floor is the present value of the minimum wealth level to achieve at the end of the current year. The strategy is rebalanced on a monthly basis, with a multiplier of 5. In the left column, the expected return of the stock is set to its base case value of 12%. In the right column, the expected return is raised to 15%.

here, since the success probability for EG1 is 100%, and that the success probability for AG has increased appreciably, to 80.7%. But the issue of drawdown is left unaddressed: the probability for EG2 is only 15.3%, certainly better than 8.7%, but still low.

As a conclusion, a GBI strategy intended to secure EG1 always reaches this objective, unless the rebalancing takes place less frequently than every month. With monthly rebalancing, EG1 is secured, except for a very large m. The largest values of m (greater than 7) entail gap risk, but the deviations are very limited in size. Thus, the choice of a multiplier value has to be made on the basis of other criteria than the achievement of EG1. Broadly speaking, a greater multiplier will improve the chances to reach ambitious wealth levels, but will increase the drawdown of the strategy. Hence, at this stage, the choice of m depends on how much upside potential the investor is ready to sacrifice in order to secure EG2. To solve this dilemma, it is of interest to consider strategies which secure both essential goals. This extension is all the more important because the current GBI strategy does not control the drawdown in a reliable way, except in the degenerate case of a zero multiplier.

4.1.3.3.   *Goals-based investing strategy securing EG1 and EG2*

As explained in Section 3.3.2.4, we protect the two essential goals by implementing a GBI strategy of the form given by Equation (3.22). The floor is the maximum of the floors associated with EG1 and EG2. For EG1, the floor on a given rebalancing date is the present value of the goal, namely $\widetilde{\mathrm{EG}}_t^1$. The floor associated with EG2 is the drawdown floor, which is 85% of the maximum wealth ever attained. The two GHPs are, respectively, the roll-over of 1-year indexed bonds and the cash account. The strategy uses as a safe asset the GHP that corresponds to the higher floor. The detailed expression for the weights of the strategy can be found in Appendix A.6.3.2. We still take a base case multiplier of 5 and assume monthly rebalancing. For clarity, we refer in what follows to this strategy as GBI2, and to the GBI strategy that protects only EG1 as GBI1.

First, Table 4.8 shows the risk allocation at date 0 implied by the GBI2 investment policy. Note that the personal bucket now contains two GHPs. The allocation to the GHP protecting EG1 is zero because the drawdown floor is higher. Indeed, it is equal to 85% of the initial

Table 4.8. Investor 1 — Initial risk allocation with GBI strategy securing EG1 and EG2.

	Value ($)	% of Total		Value ($)	% of Total		Value ($)	% of Total
Personal Bucket	1,800,000	40.0	Market Bucket	2,700,000	60.0	Aspirational Bucket	0	0
Residence	1,500,000	46.9	Equity	2,171,403	80.4			
Cash	100,000	3.1	US Fixed Income	528,597	19.6			
GHP EG1	0	0						
GHP EG2	900,000	28.1						
Adjustable Rate Mortgage	(700,000)	21.9						

Notes: This table shows the risk allocation at date 0 when the investor takes a GBI strategy of the form described by Equation (3.22) to secure EG1 and EG2, with a multiplier equal to 5. The personal risk bucket contains assets that are used to finance the investor's implicit goals and the explicitly formulated essential goal: the residence secures the goal of not being homeless, the cash reserve secures the goal of being able to afford a minimum standard of living, the GHP for G1 is a roll-over of 1-year indexed bonds, and the GHP for G2 is cash. The aspirational bucket contains in principle illiquid and concentrated positions held for wealth mobility purposes. It is empty here as these positions are liquidated at date 0. The market bucket contains all other assets (equities and bonds here). The table displays the weights of the various assets within each bucket, as well as the relative weights of the buckets.

liquid wealth, which is $3.6m: it is thus $3.06m, which is larger than $3m, the value of the floor associated with EG1. Logically, since this strategy aims at protecting two goals, it is more conservative than the one for GBI1, so the personal bucket represents a larger fraction of investor's wealth: 40% versus 33.3%.

As appears from Figure 4.13, the first benefit of the GBI2 strategy over the one for GBI1 is that it fully secures EG2: indeed, the maximum possible drawdown, across all dates and states of the world, is less than 15%. This improvement is all the more appreciable because the GBI1 rule respects the drawdown constraint with a low probability, of 8.7% only. Among all the strategies that have been tested so far, only the safe strategies, i.e. the one invested in the roll-over of indexed bonds and the one invested in cash, displayed probabilities of 100% for both essential goals (Figures 4.7 and 4.8). But the key improvement here with respect to these conservative policies is the success

Figure 4.13. Investor 1 — Success indicators with GBI strategy securing EG1 and EG2.

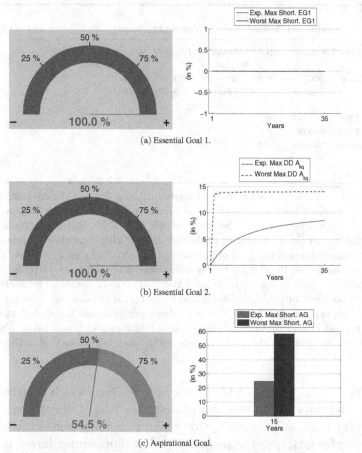

(a) Essential Goal 1.

(b) Essential Goal 2.

(c) Aspirational Goal.

Notes: Aspirational assets and existing positions in stocks and bonds are liquidated at date 0, and the proceeds are re-invested in a dynamic GBI strategy of the form described by Equation (3.22). The performance building block is the MSR portfolio, and the floor that appears in the risk budget is the maximum of the floors associated with the two goals. The floor for EG1 is the present value of the minimum wealth level to achieve at the end of the current year, and the floor for EG2 is the drawdown floor. The floor-replicating portfolio is the GHP that corresponds to the higher floor, i.e. a roll-over of 1-year indexed bonds for EG1, and the cash account for EG2. The portfolio is rebalanced every month, with a multiplier of 5. The left column shows the success probabilities for the goals, and the right column displays the expected maximum shortfall for goals EG1 and AG, and the expected maximum drawdown (see the caption of Figure 4.1 for the definition of the success indicators).

probability for AG: while safe strategies achieve this goal with a less than 10% probability, the GBI2 strategy displays a much higher probability of 54.5%. This is a consequence of the MSR portfolio being assigned a non-zero weight: this portfolio has higher expected return than the safe assets, so its presence increases the potential for performance at the strategy level.

Nevertheless, AG is less likely to be achieved with the GBI2 strategy than with the GBI1 one. Indeed, the success probability with GBI1 was 62.7%, and it is now 54.5%. This reduction reflects the opportunity cost of imposing the constraint of a 15% maximum drawdown. Indeed, the floor of the GBI2 strategy is by definition higher than that of GBI1 so the risk budget is mechanically lower. This means a lower allocation to the MSR, hence a reduced access to upside.

As for the GBI1 strategy, we study the impacts of the multiplier and the rebalancing frequency. The objective is in particular to see whether some choices of these two parameters lead to violations of the floor constraints. The success probabilities for EG1 shown in Figure 4.14 display the same pattern as for the GBI1 strategy: EG1 is secured for any choice of m less than 6, and violations arise for multipliers of 7 or more, but they remain very limited in size, with an expected shortfall less than 1%. But the most striking difference between GBI1 and GBI2 is that while GBI1 has little chance to reach EG2, the success probability for this goal is 100% for any m between 0 and 8, and it is hardly less than 100% for a multiplier of 9 or 10. Even for these two values, the expected maximum drawdown is less than 15%, which shows that the violations of the 15% constraint are caused by a few extreme scenarios. But the success probabilities for AG are always less with GBI2 than with GBI1, which is a manifestation of the lower allocation to the MSR building block.

The fact that the GBI2 investment policy allocates less to the MSR than the GBI1 one may also explain why it is less subject to gap risk when the rebalancing frequency is decreased: indeed, both essential goals are always attained with monthly or quarterly rebalancing, and the success probabilities obtained for semi-annual or annual rebalancing, while being less than 100%, are higher than those achieved with the GBI1 policy. The downside deviations from EG1 are also smaller than for GBI1, and the expected maximum drawdowns are greatly reduced. This clearly shows the usefulness

Figure 4.14. **Investor 1 — Impacts of multiplier and trading frequency on success indicators with GBI strategy securing EG1 and EG2.**

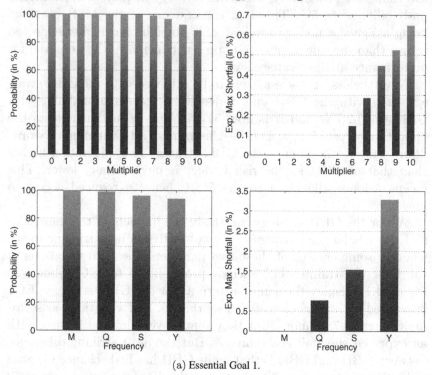

(a) Essential Goal 1.

Notes: Aspirational assets and existing positions in stocks and bonds are liquidated at date 0, and the proceeds are re-invested in a dynamic GBI strategy of the form given by Equation (3.22). The performance building block is the MSR portfolio, the first GHP is a roll-over of 1-year indexed bonds which secures EG1, and the second GHP, which secures EG2, is fully invested in cash. The floor is the maximum of the floors associated with EG1 and EG2. The former floor is the present value of the minimum wealth level to achieve at the end of the current year, and the latter floor is 85% of the maximum-to-date of wealth. The base case multiplier is 5, and the base case rebalancing period is one month. We let the multiplier vary from 0, which implies that the portfolio is fully invested in the roll-over or in cash, to 10. The rebalancing period is taken to be one month, one quarter, one semester or one year. The left column shows the success probabilities for the goals, and the right column displays the expected maximum shortfall for goals EG1 and AG, and the expected maximum drawdown (see the caption of Figure 4.1 for the definition of the success indicators).

Figure 4.14. (*Continued*)

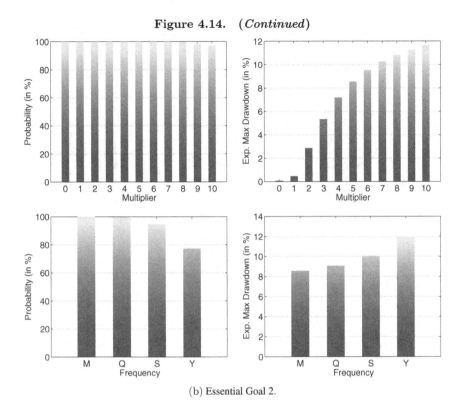

(b) Essential Goal 2.

of the drawdown control. But this reduction of drawdown comes at the cost of a decreased probability of reaching ambitious wealth levels, as can be seen from the success probabilities for AG, which are lower with GBI2 than with GBI1 for any choice of the rebalancing frequency.

In order to have a direct measure of the opportunity cost, we compute the additional initial capital which must be invested in the GBI2 strategy in order to generate the same probability of reaching AG as with the GBI1 strategy. The definition of this indicator is inspired by the monetary utility gain, which is often reported in the literature on optimal portfolio choice and is the additional initial investment needed to achieve the same expected utility as with a benchmark strategy (see e.g. Sangvinatsos and Wachter (2005) and Martellini and Milhau (2010)). Here, expected utility is replaced by the probability of reaching AG, and the benchmark is the GBI1 strategy.

Figure 4.14. (*Continued*)

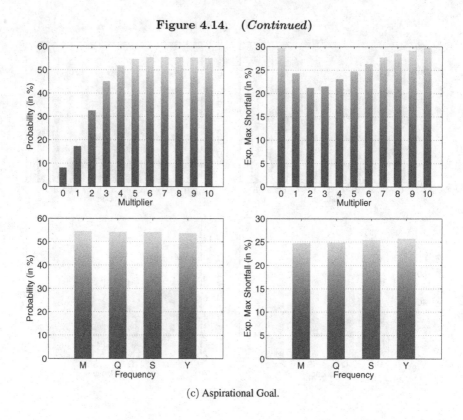

(c) Aspirational Goal.

In Figure 4.15, we calculate the success probability and the opportunity cost for various values of the maximum drawdown introduced in the GBI strategy: this parameter is the maximum loss that the investor is ready to accept, and it is used to compute the drawdown floor. By definition, a zero maximum drawdown leads to a portfolio fully invested in cash, and a 100% maximum drawdown to the GBI1 strategy, which does not attempt to cap losses. Of course, imposing a 100% maximum drawdown does not imply that the portfolio will effectively display such a large loss: the worst maximum drawdown of the GBI1 strategy is 75.3%, a value which represents the worst possible loss for a GBI2 strategy.

The figure confirms the previous explanation: indeed, the probability of reaching AG is increasing in the maximum drawdown, which means that a tighter drawdown constraint results in a lower probability of reaching ambitious goals. As a consequence, the opportunity

Figure 4.15. Investor 1 — Opportunity cost of drawdown constraint with GBI strategy securing EG1 and EG2.

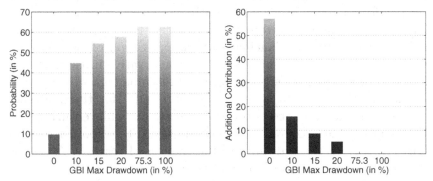

(i) Success probabilities for Aspirational Goal.   (ii) Additional initial contribution required.

Notes: Aspirational assets and existing positions in stocks and bonds are liquidated at date 0, and the proceeds are re-invested in a dynamic GBI strategy of the form given by Equation (3.22), which protects both EG1 and EG2. The portfolio is rebalanced every month, with a multiplier of 5. Panel (i) shows the probability of reaching the aspirational goal as a function of the maximum drawdown imposed in the GBI strategy. Panel (ii) displays the additional initial contribution which is necessary for the GBI strategy with the drawdown constraint to have the same success probability as the otherwise equivalent GBI strategy without this constraint. The value 75.3% on the horizontal axis is the maximum drawdown of the GBI strategy without the drawdown constraint.

cost measured in terms of additional initial wealth strongly increases when the tolerance for loss risk decreases: an investor who refuses any losses should invest in cash only, and he would have to multiply his initial investment by 1.57 in order to achieve the same success probability as if he was following the GBI1 strategy. Our base case maximum drawdown, which is 15%, yields a cost of 8.55%: this percentage is much lower than for the strategy fully invested in cash, but it is still non-negligible. This illustrates that the drawdown constraint has a significant cost in terms of performance.

As a conclusion, the GBI strategy described by Equation (3.22), which switches between the GHPs associated with the two essential goals, does secure both goals and proves to be rather robust to gap risk. This risk materialises only for high values of m (those greater than 8): it affects more the probability of reaching EG1 than that of reaching EG2, but as for the GBI strategy securing EG1 only, the deviations from the goal remain small on average. This strategy also displays improved robustness with respect to the choice of the rebalancing frequency. Indeed, it secures both goals not only when the portfolio is rebalanced every month, but also with quarterly rebalancing, while the GBI strategy dedicated to EG1 secures this goal only with monthly rebalancing. But the protection of two essential goals as opposed to one implies a more conservative investment policy, which results in lower probabilities of reaching high wealth levels. In view of these results, it is the values 6 and 7 for the multiplier that give the highest success probabilities for AG while ensuring that EG1 and EG2 are secured. The next step is to test another form of GBI strategy to try and improve the chances of reaching AG while keeping the protection of EG1 and EG2.

4.1.3.4. *Goals-based investing strategy securing EG1 and EG2 with a cap*

We recall from Section 3.3.2.5 that the idea behind the imposition of a cap is to reduce the cost of insurance against downside risk. This approach is justified by the theoretical results of Proposition 13 and Corollary 3: when a cap is imposed, the optimal strategy involves a short position in a call option written on the performance assets, and the premium received by selling this option decreases the price of the put to purchase in order to secure the goal. Equivalently, this strategy captures a larger fraction of the performance of the MSR portfolio than the strategy which does not set any upper bound on wealth.

Because AG is not affordable, while EG1 and EG2 are, it represents the investor's highest goal. So, it is reasonable to assume that the investor has no utility from reaching wealth levels in excess of this goal. Thus, we first test a GBI strategy of the form described by Equation (3.23) where the cap is the present value of AG. In order to protect both goals, we still take the floor to be the maximum of the floors, respectively, associated with EG1 and EG2, and the GHP of the strategy is the GHP that corresponds to the higher floor. In line with the definition of the cap, the "cap-hedging portfolio", which tracks the present value of the cap, is the indexed zero-coupon bond that matures at the end of 15 years and pays $7.2m in real terms. Of course, this bond is only available for the first 15 years, so we switch to the GBI2 strategy (i.e. the one protecting both essential goals)

Table 4.9. Investor 1 — Initial weights of GBI strategy with illiquid aspirational assets.

	Value ($)	% of Total		Value ($)	% of Total		Value ($)	% of Total
Personal Bucket	1,500,000	33.3	Market Bucket	1,550,000	34.5	Aspirational Bucket	1,450,000	32.2
Residence	1,500,000	51.7	Equity	1,246,546	80.4	Concentrated Stock	1,250,000	86.2
Cash	100,000	3.4	US Fixed Income	303,454	19.6	Executive Stock Option	100,000	6.9
GHP EG1	600,000	20.7				Real Asset	100,000	6.9
Adjustable Rate Mortgage	(700,000)	24.1						

Notes: This table shows the risk allocation at date 0 when the investor follows a GBI strategy of the form described by Equation (30) to secure EG1, with a multiplier equal to 5. The personal risk bucket contains assets that are used to finance the investor's implicit goals and the explicitly formulated essential goal: the residence secures the goal of not being homeless, the cash reserve secures the goal of being able to afford a minimum standard of living, and the GHP is a roll-over of 1-year indexed bonds that secures EG1. The aspirational bucket contains illiquid and concentrated positions held for wealth mobility purposes. The market bucket contains all other assets, here equities and bonds. The table displays the weights of the various assets within each bucket, as well as the relative weights of the buckets.

after the bond has expired. In the following comments, we refer to the GBI strategy with a cap as GBI3. The detailed expressions for the weights are given in Appendix A.6.3.3. The initial risk allocation is in fact the same as with the GBI2 strategy (see Table 4.9) because the allocation at date 0 to the cap-hedging portfolio is zero. Indeed, the numerical value of the threshold defined in Section 3.2.2.5 is (in millions of dollars)

$$\xi_0 = \frac{\tilde{F}_0 + \tilde{C}_0}{2} = \frac{3.06 + 4.81}{2} = 3.94$$

which is greater than the liquid wealth of $3.6m. Thus, at date 0, the investor acts as if there was no cap, and only takes care of floor protection.

It turns out from Panel (a) of Figure 4.16 that imposing a cap equal to the present value of AG leads to a lower probability of reaching this goal than with the GBI2 strategy. In particular, the

Figure 4.16.   Investor 1 — Success indicators for aspirational goal with GBI strategy securing EG1 and EG2 and imposing a cap.

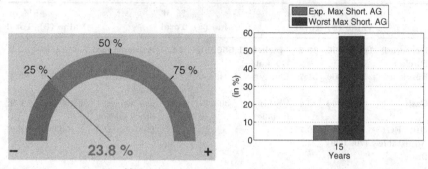

(i) Cap = present value of Aspirational Goal.

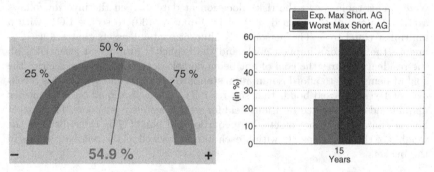

(ii) Cap = 2 × present value of Aspirational Goal.

Notes: Aspirational assets and existing positions in stocks and bonds are liquidated at date 0, and the proceeds are re-invested in a dynamic GBI strategy of the form given by Equation (3.23). The floor is the maximum of the two floors associated with goals EG1 and EG2 (present value of minimum wealth level to achieve at the end of the current year for EG1 and drawdown floor for EG2). The cap is the present value of the aspirational goal in Panel (a), and 2 or 3 times this present value in Panels (b) and (c). The floor-replicating portfolio is the GHP that corresponds to the higher floor (roll-over of 1-year indexed bonds for EG1 and cash account for EG2). The cap-replicating portfolio is the indexed zero-coupon that pays $7.2m at the end of 15 years. The portfolio is rebalanced every month, with a multiplier m of 5. The left column contains the success probabilities and the right column the expected shortfalls (see the caption of Figure 4.1 for the definition of the success indicators).

Figure 4.16. (*Continued*)

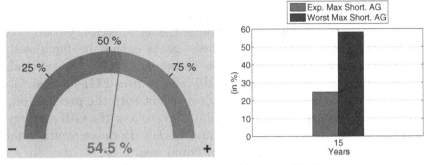

(iii) Cap = 3 × present value of Aspirational Goal.

success probability is 23.8%, versus 54.5% (see Figure 4.13) for the latter strategy, which was to be expected since risk-taking is reduced before the cap is reached. So, the reduction in success probability is not inconsistent with the fact that the strategy with a cap has in theory a higher access to the upside (see Corollary 3). Indeed, this property does not imply that imposing a cap increases the chances of reaching any wealth level: the levels in excess of the cap will never be attained, and it is only for "medium" levels that the distribution of wealth is improved. As an attempt to increase the success probability for AG, we may decide to choose the cap level in such a way that the present value of AG lies between the floor and the cap. This is what we do in Panels (b) and (c), where we set the cap equal, respectively, to 2 and 3 times the present value of AG. The effect on the probability is positive since this indicator grows to 54.9% and 54.5%, but these values do not represent a significant improvement with respect to the GBI2 strategy, for which the probability was already 54.5%.

On the other hand, leaving aside the probability of reaching a goal, a key benefit of the introduction of a cap is that it has a very significant positive impact on expected shortfall. For example, in the case of the cap taken to be at the AG level, we obtain that the expected shortfall has fallen by two-thirds, decreasing from 24.7% to 8.14%. As a result, we confirm that imposing a cap implies a reduction in the opportunity cost of downside risk protection, which in turn translates into lower expected shortfall in situations when a goal is almost reached.

4.1.3.5. *Impact of illiquid positions*

The previous analysis has mainly focused on the case where aspirational assets can be liquidated, because this is a necessary condition for the affordability of EG1. If these assets cannot be liquidated, the goal cannot be secured and has to be regarded as aspirational. Despite this change of status, we still refer to it as EG1 in what follows in order to have a terminology consistent with the previous one employed. The purpose of this section is to see how the GBI strategy behaves in the presence of an illiquid bucket. Because aspirational assets are not liquidated, the initial liquid wealth is

$$A_{\text{liq},0} = A_{\text{mkt},0} = \$2.15\text{m}.$$

First, the reference wealth to take into account to compute the risk budget is the sum of the market and the aspirational wealth levels, since the goal expressed by the investor is to keep the sum of these two quantities above \$3m plus inflation. This leads to the following formula for the risk budget:

$$\text{RB}_t = \max[0, A_{\text{liq},t} + A_{\text{asp},t} - \widetilde{\text{EG}}_t^1].$$

The total allocation to performance assets (i.e. assets contained in the market and the aspirational buckets) is the sum of the market and the aspirational wealth levels. Assuming that the market bucket is fully invested in the MSR of stocks and bonds, the total exposure to performance assets can be written as

$$q_{\text{perf},t} = q_{\text{MSR},t} + A_{\text{asp},t}.$$

According to the definition of the GBI strategy, this allocation should be equal to the cushion $m \times \text{RB}_t$. But when the cushion is less than the aspirational wealth, there is an overexposure to risky assets. If this happens, the allocation to the MSR portfolio is set to zero, in order to reduce as much as possible the size of the exposure. In all other cases, we take $q_{\text{perf},t}$ equal to the cushion, which amounts to investing $[m \times \text{RB}_t - A_{\text{asp},t}]$ in the MSR portfolio. As usual, this sum is capped to the value of liquid wealth. The amount invested in the GHP is then equal to liquid wealth minus the investment in the MSR building block.

Table 4.9 shows the weights of the GBI strategy at date 0. The inner composition of the market bucket is the MSR allocation to stocks and bonds, exactly as in the case where aspirational assets are liquid. Moreover, the amount invested in the GHP turns out to be the same as in the liquid case. Indeed, the initial cushion is (in millions of dollars)

$$m \times \mathrm{RB}_0 = 5 \times (2.15 + 1.45 - 3) = 3,$$

which is greater than $A_{\mathrm{asp},0}$ (equal to \$1.45m). Thus, the amount invested in the MSR portfolio is

$$q_{\mathrm{MSR},0} = m \times \mathrm{RB}_0 - A_{\mathrm{asp},0},$$

and that invested in the GHP is

$$q_{\mathrm{GHP},0} = A_{\mathrm{liq},0} - q_{\mathrm{MSR},0} = A_{\mathrm{mkt},0} + A_{\mathrm{asp},0} - m \times \mathrm{RB}_0,$$

which is exactly the same value as in the liquid case. This explains why the composition of the personal bucket is strictly identical in the liquid and the illiquid cases. In order to observe a difference between the two, one would have to choose a sufficiently low value of m, for the cushion to be less than $A_{\mathrm{asp},0}$. The allocation to the MSR would then be zero, while the investment in the GHP would be

$$q_{\mathrm{GHP},0} = A_{\mathrm{mkt},0},$$

while it was equal to $[A_{\mathrm{mkt},0} + A_{\mathrm{asp},0} - m \times \mathrm{RB}_0]$ when aspirational assets were liquidated.

Thus, the personal and market bucket compositions are the same in the liquid and the illiquid cases. But the relative weights of the various compartments are different. In the illiquid case, the investment in performance assets is split across the market and the aspirational buckets, so the total weight of these two buckets is 57.7%, which is the weight of the market bucket in the liquid case (see Table 4.6).

Plain GBI Strategy. We first test the GBI strategy in its "plain" form, that is, as it is described in Section 4.1.3.1. Figure 4.17 shows that the success probability for EG1 falls to 53.0%. There are two reasons why this probability is no longer 100%. The first is independent of the investment rule. The initial liquid wealth is \$2.15m (the sum of the current positions in stock and bond indices), which is less than the present value of EG1, which is \$3m. Hence, by absence of arbitrage opportunities, no strategy can reach EG1 with a 100% probability. The second reason is specific to the GBI strategy. As explained above, it implies an overexposure to performance assets

Figure 4.17. Investor 1 — Success indicators for EG1 with GBI strategy and illiquid aspirational assets.

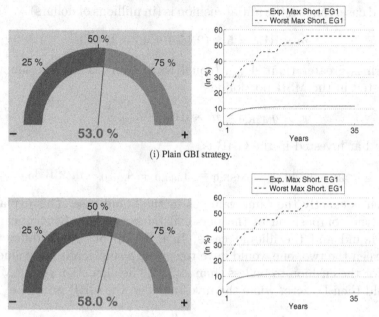

(i) Plain GBI strategy.

(ii) GBI strategy with ratchet effect.

Notes: This figure shows the success indicators for EG1 when aspirational assets cannot be liquidated, but the existing positions in stocks and bonds within the market bucket are liquidated and re-invested in a dynamic GBI strategy of the form described by Equation (3.20). In Panel (ii), a ratchet effect is added to the strategy, that is, the portfolio switches to the GHP (a roll-over of 1-year indexed bonds) as soon as market wealth hits the present value of the goal. The portfolio is rebalanced on a monthly basis, with a multiplier of 5. The left column shows the success probabilities, and the right column displays the expected maximum shortfall (see the caption of Figure 4.1 for the definition of the success indicators).

whenever the cushion is lower than the aspirational wealth. As a consequence, the volatility of the ratio $(A_{\text{liq},t} + A_{\text{asp},t})/\widetilde{\text{EG}}_t^1$ does not shrink to zero when the ratio approaches 1, that is, when wealth approaches the floor. For this reason, we would expect violations of the floor, even if the initial liquid wealth was greater than \$2.15m (see the discussion in Section 3.3.2.1).

GBI Strategy with Ratchet Effect. The standard GBI strategy may, by chance, reach the present value at some date, even if it starts from a lower level at date 0. The goal would then change status by becoming affordable, but it is not secured by the strategy, because of the inability to cancel the exposure to performance assets when the risk budget shrinks to zero. In order to avoid breaching the floor after it has been reached, we implement a modified version of the GBI strategy which incorporates a "ratchet" effect: as soon as liquid wealth hits the present value of the goal, the goal is secured by investing liquid wealth in the GHP only. Hence, the access to the upside potential of performance assets is lost after the first hitting time, but this performance is used in the first phase to reach the non-affordable goal.[4]

The effect on the success probability is positive, but it is mild: the probability grows from 53.0% to 58.0%. This suggests that the lack of success in reaching EG1 with the plain GBI strategy is primarily due to the insufficient level of liquid wealth compared to the goal value. The other factor which contributed to the floor violations was the fact that the GBI strategy does not secure the goal after its present value has been hit, but it turns out that avoiding subsequent violations through ratcheting has only a small positive effect. This makes a case for the liquidation of aspirational assets in order to make the first goal affordable.

Partial Liquidation of Aspirational Assets. In order to address the issue of insufficient liquid wealth at date 0, one can attempt to liquidate a fraction of the aspirational assets in order to have liquid wealth just equal to the goal present value. After the partial liquidation, liquid and aspirational wealth values are

$$A_{\text{liq},0} = \$3\text{m}, \quad A_{\text{asp},0} = \$0.6.$$

Liquid wealth is exactly the minimum capital required to secure the goal, so the goal becomes affordable again. Figure 4.18 shows the impact of the multiplier on the success probabilities and expected shortfalls. It can be compared to Figure 4.11, where the aspirational bucket was entirely liquidated at date 0. The various indicators display a similar pattern: the probabilities of reaching essential goals decrease as the multiplier grows, while the expected shortfall tends to increase.

---

[4]Another choice of investment policy for the first phase would be the growth-optimal policy because under some assumptions, this strategy minimises the expected time to reach the goal (see Section 3.2.1).

Figure 4.18. Investor 1 — Impact of multiplier on success indicators with GBI strategy and partially liquid assets.

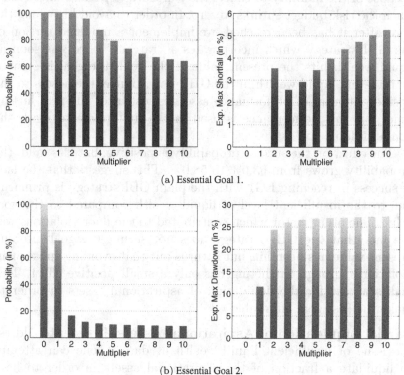

(a) Essential Goal 1.

(b) Essential Goal 2.

Notes: This figure shows the impact of the multiplier on the success indicators with a dynamic GBI strategy of the form given by Equation (3.22). Existing positions in stocks and bonds are liquidated at date 0, and aspirational assets are partially liquidated: the amount liquidated is equal to the difference between the present value of EG1 ($3m) and the current liquid wealth ($2.15m). The proceeds of the liquidation are re-invested in the GBI strategy. The performance building block is the MSR portfolio, and the GHP is a roll-over of 1-year indexed bonds which secures EG1. The floor is the present value of the minimum wealth level to achieve at the end of the current year. The portfolio is rebalanced every month. The left column shows the success probabilities for the goals, and the right column displays the expected maximum shortfall for goals EG1 and AG, and the expected maximum drawdown (see the caption of Figure 4.1 for the definition of the success indicators).

Figure 4.18. (*Continued*)

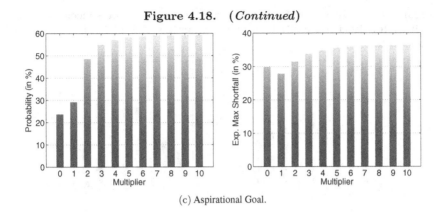

(c) Aspirational Goal.

The main difference is that gap risk for EG1 arises for a multiplier of 3 in the partially liquid case, while it does not arise until a multiplier of 7 in the liquid case. For instance, with a multiplier of 5, the success probability is only 79.2%. This is due to the lower level of liquid wealth in the former case. Indeed, a partial liquidation of the aspirational bucket leaves an initial wealth of $3m, instead of $3.6m with a complete liquidation. Thus, the safety margin available to absorb adverse shocks on the value of the performance portfolio is lower, and the portfolio is more sensitive to gap risk.

GBI Strategy with Overlay. As explained above, a drawback of the plain GBI strategy is that it implies an overexposure to risky assets (that is, assets not dedicated to the hedging of essential goals) when the cushion is less than the value of the aspirational bucket. This overexposure could be reduced, or even completely eliminated, if it was possible to sell short the aspirational assets within the liquid portfolio. This possibility is not completely unrealistic as far as the illiquid stock (which aggregates the concentrated stock and the executive stock options) is concerned, but it is certainly ruled out for investment real estate. Thus, we consider the following cases: first, the illiquid stock can be sold short (which is the ideal situation); second, this short sale is not possible and the investor has to resort to an imperfect substitute.

In all cases, we set a limit on the size of the short sale: it is the value of the illiquid stock position. So, when the cushion exceeds the aspirational wealth, a short position of size $[m \times \mathrm{RB}_t - A_{\mathrm{asp},t}]$ is taken in the shortable asset, up to a cap. The detailed expression

Figure 4.19. Investor 1 — Impact of multiplier on success probabilities for EG1 with GBI strategy shorting the illiquid stock or a substitute.

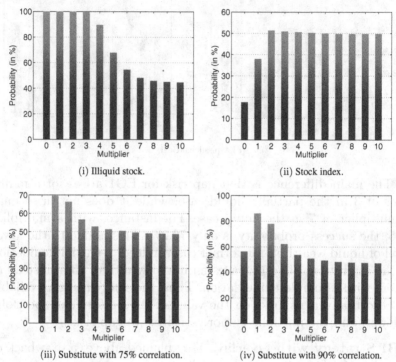

(i) Illiquid stock.   (ii) Stock index.

(iii) Substitute with 75% correlation.   (iv) Substitute with 90% correlation.

Notes: This figure shows the impact of the multiplier on the success indicators with a dynamic GBI strategy of the form described in Equation (3.22). Existing positions in stocks and bonds are liquidated at date 0, but aspirational assets are illiquid. The strategy shorts the illiquid stock or a substitute when its cushion is less than the aspirational wealth. In Panel (i), the shortable asset is the illiquid stock itself; in Panel (ii) it is the stock index, which has a correlation of 50% with this stock; in Panels (iii) and (iv) it is a substitute with higher correlation (75% or 90%). The portfolio is rebalanced every month.

of the weights is given in Appendix A.6.3.4. It should be noted that with this specification, the strategy is overexposed to risky assets only when the cushion is less than the value of the position held in real estate. Thus, overexposure is less frequent, and of smaller size, than when short sales are prohibited. But it cannot be completely eliminated because of the non-tradable position in real estate.

Figure 4.19 shows the success probability for EG1 as a function of the multiplier, for various choices of the shortable asset. When the illiquid stock itself can be sold short, the situation is better than when short sales are ruled out for all values of the multiplier ranging from 0 to 3: indeed, no violation of the floor is observed. The explanation depends on the value of m. For a zero multiplier, the cushion is zero, hence less than the value of the investment real estate position. Thus, the investor has a systematic overexposure to risky assets. As a consequence, nothing is invested in the MSR portfolio, and it follows from the formulas in Appendix A.6.3.4 that the dollar amount invested in the GHP is

$$q_{\text{Ft}} = A_{\text{liq},t} + A_{X,t},$$

where $A_{X,t}$ is the value of the illiquid stock position. At the initial date, this amount is, in millions of dollars,

$$q_{F0} = 2.15 + 1.25 + 0.1 = 3.5.$$

It is greater than the goal present value, which is of \$3m. Thus, the possibility of selling short the illiquid stock makes the goal of maintaining a minimum level of wealth of \$3m affordable. It turns out in our simulations that the condition $q_{\text{Ft}} \geq \widetilde{\text{EG}}_t^1$ is satisfied at all rebalancing dates. Hence, at each of these dates, the investor can afford the roll-over of bonds that secure the essential goal, and the success probability is 100%.

For multiplier values of 1, 2 or 3, the probability of being overexposed is small, because the position in real estate is only \$100,000, which represents a relatively small amount. In our simulations, the probability of being overexposed at one rebalancing date at least is less than 1%. For larger multiplier values, gap risk arises. It should be noted that this risk is made more important by the short position: indeed, violations can be caused not only by a bad return on the MSR portfolio but also by a good return on the shorted asset. That is why, for a multiplier greater than 7, the success probability is less than 50%.

If short sales of the illiquid stock are not possible, one can envision the use of a substitute. From Figure 4.19, the stock index appears to be a poor substitute: the probability of reaching EG1 is hardly 50%. It should be noted that for any choice of the shortable asset, the liquid wealth may become negative if the asset in question displays good returns. But when the asset is the illiquid stock itself, the returns in the liquid portfolio and in the aspirational buckets exactly offset each other, and the sum of the liquid and the aspirational wealth levels remains non-negative. This is no longer the case when the returns on the shortable asset do not perfectly replicate those of the illiquid stock. As a result, not only the liquid wealth, but the sum of the liquid and the aspirational wealths may become negative as well. Of course, in these scenarios, EG1 is missed. This has a negative impact on the probability of reaching this goal, as can be seen from the figure.

In order to better replicate the returns on the illiquid stock, an idea is to sell short a stock index that is better correlated than the broad stock index. Indeed, the correlation between the broad index and the illiquid stock is 50%, but a sector index representative of the activity sector of the concentrated stock is likely to have a higher correlation. We model this increase in the correlation by taking as a shortable asset an index with a correlation of 75% or 90% with the illiquid stock. Figure 4.19 shows that the success probability is increasing in the correlation, and higher than what is achieved with the broad index, but the change is apparent only for the lowest multiplier values, i.e. the values between 0 and 3. In any case, however, the probability is less than 100%, which indicates that the goal is never secured.

As a conclusion, the presence of an illiquid aspirational bucket makes the "EG1" unaffordable, which turns this goal into an aspirational one. As a result, no strategy can secure the goal, and the decrease in the success probability is severe: for the tested GBI strategies, the probability falls below 60% (it was exactly 60% with the current strategy; see Figure 4.1). Affordability can be recovered if the investor can liquidate a fraction of his aspirational assets, but this leaves him with substantial gap risk, unless the multiplier is set to a level less than 3. The existence of the illiquid bucket raises also an issue specific to the GBI strategy: the strategy is overexposed to risky assets when the risk budget is close to zero. This overexposure can be reduced by taking a short position as a substitute for an aspirational asset, but the substitute must have a high correlation with the asset, and as for the partial liquidation, gap risk creates frequent deviations from the goal for large multiplier values.

4.1.3.6. *Impact of taxes*

The last robustness test that we perform relates to the impact of taxes (see Section 2.3 for a general introduction to the question of taxes). We are interested in checking whether the protection of EG1 is still effective after taking taxes into account.

The assets involved in the GBI strategy aiming to secure EG1 are the stock and the bond indices and the GHP, which is an annual roll-over of 1-year indexed bonds. We assume that the dividends and the coupons paid by the constituents of the two indices are re-invested in the indices themselves, so that none of the three assets pays dividends. Hence, taxes only arise from capital gains. In detail, the sources of taxes are as follows:

- the rebalancing of the MSR towards constant weights;
- the roll-over operations within the GHP: at the end of each year, the position in the GHP is virtually liquidated, which possibly generates profits;
- the rebalancing between the building blocks (MSR portfolio and GHP).

As explained in Section 2.3, we apply a 20% tax rate on all capital gains, and we use the "Last In First Out" (LIFO) algorithm to compute the taxable gains (see Appendix A.6.5 for details).

To account for the presence of taxes in the design of the GBI strategy, we raise the floor by an amount equal to a tax provision, as described in Section 3.3.3.2: the provision is computed as the amount of taxes accrued since the beginning of the year. It should be emphasised that it is not equal to the present value of the annual tax payment, so that the GBI strategy might not reach the goal with certainty. This can be verified in Figure 4.20, where we look at the impact of the multiplier on the success probabilities for EG1. While no violation of the minimum wealth constraint is observed for a multiplier of 1, a few deviations from the goal appear for multipliers of 3 and 5. For a value of 3, the probability of missing EG1 is only 0.2%, which is close to negligible. For a value of 5, the shortfall probability is more significant, reaching 3.1%, but the deviations are of limited size, with an expected shortfall less than 1%.

In Figure 4.21, we let the tax rate vary across the values 0, 10% and 20%. With a multiplier of 1, there is no deviation from the goal, and with a value of 3, deviations are so rare that the success probability is indistinguishable from 100%. Only the graph of expected shortfalls reveals that some deviations occur when the tax rate

Figure 4.20.   Investor 1 — Impact of multiplier on success indicators for EG1 with GBI strategy in the presence of taxes.

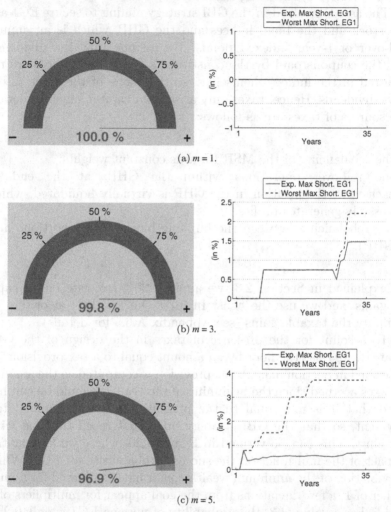

(a) $m = 1$.

(b) $m = 3$.

(c) $m = 5$.

Notes: This figure shows the impact of the multiplier on the success indicators for EG1 with a dynamic GBI strategy which aims at securing EG1, when a 20% tax rate is applied to gains on the stock and the bond indices and gains on the roll-over operations on 1-year indexed bonds. Existing positions in stocks and bonds and aspirational assets are liquidated at date 0. The performance building block is the MSR and the GHP is a roll-over of 1-year indexed bonds with a face value of $3m. The floor is the present value of the minimum wealth level to achieve at the end of the current year, plus a tax provision. The multiplier is set to 1, 3 or 5. The left column shows the success probabilities and the right column shows the expected and worst maximum shortfalls.

Figure 4.21. Investor 1 — Impact of tax rate on success indicators for EG1 with GBI strategy.

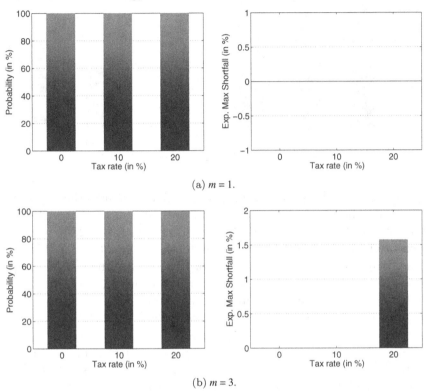

(a) $m = 1$.

(b) $m = 3$.

Notes: This figure shows the impact of the tax rate on the success indicators for EG1 with a dynamic GBI strategy which aims at securing EG1. Taxes are applied to gains on the stock and the bond indices and gains on the roll-over of 1-year indexed bonds. Existing positions in stocks and bonds and aspirational assets are liquidated at date 0. The performance building block is the MSR and the GHP is a roll-over of 1-year indexed bonds with a face value of $3m. The floor is the present value of the minimum wealth level to achieve at the end of the current year, plus a tax provision. The multiplier is set to 1, 3 or 5. The left column shows the success probabilities and the right column shows the expected maximum shortfalls.

is 20%. It is only with the highest tax rate (20%) and the most aggressive strategy (corresponding to a multiplier of 5) that the shortfall probability becomes non-negligible.

To complete this study, Figure 4.22 shows the impact of the tax rate on the success indicators for the aspirational goal. For the three values of the multiplier, the effect is the same: a higher tax rate

Figure 4.21. (*Continued*)

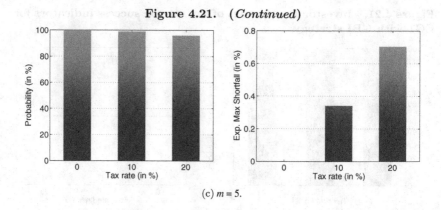

(c) $m = 5$.

lowers the probability of reaching the goal and increases the expected shortfall. The impact is material, but not substantial. For instance, for a value of 5, the success probability decreases from 62.7% with no taxes to 61.5% with a 20% rate. A potential explanation for this low sensitivity with respect to the level of taxes is that the GBI strategy leads by definition to selling the performance assets (stock and bond indices) on the downside (that is, when the risk budget shrinks), so that it is unlikely that profits will be made from these operations, and the contribution to taxes is small.

As a conclusion, the GBI strategy is relatively robust to the impact of taxes in the sense that it still secures the essential goal, except for high values of the tax rate and the multiplier.

4.2.   Case Study 2 (HNW Retiree)

The second case study is that of a married and just retired couple. The husband and wife both are 67 years old and have no long-term care or life insurance coverage to start with. They have enough savings and retirement income to fund some of their goals, but, as we explain in what follows, some goals remain aspirational because they cannot be fully funded.

4.2.1.   *Current allocation and goals*

4.2.1.1.   *Description of risk buckets*

The detailed composition of the current risk and asset allocation is given in Table 4.10. The initial net worth of the household is

Figure 4.22. Investor 1 — Impact of tax rate on success indicators for aspirational goal with GBI strategy.

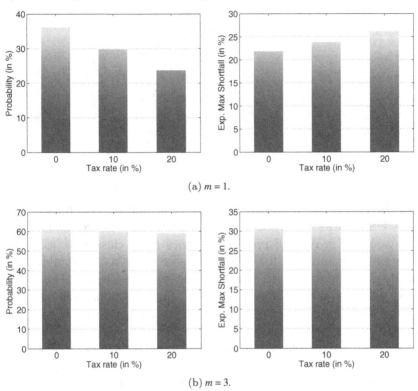

(a) $m = 1$.

(b) $m = 3$.

Notes: This figure shows the impact of the tax rate on the success indicators for an Aspirational Goal with a dynamic GBI strategy which aims at securing EG1. Taxes are applied to gains on the stock and the bond indices and gains on the roll-over of 1-year indexed bonds. Existing positions in stocks and bonds and aspirational assets are liquidated at date 0. The performance building block is the MSR portfolio and the GHP is a roll-over of 1-year indexed bonds with a face value of $3m. The floor is the present value of the minimum wealth level to achieve at the end of the current year, plus a tax provision. The multiplier is set to 1, 3 or 5. The left column shows the success probabilities and the right column shows the expected maximum shortfalls.

equal to $2,750,000 and consists of $1,350,000 in personal assets and $1,400,000 in market assets that can be sold to design a bespoke GBI strategy. The personal risk bucket is divided into a residence whose value is equal to $900,000 and $450,000 in cash. The personal risk bucket will be considered illiquid, and therefore

Figure 4.22. (*Continued*)

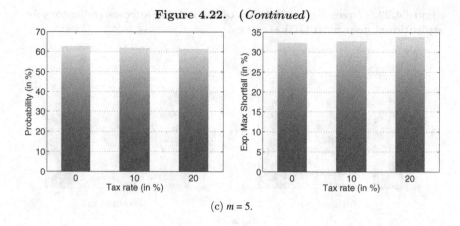

(c) *m* = 5.

modelled as a buy-and-hold strategy. The market risk bucket contains US equities (55%), US fixed-income (30%), hedge funds (10%) and cash (5%). We will proxy the equity asset class as a broad US equity index and the fixed-income asset class as a sovereign US bond index, and assume that both classes are liquid. The hedge fund will also be assumed liquid so that the household can liquidate their entire market wealth to form a goals-based portfolio invested in the MSR portfolio and one or more GHP(s). Note that unlike in the previous case study, the investor owns no aspirational assets.

The household receives an income of $65,000 (pre-tax) per year which consists of $30,000 from the social security and $35,000 from a personal pension (no Cost Of Living Adjustment). This income is taxed with a 20% rate. The same tax rate will be used for the capital gains obtained from rebalancing and receiving bond coupons.

4.2.1.2.   *Goals and goal-hedging portfolios*

The household has three explicitly formulated consumption goals. G1 is a consumption-based goal that consists of protecting a minimum lifestyle on retirement: the investor wants to afford an annual expense of $80,000 growing at the annual rate of 2.5% between ages 67 and 93 (that is, at horizons comprising between 1 and 26 years). The goal value is thus given by

$$G_t^1 = G_0^1 \times 1.025^t \quad \text{for } t = 1, \ldots, 26,$$

Table 4.10.   Investor 2 — Current risk and asset allocation and goals.

(a) Risk and asset allocation.

	Value ($)	% of Total		Value ($)	% of Total		Value ($)	% of Total
Personal Bucket	1,350,000	47.3	Market Bucket	1,400,000	52.7	Aspirational Bucket	0	0
Residence	900,000	66.7	US Equity	770,000	55.0			
Cash	450,000	33.3	US Fixed Income	420,000	30.0			
			Hedge Fund	140,000	10.0			
			Cash	70,000	5.0			

(b) Goals.

Name	Goal	Time horizon (years)	Threshold
Goal 1	Retirement Lifestyle	1–26	$80,000 (inflation-adjusted 2.5%)
Goal 2	Long-term Care Contingencies	24–29	$100,000 (inflation-adjusted 4.5%)
Goal 3	Retirement Lifestyle	1–26	$40,000 (inflation-adjusted 2.5%)
Goal 4	Bequest to Children	29	Surplus Assets

Notes: Panel (a) describes the current risk and asset allocation of Investor 2. Panel (b) describes his goals, which are ranked by order of decreasing priority from the top to the bottom.

where $G_0^1 = \$80,000$. The GHP for this goal is a coupon-paying bond that pays fixed annual coupons equal to $G_1^1, \ldots, G_{26}^1$. Its price on date t is equal to the present value of the goal, that is   .

$$GHP_{G1,t} = \sum_{\substack{s=1 \\ s>t}}^{26} G_s^1 \times b_{t,s}.$$

We recall that $b_{t,s}$ is the price at date s of the nominal zero-coupon which pays \$1 at date t. By Proposition 4, G1 is affordable if, and only if, the wealth available to finance the consumption stream is greater than or equal to $GHP_{G1,0}$.

The second goal by decreasing order of priority is G2. Like G1, it can be seen as a consumption-based goal, but unlike the previous goal, it occurs only with a probability p less than 100%. This expenditure is meant to finance long-term care contingencies (LTCC): the horizon ranges from year 24 (when the husband reaches age 91) to year 29 (when his wife turns 96) with a face value of $100,000 at the initial time. The working assumptions are as follows. When the couple reaches age 90, the husband will need a nursing home for 3 years and then pass away. Then, his wife will need 3 years of home care, starting at age 93 until she reaches 96 and dies. In our study we consider the following value $p = 65.39\%$ for G2 to occur. This value has been tabulated to reflect the need for LTCC of a couple that is 90 years old. The cost of this care is $100,000 per year today, and rises 4.5% per year in subsequent years. Eventually, the goal value is

$$G_t^2 = \begin{cases} G_0^2 \times 1.045^t & \text{for } t = 24, \ldots, 29 \text{ with probability } p \\ 0 & \text{with probability } (1-p) \end{cases},$$

where $G_0^2 = \$100,000$. The price of this consumption stream on date t is the price of a bond with random coupons equal to $G_{24}^1, \ldots, G_{29}^1$. It is given on date t by

$$P_{\text{G2},t} = G_0^2 \times p \sum_{\substack{s=24 \\ s>t}}^{29} 1.045^s \times b_{t,s}.$$

For simplicity, we assume that the actuarial risk is independent from the financial risk under the risk-neutral probability, so that the risk-neutral probability for the LTCC coincides with the historical probability. The price $P_{\text{G2},t}$ is the theoretical present value of G2. However, because the bond coupons are positive only in those states of the world where the couple needs a nursing home, it is not feasible to replicate the bond by matching interest rate sensitivities, and one would also need to use securities with an exposure to health risk.

Because such securities may be hard to find, we consider alternative approaches to deal with random consumption goals. The first is to design a GHP with deterministic coupons that can cover the random consumption streams in all states of the world. This corresponds to *super-replication* as opposed to *replication*. The price of the bond that covers each stream at date t is given by

$$\text{GHP}_{\text{G2},t}^{\text{surrep}} = G_0^2 \sum_{\substack{s=24 \\ s>t}}^{29} 1.045^s \times b_{t,s}.$$

If one invests in such a GHP, then G2 would be super-replicated since $P_{\text{G2},t}$ is less than or equal to $\text{GHP}_{\text{G2},t}^{\text{surrep}}$.

A second approach to secure the LTCC is to buy insurance. As explained in Section 2.4.1, using insurance can be well-suited for goals with uncertain cash flows since it might lead to cheaper strategies than a full super-replication of the random cash flows. In what follows, we will consider an insurance policy where the conditions include an annual premium of \$11,476 for a contract that covers half of the LTCC expenses. This annual premium is constant for life but premiums are no longer due once a claim is made at year 24. The insurance policy yearly benefit is \$50,000 today, and rises 4.5% per year in subsequent years. In summary, the couple pays \$11,476 per year in premiums for 23 years. Over the subsequent 6 years, either they remain healthy and keep paying the premiums, or they file an insurance claim, which gives them the right to stop paying the premiums and to receive half of their LTCC expenses from the insurer. The second possibility occurs with probability p. The premiums have been computed so that the following identity is satisfied with a load equal to 25%:

$$\text{PV(Benefits)} = (1 - \text{load}) \times \text{PV(premiums)}.$$

Thus, for every dollar of premium, the insured can (in present terms) expect to receive 75 cents of benefits. This 25% estimate for the load is consistent with standard practice, as cited by Brown and Finkelstein (2007). In the case of insurance, the GHP must be a bond that pays fixed coupons equal to the annual premiums, that is \$11,476 during the first 23 years, and pays fixed coupons over the last 6 years that cover the worst case scenario between paying the premiums without claiming insurance, or claiming insurance and paying the LTCC expenses that are not covered by the insurance. Since the insurance covers 50% of the LTCC expenses, the worst case scenario is to claim insurance. The price of the super-replicating GHP is therefore given by

$$\text{GHP}^{\text{assur}}_{\text{G2},t} = Q_0^2 \sum_{\substack{s=1 \\ s>t}}^{23} b_{t,s} + \frac{G_0^2}{2} \sum_{\substack{s=24 \\ s>t}}^{29} 1.045^s \times b_{t,s},$$

where $Q_0^2 = \$11,476$ represents the annual premium paid to the insurer. With the parameters of the case study, Table 4.11 shows that $P_{\text{G2},t}$ is less than $\text{GHP}^{\text{assur}}_{\text{G2},t}$, which is itself less than $\text{GHP}^{\text{super-rep}}_{\text{G2},t}$. This means that the strategy involving the insurance is cheaper than the strategy with full super-replication of G2.

The goal with the lowest priority rank is G3. It is also a consumption-based goal very similar to G1, needed to improve the retirement lifestyle. The level of G3 is $40,000 per year, growing at the annual rate of 2.5% between ages 67 and 93 (that is, at horizons comprising between 1 and 26 years). The nominal value of the goal is thus

$$G_t^3 = G_0^3 \times 1.025^t \quad \text{for } t = 1, \ldots, 26,$$

with $G_0^3 = \$40,000$. The present value of this goal is the price of a bond that pays fixed annual coupons equal to $G_1^3, \ldots, G_{26}^3$. Its price on date t is equal to the present value of the goal, that is

$$\text{GHP}_{\text{G3},t} = \sum_{\substack{s=1 \\ s>t}}^{26} G_s^3 \times b_{t,s}.$$

4.2.1.3. *Funding status of goals*

The first column of Table 4.11 looks at the goal affordability without using the income as a way to secure the goals. We notice that G1 and G2 require $1,824,302 to be secured without any income, which is lower than the total liquid wealth (including the present value of guaranteed lifetime income). If we add the minimum requirement for G3, then this sum exceeds the initial liquid wealth. Therefore, using

Table 4.11.   Investor 2 — Funding status of goals.

(i) Value of assets (in $).

Market wealth	1,400,000
Present value of guaranteed lifetime income	755,405
Total	**2,155,405**

(ii) Minimum capital required to secure one or more goal(s) (in $).

	Total Value (super-replication)	Net Value (super-replication)	Net Value (insurance)
Goal 1	1,461,467	732,093	732,093
Goal 2	362,835	336,805	309,032
G1 and G2	**1,824,302**	**1,068,898**	**1,041,125**
Goal 3	730,734	730,734	730,734
G1, G2 and G3	**2,555,036**	**1,799,632**	**1,771,859**

Notes: The assets of Investor 2 consist of liquid market assets and a claim on guaranteed lifetime income. Panel (ii) shows the minimum capital required to secure G1, G2 and G3 individually or jointly in three situations. In the first situation, the investor relies on both market wealth and income to secure the goals. In the second and third situations, the investor uses income to partially secure G1 and G2 (the present value of future income becomes equal to 0). In the second situation, G2 is fully super-replicated while in the third case, the same goal is 50% covered by insurance, and the other 50% is super-replicated. We notice that only G1 and G2 are affordable, hence can be considered as essential whereas G3 will remain aspirational. Also, we notice that the minimum capital required to secure the long-term care contingencies, which correspond to G2, is lower with the insurance.

Proposition 6, we can conclude that G1 and G2 are jointly affordable and that G3 will remain aspirational. In summary:

- G1 is affordable with liquid wealth and can thus be treated as an essential goal (referred to as EG1);
- G2 is affordable with liquid wealth jointly with EG1 and can thus be treated as an essential goal (referred to as EG2);
- G3 is not affordable jointly with EG1 and EG2, and thus represents an aspirational goal (referred to as AG1, while AG2 will refer to the goal concerning the bequest to the children).

If G1 and G2 are secured with income, then the super-replication or the insurance approach for G2 both lead to a minimum capital requirement that is lower than the initial liquid market wealth of $1.4 million. The use of income to secure the two essential goals is justified in Sections 2.2.4.5 and 2.2.4.6. In a nutshell, by doing so the couple leaves a higher fraction of liquid wealth available to invest in performance assets and increase their chances of reaching aspirational goals.

4.2.1.4. *Decision rules for goal payment*

In order to increase the probability of reaching all their essential goals, at a given time, the couple should pay their non-essential goals only if they are left with enough wealth to secure all the essential goals until the end of their lives. Hence, AG1 is paid in full at date t if the wealth on date t after paying the essential goals, but before paying the non-essential goals (and net of income and mortgage repayment) is greater than $\text{MCR}_{EG,t} + \text{AG1}_t$, where $\text{MCR}_{EG,t}$ is the minimum capital requirement for securing both essential goals and AG1_t represents the non-essential goal expenses of the aspirational goal at date t. The minimum capital requirement at a given date t is obtained by summing up the GHP values at the same date of all the essential goals.

In case the available wealth is not sufficient to pay a goal in full, the investor only pays the fraction of the goal such that the wealth after the payment is greater than the minimum capital level.

4.2.2. *Strategies securing essential goal(s)*

4.2.2.1. *Current strategy*

The current strategy is a fixed-mix that keeps the asset weights within the liquid bucket (US equity, US fixed-income, hedge fund and cash) equal to their initial values at the beginning of each year. We assume that at each goal payment date, the household pays the goal if there is enough liquid wealth. Otherwise it pays the largest possible fraction of the goal that can be covered by the liquid wealth. We report the probabilities of reaching goals with the current strategy in Figure 4.23.

Figure 4.23. Investor 2 — Success indicators for current strategy.

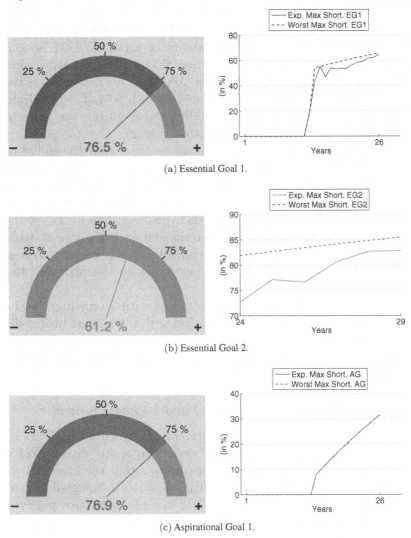

(a) Essential Goal 1.

(b) Essential Goal 2.

(c) Aspirational Goal 1.

Notes: The half circles represent the success probabilities for each goal: the probability is estimated as the percentage of scenarios in which the goal was reached. The expected maximum shortfall on date t is the expectation of the maximum relative deviation from the goal recorded by date t, conditional on the event of such a deviation. The worst maximum shortfall is defined as the worst relative loss recorded by date t across all dates and paths. The "current strategy" is a fixed-mix policy with annual rebalancing towards the current market allocation.

The goal with the highest probability of achievement (at 76.9%) is the aspirational goal. It shares the same cash-flow dates as EG1, but its level is only half that of EG1, so it can be met more often than EG1. Indeed the probability of attaining EG1 is equal to 76.5%, which is slightly lower than that of AG1. When looking at the expected shortfall figures for AG1 and EG1, we notice that the default occurs in the same year 13 which is half way through the payment period of both goals. From year 13 on, the expected loss increases until the last payment on year 26.

On the other hand, EG2 payment dates occur near the end of the period, from year 24 to year 29. Therefore, despite the importance of this goal, it will be harder to achieve given that the liquid wealth will have been already spent on the two other goals before year 24. We observe a probability of achieving their goal equal to 61.2%, with a strictly positive expected shortfall on the first date of payment, which shows that the average investor who follows the current strategy cannot even fully afford the LTCC expenses on the first year they have to be paid.

Both essential goals cannot be attained with a very high level of confidence, and the goal that is satisfied with the highest probability is the least essential to the investor. These two drawbacks of the current strategy will be addressed with a GBI solution described in the following sections.

4.2.2.2. *Protecting essential goals 1 and 2 without insurance*

In this section, we propose to secure the two essential goals with a GBI solution. We use all received income to secure either EG1 or EG2 in order to reduce the future cash flows that the investors will have to pay, hence reducing the initial position in the goal-hedging portfolios. In this section, we do not use the insurance policy to protect the household against the risk of needing long-term care. Therefore, we have to super-replicate EG2 using $\text{GHP}_{G2,t}^{\text{super}-\text{rep}}$ as explained in Section 4.2.1.2. The results for this GBI strategy are provided in Figure 4.24.

The success indicators for the strategy securing EG1 and EG2 are equal to 100%, which shows that in each of our 1,000 Monte Carlo scenarios, the household can afford their retirement lifestyle (EG1) and their long-term care contingencies (EG2). However, the

Figure 4.24. Investor 2 — Success indicators for strategy securing EG1 and EG2 in the absence of insurance for EG2.

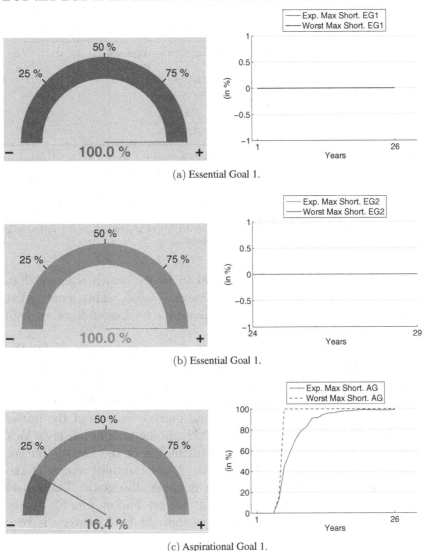

(a) Essential Goal 1.

(b) Essential Goal 1.

(c) Aspirational Goal 1.

Notes: This figure shows the success probabilities (left column) and the expected and the worst maximum shortfalls (right column) for a strategy securing EG1 and EG2. Protection of EG2 is achieved through super-replication of the long-term contingencies claims. The portfolio is buy-and-hold in the bond that pays the cash flows of EG1 and EG2.

Table 4.12.　Investor 2 — Initial risk allocation of strategy securing EG1 and EG2 in the absence of insurance for EG2.

	Value ($)	% of Total		Value ($)	% of Total		Value ($)	% of Total
Personal Bucket	2,418,898	88.00	Market Bucket	331,102	12.0	Aspirational Bucket	0	0
Residence	900,000	37.2	US Equity	266,280	80.4			
Cash	450,000	18.6	US Fixed Income	64,822	19.6			
GHP: EG1+EG2	1,068,898	44.2						

Notes: This table shows the risk allocation at date 0 when the investor holds buy-and-hold positions in the MSR portfolio and the GHP for EG1 and EG2, which is a bond that delivers the goal cash flows. The cash flows are $80,000 per year from year 1 to year 26 and $100,000 per year from year 24 to year 29. The personal bucket contains the assets that are used to finance the investor's essential goals. The aspirational bucket is empty because income is used to finance EG1 and EG2 at the end of each year. The market bucket contains all other assets (equities and bonds here). The table displays the weights of the various assets within each bucket, as well as the relative weights of the buckets.

probability of reaching AG1 is equal to 16.4%, which is lower than that obtained with the current strategy (76.9%). This means that after paying EG1 and EG2, the investors no longer have enough wealth available to pay for AG1.

Failing to pay for AG1 occurs earlier in the period compared to the current strategy because in a GBI strategy a significant percentage of the initial wealth is used to invest in GHP, and the non-essential goals can no longer be financed. Table 4.12 shows the percentage of wealth invested in the personal and market buckets at the initial date. In order to secure EG1 and EG2, the household needs to lock up $1,068,898. Therefore, the investment left in the market bucket is equal to $331,102 which represents 12% of the total wealth of the household that is free to cover the non-essential goals. The initial percentage of wealth invested in the market bucket was 52.7% for the current strategy, which illustrates that the GBI strategy is very different from the current allocation.

4.2.2.3.　*Protecting essential goals 1 and 2 with LTCC insurance*

We now assume that instead of fully super-replicating the long-term care contingencies expenses as in Section 4.2.2.2, the household buys an insurance policy that covers half of their expenses in case they need long-term care. Again, we use income to partially secure EG1

Figure 4.25. Investor 2 — Success indicators for strategy securing EG1 and EG2 when insurance is used for EG2.

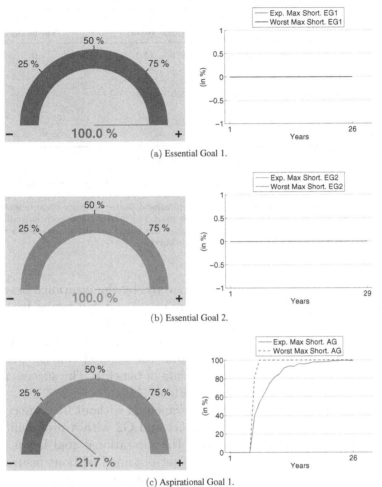

(a) Essential Goal 1.

(b) Essential Goal 2.

(c) Aspirational Goal 1.

Notes: This figure shows the success probabilities (left column) and the expected and the worst maximum shortfalls (right column) for a strategy securing EG1 and EG2 when 50% of the long-term care contingencies claims (EG2) are covered by insurance and the remaining 50% are super-replicated. The portfolio is buy-and-hold in the bond that pays the cash flows of EG1 and EG2.

and what is left to cover in EG2. As explained in Section 4.2.1.2, the value of the goal-hedging portfolio is now given by $\text{GHP}_{\text{G2},t}^{\text{assur}}$ and is computed as the sum of two components: the present value of the fixed policy premiums paid over the first 23 years, and the present

Table 4.13.   Investor 2 — Initial risk allocation of strategy securing EG1 and EG2 in the presence of insurance for EG2.

	Value ($)	% of Total		Value ($)	% of Total		Value ($)	% of Total
Personal Bucket	2,391,125	86.9	Market Bucket	358,875	13.1	Aspirational Bucket	0	0
Residence	900,000	37.7	US Equity	288,616	80.4			
Cash	450,000	18.8	Income Income	70,259	19.6			
GHP: EG1+EG2	1,041,125	43.5						

Notes: This table shows the risk allocation at date 0 when the investor holds buy-and-hold positions in the MSR portfolio and the GHP for EG1 and EG2, which is a bond that delivers the goal cash flows ($80,000 per year from year 1 to year 26, and $50,000 per year from year 24 to year 29 plus the insurance annuities). The personal bucket contains the assets that are used to finance investor's essential goals. The aspirational bucket is empty because income is used to secure EG1 and EG2 at the end of each year. The market bucket contains all other assets (equities and bonds here). The table displays the weights of the various assets within each bucket, as well as the relative weights of the buckets.

value of the expenses that are not covered by the insurance between years 24 and 29. If the insurance policy is not too expensive, this strategy is cheaper and therefore enables the investor to get more upside. In our simulation, we have considered a load of 25% meaning that for every dollar of premium, the insured can (in present value terms) expect to receive 75 cents of benefits. The success metrics for this strategy are shown in Figure 4.25.

Similar to the GBI strategy implemented without insurance, this strategy can secure both essential G1 and G2 with a probability of 100%. The probability of securing the aspirational goal is equal to 21.7%, which is 5.3% higher than that obtained without insurance. The explanation for improving the performance with respect to AG1 is that insurance reduces the cost of EG2, freeing up more wealth to pay for the cash flows of AG1. As shown in Table 4.13, the sum of both GHP values for the two essential goals is equal to $1,041,125 with insurance, which is slightly lower than the amount of $1,068,898 obtained without insurance. The difference is not very high because the coverage of the insurance is equal to 50%, hence the remaining half of the expenses still has to be covered by a super-replication strategy.

In Figure 4.26, we show the terminal wealth distribution for both strategies. We notice that they share the same minimum and median

Figure 4.26. Investor 2 — Distribution of terminal wealth for strategies securing EG1 and EG2.

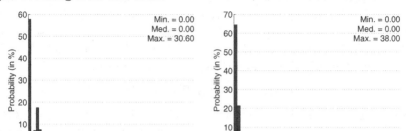

Notes: This figure shows the distribution of the terminal wealth at the end of year 29 with two strategies for the long-term care contingencies claims: super-replication in left column and insurance in right column. The portfolio is buy-and-hold in the bond that pays the cash flows of EG1 and EG2.

wealth — equal to 0. Indeed, since AG1 is not affordable, both strategies will pay cash flows until the household runs out of wealth. This should happen more than 50% of the time since the probability that the investors will face LTCC expenses is equal to 65.39%. In that case, the household will be spending a substantial amount of wealth in their last 6 years of life. In the other 34.61% of the time, they will not spend anything for LTCC and end their life with a significant surplus (a maximum of $30m or $38m depending on the strategies according to Figure 4.26) which represents the bequest left to the children. In order to have a control on the minimum bequest level to the children, we can add a wealth-based goal to the strategy. This is the content of the next section.

4.2.2.4. *Introduction of a minimum wealth constraint*

We now consider the introduction of an additional goal, which is to secure at the 29-year horizon an amount of wealth equal to the initial liquid capital, that is $1,400,000. This wealth-based goal models the second aspirational goal of the household, which is a bequest objective: the investor wants to leave a certain amount of money to his children. We refer to it as Goal 4 (G4).

As can be seen from Figure 4.26, the median wealth is equal to zero with and without insurance, which means that at least half of the scenarios lead to final wealth levels that remain below the target of $1.4m, so the strategy fails to secure this wealth-based goal. Before designing a new strategy that takes G4 into account, the first question that we should address is to know whether or not this new goal is jointly affordable with the more essential goals EG1 and EG2. So, we must first qualify the affordability of G4. By absence of arbitrage opportunities, if the goals EG1 and EG2 are reached with certainty, then the liquid wealth at the initial date must satisfy

$$A_0 \geq \text{GHP}_{G1,0} + \text{GHP}_{G2,0} + A_0 b_{0,29},$$

where $\text{GHP}_{G1,0}$ is the value of the goal-hedging portfolio for EG1, $\text{GHP}_{G2,0}$ the value of the goal-hedging portfolio for EG2 (either equal to $\text{GHP}_{G2,0}^{\text{assur}}$ if we use insurance or equal to $\text{GHP}_{G2,0}^{\text{super}-\text{rep}}$ in the absence of insurance), A_0 is the initial wealth (\$1,400,000) and $b_{0,29}$ is the price of a zero-coupon bond maturing at date 29. Conversely, if the inequality holds, then the investor can afford the bonds that finance EG1 and EG2, plus a zero-coupon that will deliver A_0 on date 29. Hence, the above inequality is a necessary and sufficient condition for the goals EG1, EG2 and G4 to be jointly affordable. In Table 4.14, we observe that the present value of securing \$1,400,000 at year 29 is equal to \$214,792, which shows that EG1, EG2 and G4 are jointly affordable. Indeed, in the net value version (where income is used to secure EG1 and EG2) we find that the right-hand side of the above inequality is equal to \$1,283,690 in the strategy without insurance and to \$1,255,250 in the strategy with insurance. Both minimum capital requirements fall below the initial liquid wealth A_0. Therefore, G4 is affordable with liquid wealth jointly with EG1 and EG2, and can thus be treated as an EG3. The detailed initial risk allocations with strategies securing EG1, EG2 and EG3 are given in Table 4.15.

Figure 4.27 shows that the GBI strategy securing the three essential goals EG1, EG2 and EG3 achieves its target, whether the household buys an insurance policy or not. There is a 100% chance to attain the three essential goals. However, the aspirational goal becomes impossible to attain with both strategies. In order to see how the two approaches for handling EG2 differ, we look in Figure 4.28 at the distribution of terminal wealth and at the shortfall indicator for AG1. It turns out that the strategy without insurance fails on average to pay AG1 on the second date, whereas the strategy that uses insurance can afford the first and second payments. This comes from the higher cost of super-replication compared to the cost of insurance. When looking at terminal wealth, we see that the minimum wealth coincides with the median wealth and is equal to \$1.4m. The maximum wealth

Table 4.14. **Investor 2 — Funding status of goals in the presence of a minimum wealth goal.**

(i) Value of assets (in $).

Market wealth	1,400,000
Present value of guaranteed lifetime income	755,405
Total	**2,155,405**

(ii) Minimum capital required to secure one or more goal(s) (in $).

	Total Value	Net Value (super-replication)	Net Value (insurance)
EG1	1,461,467	732,093	732,093
EG2	362,835	336,805	309,032
Goal 4	214,792	214,792	214,792
EG1, EG2 and G4	**2,039,094**	**1,283,690**	**1,255,917**
AG1	730,734	730,734	730,734
EG1, EG2, G4 and AG1	**2,769,828**	**2,014,424**	**1,986,651**

Notes: The assets of Investor 2 consist of liquid market assets and a claim on guaranteed lifetime income. Panel (ii) shows the minimum capital required to secure each goal individually or jointly in three situations (the last two situations use income to secure EG1 and EG2, hence reduce to zero the present value of income after netting operations). The minimum wealth goal, denoted by G4, is affordable together with EG1 and EG2, so it can be treated as a third essential goal, EG3.

is higher for the super-replication strategy because in the case the household does not have to pay for LTCC, the super-replication of the strategy leaves them with a lot of wealth towards the end of their life. When the household uses insurance, they only super-replicate one half of the LTCC expenses, which will give them 50% less extra wealth in case they do not have to pay for LTCC. Moreover, if they remain healthy, they will have to keep paying the insurance premiums. This explains why the maximum terminal wealth level is higher for the strategy without insurance, and differs from the strategy with insurance by a factor close to 2.

4.2.3. Impact of taxes

To see if the results obtained in Section 4.2.2.2 remain robust in the presence of taxes, we now consider a uniform tax rate ζ equal to 20%,

Table 4.15. Investor 2 — Initial risk allocations with strategies securing EG1, EG2 and EG3.

(a) EG2 protected without insurance.

	Value ($)	% of Total		Value ($)	% of Total		Value ($)	% of Total
Personal Bucket	2,633,690	95.8	Market Bucket	116,310	4.2	Aspirational Bucket	0	0
Residence	900,000	34.2	US Equity	93,539	80.4			
Cash	450,000	17.1	US Fixed Income	22,771	19.6			
GHP: EG1+ EG2+EG3	1,283,690	48.7						

(b) EG2 protected with insurance.

	Value ($)	% of Total		Value ($)	% of Total		Value ($)	% of Total
Personal Bucket	2,605,917	94.8	Market Bucket	144,083	5.2	Aspirational Bucket	0	0
Residence	900,000	34.6	US Equity	115,875	80.4			
Cash	450,000	17.3	US Fixed Income	28,208	19.6			
GHP: EG1+ EG2+EG3	1,255,917	48.2						

Notes: This table shows the risk allocation at date 0 for two strategies securing EG1, EG2 and EG3. In Panel (a), the investor purchases a bond that pays the cash flows of EG1 and EG2 and delivers the minimum wealth level that corresponds to EG3 in year 29. In Panel (b), the investor partially secures EG2 with insurance, and purchases a bond that pays the cash flows for EG1, EG2 and delivers the minimum wealth level that corresponds to EG3 in year 29. The minimum wealth at date 29 has been set equal to the initial market wealth, i.e. equal to $1.4million.

and adopt the LIFO convention to compute the taxable gains (see Appendix A.6.5 for mathematical details). We run the robustness check on the strategy that secures both EG1 and EG2. This will adjust the previous GHP computations to take into account taxes in the GBI strategy.

4.2.3.1. *Adjustment to GHP for goal 1*

In this case study, taxes arise from the selling operations in the stock and the bond indices held within the PSP building block and from the coupons paid by the bonds that secure EG1 and EG2, coupons which are equal to the consumption expenses.

Figure 4.27. Investor 2 — Success indicators for strategy securing EG1, EG2 and EG3 with either super-replication (left column) or insurance (right column) for EG2.

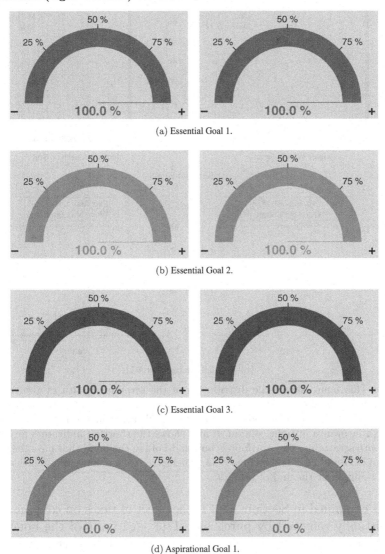

Notes: This figure shows the success probabilities with two strategies securing all three essential goals. Protection of EG2 is achieved through super-replication in the left column, and insurance in the right column. The portfolio is buy-and-hold in the bond that pays the cash flows of EG1 and EG2 and secures EG3, which is to reach a minimum wealth of $1.4 million at the end of year 29.

Figure 4.28.   Investor 2 — Distribution of terminal wealth and short-fall indicators for strategies securing EG1, EG2 and EG3.

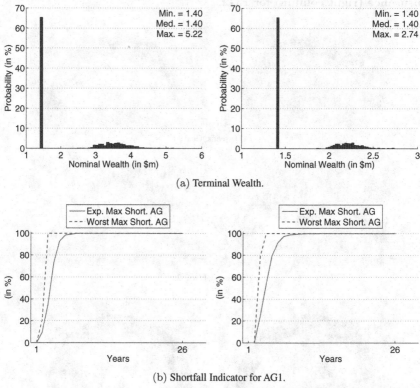

(a) Terminal Wealth.

(b) Shortfall Indicator for AG1.

Notes: This figure shows the distribution of the terminal wealth at the end of year 29 considering two strategies for the long-term care contingencies claims. Protection of EG2 is achieved through super-replication in the left column and through insurance in right column. It also shows the shortfall indicators for AG1 with both strategies. The portfolio is buy-and-hold in the bond that pays the cash flows of EG1 and EG2 and secures EG3, which is to reach a minimum wealth equal to $1.4 million at the end of year 29.

As explained in Section 3.3.3.1, the effect of taxes on coupons can be virtually removed by purchasing $1/(1 - \zeta)$ units of the bond. In other words, for the goal to be secured with certainty, the investor's wealth at the initial date must satisfy

$$A_0 \geq \frac{1}{1 - \zeta}(\text{GHP}_{\text{G1},0} + \text{GHP}_{\text{G2},0}),$$

where we recall that $\text{GHP}_{\text{G1},0}$ is the present value of retirement lifestyle expenses and $\text{GHP}_{\text{G2},0}$ is the value of the goal-hedging portfolio securing the long-term care contingencies (either equal to GHP$^{\text{assur}}_{\text{G2,0}}$ if we use the insurance or equal to GHP$^{\text{surrep}}_{\text{G2,0}}$ in the absence of insurance). Thus, in the presence of taxes, the values of the GHPs for G1 and G2 are simply given by

$$\text{GHP}_{Gj,tax,0} = \frac{1}{1-\zeta}\text{GHP}_{Gj,0} \quad \text{for } j = 1 \text{ and } 2.$$

The tax rate being positive, it is clear that these GHPs are more expensive than the ones that secure the goals in the absence of taxes, leading to more costly GBI policies to attain the same level of goal achievement. The performance-seeking allocation of our portfolio which is represented by the MSR portfolio can also lead to additional taxes from periodical rebalancing. These taxes are not hedged by the adjustment to the GHP value so the taxes generated by selling operations can in theory cause violations of the essential goal.

To verify that EG1 and EG2 remain jointly affordable in the presence of taxes, we go back to Table 4.11 and multiply the minimum capital required by 1.25 (the value of the multiplicative factor $1/(1 - \zeta)$ with a 20% tax rate). We obtain the following values:

No Insurance: $1.25 \times \$1,068,898 = \$1,336,122.5,$

Insurance: $1.25 \times \$1,041,125 = \$1,301,406.5.$

These minimum capital levels can be secured at the initial date since the liquid wealth is equal to \$1,400,000 at date 0. Therefore, the two goals remain jointly affordable, but the risk budget which corresponds to the difference between the liquid wealth and the minimum capital required to secure the essential goals has become very small. Therefore, G4 can no longer be affordable together with EG1 and EG2, and the aspirational goal AG1 will have to remain aspirational.

4.2.3.2. *Test of strategies securing essential goals 1 and 2*

As expected, the risk budget resulting from the introduction of taxes is too small to enable the household to afford AG1. In Figure 4.29, we have tested the strategy that secures both EG1 and EG2 without insurance for EG2. We observe that the probability of reaching AG1 is equal to 0. However, the probabilities of achieving both EG1 and EG2 remain equal to 100%, which shows that GBI strategies

Figure 4.29. Investor 2 — Success indicators for strategy securing EG1 and EG2, without taxes (left column) and with a 20% tax rate (right column).

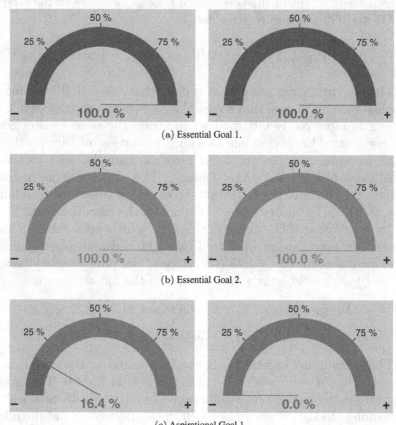

(a) Essential Goal 1.

(b) Essential Goal 2.

(c) Aspirational Goal 1.

Notes: This figure shows the success probabilities for the strategy for securing EG1 and EG2, when protection of EG2 is achieved through super-replication. There are no taxes in the left column, while a 20% rate is applied to gains from selling securities and to bond coupons in the right column. The portfolio is buy-and-hold in the bond that pays the cash flows of EG1 and EG2.

are robust to the introduction of taxes as long as the minimum capital required is updated accordingly. Here, taxes coming from selling operations in the MSR portfolio do not cause violations. We do not report the results of the strategy with insurance in the presence of taxes since they are very similar to those of the strategy without insurance.

4.3.   Case Study 3 (Affluent Accumulator)

The third case study relates to a younger investor (45 years old), with potential to move up the wealth level. As in the previous two case studies, the investor has both essential and aspirational goals.

4.3.1.   *Current allocation and goals*

4.3.1.1.   *Description of risk buckets*

Table 4.16 shows the current risk and asset allocation of the investor. The personal risk bucket consists of the principal residence, whose current value is $300,000, and a cash account of value $10,000. As in the other two case studies, these assets are used to finance essential needs which are, respectively, not to be homeless and to afford a minimum standard of living. Thus, we will assume a buy-and-hold allocation to these assets. The investor must also repay a fixed-rate mortgage loan. We assume a constant-annuity scheme with a borrowing rate of 4%. The expression for the constant annuity l is derived in Appendix A.5.2 and reads

$$\ell = \frac{r}{1 - (1+r)^{-T}} \times L.$$

Here, r is 4%, L is the principal of the loan, of $250,000, and the maturity T is 20 years. Numerically, the constant annuity is $18,395.

As can be seen from Table 4.16, the market risk bucket is dominated by equities, which represent 63.8% of market wealth. The remainder of this bucket is invested in US fixed-income instruments (31.9%) and cash (4.3%). These proportions are similar to those of the investor in the first case study (see Section 4.1), but here, the investor owns no aspirational assets. We will proxy the equity asset class as a broad US equity index and the fixed-income asset class as a sovereign US bond index, and assume that both classes are liquid.

In addition to these assets and liabilities, the investor is also endowed with a positive net income stream: every year, he receives $25,000 after taxes, an amount that grows by 2.5% every year. Mathematically, the income received in year t is

$$y_t = \begin{cases} y_0 \times 1.025^t & \text{for } t = 1, \ldots, 20 \\ 0 & \text{otherwise} \end{cases}.$$

Table 4.16.   Investor 3 — Current risk and asset allocation and goals.

(a) Risk and asset allocation.

	Value ($)	% of Total		Value ($)	% of Total		Value ($)	% of Total
Personal Bucket	60,000	6.0	Market Bucket	940,000	94.0	Aspirational Bucket	0	0
Residence	300,000	53.6	Equity	600,000	63.8			
Cash	10,000	1.8	US Fixed Income	300,000	31.9			
Adjustable Rate Mortgage	(250,000)	44.6	Cash	40,000	4.3			

(b) Goals.

Priority	Goal	Time horizon (years)	Threshold
Goal 0	Mortgage amortisation	1–20	$18,395/year (constant)
Goal 1	Retirement lifestyle	21–50	$90,000/year (inflation-adjusted)
Goal 2	Children's education	11–14	$50,000/year (inflation-adjusted)
Goal 3	House purchase	5	$300,000 (inflation-adjusted)

Notes: Panel (a) describes the current risk and asset allocation of Investor 3. Panel (b) describes his goals, which are ranked by order of decreasing priority from the top to the bottom.

4.3.1.2.   *Goals and goal-hedging portfolios*

First of all, it should be noted that mortgage amortisation represents an implicit essential goal (referred to as Goal 0 in Table 4.16): indeed, the annual down payment is a payment that the investor can neither cancel nor postpone. The present value of this goal equals the face value of the loan of $250,000.

Besides, the investor has three explicitly formulated goals. G1 is a consumption-based goal that consists of protecting a minimum lifestyle during retirement: the investor wants to afford an annual expense of $90,000 growing at the annual rate of 2.5% between ages 66 and 95 (that is, at horizons comprising between 21 and 50 years). The annual expense is fixed in real terms, which means that it is adjusted for inflation. The nominal goal value is thus

$$G_t^1 = \begin{cases} G_0^1 \times 1.025^t & \text{for } t = 21, \ldots, 50 \\ 0 & \text{otherwise} \end{cases},$$

where $G_0^1 = \$90{,}000$. The GHP for this goal is a coupon-paying bond that pays fixed annual coupons equal to $G_1^1, \ldots, G_{50}^1$. Its price on date t is equal to the present value of the goal, that is

$$\text{GHP}_{G1,t} = \tilde{G}_t^1 = \sum_{\substack{s=21 \\ s>t}}^{50} G_s^1 \times b_{t,s}.$$

We recall that $b_{t,s}$ denotes the price on date s of the nominal zero-coupon which pays \$1 at date t. By Proposition 4, G1 is affordable if, and only if, the amount of wealth available to finance the consumption stream is greater than or equal to $\text{GHP}_{G1,0}$.

The next goal by order of decreasing priority is G2. Like G1, it is a consumption-based goal. This expenditure is meant to finance children's education: the horizon ranges from 11 and 14 years, and the face value is \$50,000. As for G1, the annual expenditure grows at the annual rate of 2.5%, so the nominal goal value in year t is

$$G_t^2 = \begin{cases} G_0^2 \times 1.025^t & \text{for } t = 11, \ldots, 14 \\ 0 & \text{otherwise} \end{cases},$$

where $G_0^2 = \$50{,}000$. The minimum capital to invest at date t to finance this consumption stream is

$$\text{GHP}_{G2,t} = \tilde{G}_t^2 = \sum_{\substack{s=11 \\ s>t}}^{14} G_s^2 \times b_{t,s}.$$

The goal with the lowest priority rank is G3. It is also a consumption-based goal, which is to purchase a house at the horizon of 5 years. The real value of the goal is \$300,000, and the nominal value grows at the annual rate of 2.5%, so it is given in year t by

$$G_t^3 = \begin{cases} G_0^3 \times 1.025^t & \text{for } t = 5 \\ 0 & \text{otherwise} \end{cases},$$

with $G_0^3 = \$300{,}000$. The present value of this goal is the price of a nominal zero-coupon that pays off \$300,000 at the 5-year horizon. At date t, we have

$$\text{GHP}_{\text{AG},t} = \tilde{G}_t^3 = G_5^3 \times b_{t,5} \times \mathbb{I}_{\{t<5\}}.$$

4.3.1.3. *Funding status of goals*

At the first level of analysis, it is possible to look at the affordability of goals by abstracting away from income. If the investor relies only on liquid wealth to achieve his consumption goals, a necessary and sufficient affordability criterion is given by Proposition 6: the initial capital must be larger than the sum of the present values of goals. Panels (i) and (ii) in Table 4.17 show, respectively, the asset side and the liability side of the balance sheet, and the second column of Panel (ii) contains the cumulated sum of the present values of goals. The other columns will be commented on later. Liquid wealth of \$940,000 is sufficient to afford the most important goal (G1), but not to afford jointly G1 and G2, because G1 requires \$810,256 but G1 and G2 require \$980,149. However, if future savings could be turned into liquid wealth, G2 would become affordable since liquid wealth would become \$1,121,506. In what follows, we will rule out this possibility because selling a claim on future savings would mean that the investor is allowed to borrow against future income. As a conclusion, if the investor does not use income to finance the goals:

- G1 is affordable with liquid wealth alone, and can thus be treated as an essential goal (henceforth referred to as EG1);
- G2 and G3 are not affordable jointly with EG1, and thus represent aspirational goals.

But as explained in Sections 2.2.4.5 and 2.2.4.6, it is better for the investor to use income to secure the goal, so as to leave a greater fraction of liquid wealth available to invest in performance assets and increase his chances of reaching non-essential goals. With this approach, the investor must purchase an option whose payoff covers the fraction of the goal that is not financed by income. Among the various strategies described in Sections 2.2.4.5 and 2.2.4.6, we

Table 4.17. Investor 3 — Funding status of goals.

(i) Value of assets (in $).

Market wealth	940,000
Present value of future savings	181,506
Total	**1,121,506**

(ii) Minimum capital required to secure one or more goal(s) (in $).

	Liquid wealth only	Income and zero re-investment rate	Income and compound option	Income and forward contracts
Goal 1	810,256	709,181	V_0	628,750
Goal 2	169,893	169,893	169,893	169,893
G1 and G2	**980,149**	**879,074**	**169,893 + V_0**	**798,643**
Goal 3	305,274	305,274	305,274	305,274
G1, G2 and G3	**1,285,424**	**1,184,348**	**475,167 + V_0**	**1,103,917**

Notes: The assets of Investor 3 consist of liquid market assets and a claim on future savings net of mortgage annuities. Panel (ii) shows the minimum capital required to secure G1, G2 and G3 individually or jointly in four situations. In the second column, the investor relies only on liquid wealth. In the third column, he uses income to secure G1, assuming a zero re-investment rate for future income payments, and purchases an option to make up for the excess of consumption over income. In the fourth column, he uses income and a compound option, the price of which is denoted by V_0 (see Proposition 8). In the fifth column, he uses income assuming that future income will be re-invested at the forward rate fixed at date 0, and purchases an option to make up for the excess consumption. Goals are ranked by decreasing order of priority.

only test the simplest ones, which do not involve compound options. Specifically, we consider the strategies referred to as INC-ZER-RET and INC-FWD in Section 2.2.4.6.

The strategy INC-ZER-RET assumes that future income is invested at a zero rate for a period equal to the time to retirement. A step-by-step description is as follows:

- At date 0, the investor purchases an option that matures on the retirement date and pays the excess of the goal present value over the cumulated value of income capitalised at a zero rate. This payoff occurs at date 21, that is at the end of the 21st year, and with the notations of Section 2.2.4.6, it is given by

$$U_{\text{ret},21,0} = \left(\tilde{G}_{21-}^1 - \sum_{k=1}^{20} y_k \right)^+.$$

The remainder of wealth is invested in a performance-seeking portfolio, which we take to be the MSR portfolio of stock and bond indices;

- At the end of year j, where j ranges from 1 to 20, the investor purchases an option that pays, on date 21,

$$U_{\text{ret},21,j} = \left(\tilde{G}_{21-}^1 - \sum_{k=j+1}^{20} y_k \right)^+.$$

As explained in Section 2.2.4.6, this option is fully financed by the option purchased at the previous date and the received income. The remaining amount is invested in the MSR portfolio;

- As of date 20, the investor holds a long position in the bond that delivers the cash flows of the goal, which fully secures this goal.

In the context of our simulations, the pricing of the options is greatly simplified because it happens that $\tilde{G}_{21-}^1$ is greater than the cumulative income with probability 1. As a result, a long position in each option is equivalent to a long position in the bond that pays the goal cash flows, plus a short position in a zero-coupon bond that pays the cumulative income upon retirement, on date 21. As a result, at each income date j, the investor can increase the dollar allocation to the MSR portfolio by the amount

$$U_{\text{ret},j,j-1} + y_j - U_{\text{ret},j,j} = (1 - b_{j,21})y_j,$$

where $b_{j,21}$ is the price of the pure discount bond that pays \$1 on the retirement date. This price is less than \$1, since nominal rates are assumed to stay non-negative throughout our simulations.

The minimum initial capital required to implement this strategy is the price of the first option. With the assumed parameter values, it is \$709,181, which of course is less expensive than the bond that pays the cash flows for the goal. Interestingly, G2 becomes jointly affordable with G1 if this strategy is followed, because the total capital requirement to fund both goals is \$879,074, which is less than the available \$940,000. As a consequence, G2 can be treated as an essential or important goal, depending on the decision to secure it or not. However, G3 is still not affordable jointly with the two more priority goals.

The second strategy to secure the essential goal, referred to as INC-FWD, uses forward contracts and proceeds as follows:

- At date 0, the investor enters forward contracts to fix the investment rate for a loan starting at date $j = 1, \ldots, 20$ and finishing at date 21. This rate is the forward rate $f_{j,21-j}$, which can be expressed as a function of zero-coupon prices:

$$f_{j,21-j} = \left(\frac{b_{0,j}}{b_{0,21}} \right)^{\frac{1}{21-j}} - 1.$$

The deficit to finance at date 21 will thus be

$$W_{21} = \left(\tilde{G}_{21-}^1 - \sum_{k=1}^{20} y_k (1 + f_{k,21-k})^{21-k} \right)^+ .$$

It is covered by purchasing an option of price W_0. Any remaining wealth is invested in the same performance portfolio as before, namely the MSR portfolio of stock and bond indices;

- At each income date $j = 1, \ldots, 20$, the received income is invested at the forward rate;
- At date 21, the investor is able to purchase the bond paying the cash flows for the goal by combining the option payoff and the cumulative income. Thus, the goal is secured.

It should be noted that with this strategy, unlike INC-ZER-RET, there is no additional investment in the MSR portfolio when an income inflow is cashed in: income is entirely invested in a separate account and grows at the forward rate. The initial cost of the protection is the option price, W_0, which is numerically equal to \$628,750. This strategy is cheaper than INC-ZER-RET, but the reduction in cost is not sufficient to make G3 affordable. As a conclusion, if the investor uses income to protect EG1:

- G2 is jointly affordable with EG1 and will be subsequently regarded as an important goal (IG);
- G3 is not jointly affordable with EG1 and IG and thus represents an aspirational goal (referred to as AG in what follows).

4.3.1.4. *Decision rules for goal payment*

The willingness to protect EG1 has implications for the payment of the other goals. Indeed, in the context of this case study, the chronological order of goals is exactly the reverse of the priority order. As a consequence, the payment of AG, which is the goal with the lowest priority, could lead in some trajectories to downgrade the funding status of EG1 and turn it into a non-affordable goal. For all strategies that aim to protect EG1, we thus adopt a payment rule that preserves the funding status of this goal. Moreover, if IG is funded at the 5-year horizon, we require that the payment of AG should not turn IG into a non-affordable goal. But since IG is not explicitly secured, it may be the case that it is no longer funded after 5 years. In this case, only the condition on EG1 is taken into account.

The minimum capital requirement for EG1 depends on the strategy and the decision whether to use income or not to protect the goal. With strategy INC-ZER-RET, the minimum wealth requirement is the price of the option needed to secure the fraction of the goal that is not covered by income, that is

$$U_{\text{ret},t} = \mathbb{E}_t \left[\frac{M_{21}}{M_t} \left(\widetilde{\text{EG}}_{21-}^1 - \sum_{\substack{k=1 \\ k>t}}^{20} y_k \right)^+ \right].$$

Recall that M is the pricing kernel, which serves to price future payoffs (see Section 2.1.1). IG is paid in full at date t if the wealth of date t before any goal payment (but net of income and mortgage repayment) is greater than $U_{\text{ret},t} + \text{IG}_t$. For AG, the condition is more severe as it states that IG must stay funded, too. Hence, the condition is to have wealth after income and mortgage repayment greater than $U_{\text{ret},t} + \text{IG}_t + \text{AG}_t$. With strategy INC-FWD, the conditions have a similar form, but the minimum capital requirement for EG1, $U_{\text{ret},t}$, is now replaced by

$$W_t = \mathbb{E}_t \left[\frac{M_{21}}{M_t} \left(\widetilde{\text{EG}}_{21-}^1 - \sum_{k=1}^{20} y_k (1 + f_{k,21-k})^{21-k} \right)^+ \right].$$

In case the available wealth is not sufficient to pay for a goal in full, the investor only pays the largest fraction of the goal such that the wealth after the payment is greater than the minimum required capital.

4.3.1.5. *Current strategy*

As in the previous case studies, we start by computing the success indicators achieved with the current strategy, which is a fixed-mix policy that maintains constant weights within the liquid bucket. Since this strategy does not aim at protecting any goal, we do not apply the decision rules given in Section 4.3.1.4, and we simply assume that at each goal horizon, the investor pays the largest fraction of the goal that is covered by liquid wealth. That is, if t is a goal horizon and $A_{\text{liq},t-}$ is the liquid wealth before any goal payment, the effective consumption expense is the minimum of G_t and $A_{\text{liq},t-}$.

From the success indicators shown in Figure 4.30, it turns out that the aspirational goal, which is the goal with the shortest horizon (5 years), is reached with certainty. This can be explained by the fact that the average annual arithmetic return of the simulated fixed-mix portfolio over the first five years is 10.40%, which is much larger than the inflation rate of 2.5%.[5] As a result, the expected wealth after five years before savings and consumption is approximately \$1.54m, which is comfortably larger than the aspirational goal value, of \$339,420 including inflation adjustment. These numbers give a sense of why wealth after five years is always larger than the aspirational goal value, hence why the goal is always attained.

Similarly, the important goal is always attained. Again, this is because the face value of this goal is relatively low compared to the available liquid wealth. Indeed, the average wealth after 11 years (still before savings and consumption) is \$2.21m, while the goal threshold is only \$50,000. Even though this amount is to be paid every year for four consecutive years, it is not difficult to guess that the consumption objective will always be attained.

The situation is different with the essential goal, which is missed with a significant probability, of 19.7%. The examination of maximum shortfalls shows that the deviations from the goal start to occur at the end of the first three years of retirement. In other words, the investor can afford the goal for the first two years with certainty, but the fixed-mix policy does not guarantee the achievement of the goal thereafter. It is also worth noting that the expected shortfall grows

---

[5]The average annual arithmetic return at horizon T is defined as $\left(\frac{\mathbb{E}[A_{\text{liq},T}]}{A_0}\right)^{1/T} - 1$.

Figure 4.30.   Investor 3 — Success indicators with current strategy.

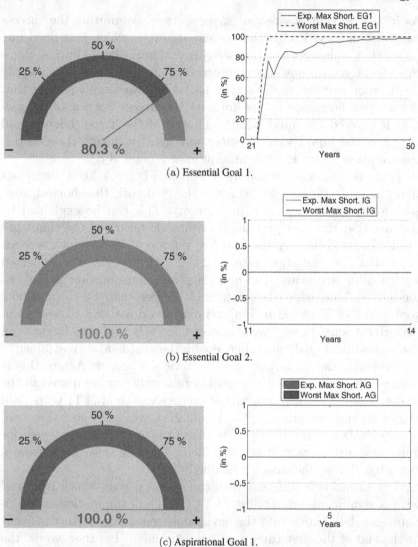

(a) Essential Goal 1.

(b) Essential Goal 2.

(c) Aspirational Goal 1.

Notes: The half circles represent the success probabilities for each goal: the probability is estimated as the percentage of scenarios in which the goal was reached. The expected maximum shortfall on date t is the expectation of the value of the maximum relative deviation from the goal recorded by date t, conditional on the event of such a deviation. The worst maximum shortfall is defined as the worst relative loss recorded by date t across all dates and scenarios. The "current strategy" is a fixed-mix policy with annual rebalancing towards the current market allocation.

very rapidly, to reach and exceed 70% after 2 years. These numbers reflect a very substantial shortfall risk, which motivates the design of strategies that secure consumption objectives. This is what we turn to in the next section.

4.3.2. *Strategies securing essential goal(s)*

4.3.2.1. *Protecting essential goal 1 with liquid wealth*

To secure EG1, the first option is to purchase a bond that pays the cash flows for the goals. This strategy (referred to as LIQ) relies only on liquid wealth to secure the goal, and disregards the presence of income: it could be adopted by an investor receiving no income and otherwise having the same characteristics as Investor 3. The bond is the GHP, and as shown previously (see Table 4.17), it is affordable with liquid wealth alone. The remainder of liquid wealth is invested in a performance block, which we take to be the MSR portfolio of stocks and bonds. As appears from Table 4.18, most assets are held in the form of safe assets within the personal bucket: this bucket represents 73.7% of total assets. The remaining part is held in the form of a claim on future savings and market assets. Following the definition of the aspirational bucket given in Section 2.5.3.2, the present value of future savings is assigned to this bucket because it is not a traded asset, and it does not have a publicly available price. Because the mortgage annuities are a constrained payment, they are subtracted from the annual savings in the computation of the present value of savings: it is as if the investor was receiving a diminished income. The present value of savings accounts for 15.3% of the total, while market assets (equities and bonds) represent only 11.0%. The small weight of market assets shows that the strategy is highly conservative.

The corresponding success probabilities and shortfall indicators are reported in Figure 4.31. The most striking observation is that AG is reached in only 1.5% states of the world. Indeed, in these trajectories, the investor gives up on some fraction of this goal because paying for the goal in full would compromise the ability to finance EG1 and IG. The associated deviations are also severe: on average, the investor finances less than 75% of the goal. These poor performances with respect to AG are not surprising in view of the risk allocation of Table 4.18: protecting EG1 with a bond exhausts most of the initial wealth, which leaves little cash available to invest in performance-seeking assets. The decision rule also has a negative impact on

Figure 4.31. Investor 3 — Success indicators with strategy securing EG1 with liquid wealth only.

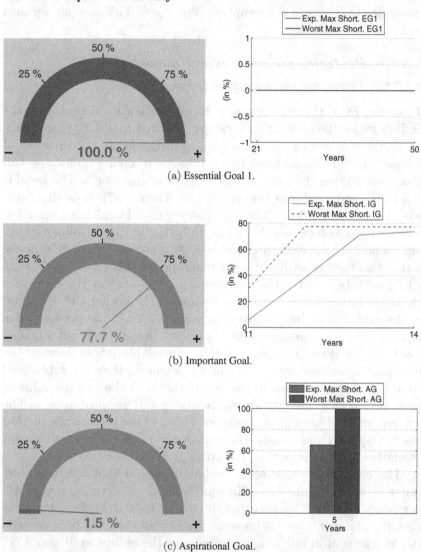

(a) Essential Goal 1.

(b) Important Goal.

(c) Aspirational Goal.

Notes: This figure shows the success probabilities (left column) and the expected and the worst maximum shortfalls (right column) for a strategy securing EG1 with liquid wealth only. The portfolio is buy-and-hold in the MSR of stocks and bonds and the bond that pays the cash flows of EG1. (Success indicators are defined in the caption of Figure 4.30.)

Table 4.18. **Investor 3 — Initial risk allocation with strategy securing EG1 with liquid wealth only.**

	Value ($)	% of Total		Value ($)	% of Total		Value ($)	% of Total
Personal Bucket	870,256	73.7	Market Bucket	129,744	11.0	Aspirational Bucket	181,506	15.3
Residence	300,000	21.9	Equity	104,343	80.4	Present value of savings	181,506	100.0
Cash	10,000	0.7	US Fixed Income	25,401	19.6			
GHP EG1	810,256	59.1						
Adjustable Rate Mortgage	(250,000)	18.2						

Notes: This table shows the risk allocation at date 0 when the investor holds buy-and-hold positions in the MSR and the GHP for EG1, which is a bond that delivers the goal cash flows ($90,000 per year from year 21 to year 50). The personal bucket contains the assets that are used to finance the investor's essential goals. The aspirational bucket contains assets held for wealth mobility purposes: it consists here of a claim on future savings net of mortgage annuities. The market bucket contains all other assets (equities and bonds here). The table displays the weights of the various assets within each bucket, as well as the relative weights of the buckets.

IG: this goal is reached with a probability of 77.7% only, while it was systematically attained with the current strategy.

4.3.2.2. *Protecting essential goal 1 with income*

In order to allocate more to performance-seeking assets, the investor must rely at least in part on future income. Strategy INC-ZER-RET assumes a zero re-investment rate for future income, and, in every year of his working life, the investor secures the fraction of the goal that is not covered by income by purchasing a suitable option. The risk allocation is shown in Table 4.19. As implied by the theoretical analysis (see Section 2.2.4.6), the new GHP is less expensive than the bond paying $90,000 per year: its price, $U_{ret,0}$, is $709,181, while the bond price, $\tilde{G}_0$, is $810,256. This decrease in the price of the GHP implies a decrease in the personal bucket size by the same amount and a related increase in the market bucket size. The difference between the two values is $101,075, which is less than the present value of future savings ($181,506). This is a verification of

Table 4.19. Investor 3 — Initial risk allocation with strategy securing EG1 with income, assuming a zero re-investment rate.

	Value ($)	% of Total		Value ($)	% of Total		Value ($)	% of Total
Personal Bucket	769,181	76.9	Market Bucket	230,819	23.1	Aspirational Bucket	0	0
Residence	300,000	23.6	Equity	185,630	80.4			
Cash	10,000	0.8	US Fixed Income	45,189	19.6			
GHP EG1	709,181	55.9						
Adjustable Rate Mortgage	(250,000)	19.7						

Notes: This table shows the risk allocation at date 0 when the investor partially secures EG1 with income, assumed to be re-invested at a zero rate. The remaining fraction of the goal is secured by purchasing an option (referred to as GHP EG1 in the table). The personal bucket contains the assets that are used to finance investor's essential goals. The aspirational bucket is empty because income is entirely dedicated to the protection of an essential goal. The market bucket contains all other assets (equities and bonds here). The table displays the weights of the various assets within each bucket, as well as the relative weights of the buckets.

the general property

$$\tilde{G}_0 - \tilde{H}_0 \leq U_{\text{ret},0},$$

which follows from the inequalities $\tilde{G}_0 - \tilde{H}_0 \leq V_0$ and $U_{\text{ret},0} \leq V_0$ established in Sections 2.2.4.4 and 2.2.4.6. Even if the protection of the goal was done optimally, that is, by the means of the cheapest replicating strategy of Proposition 8, the increase in the market bucket size would still be less than the present value of savings, because $\tilde{G}_0 - \tilde{H}_0$ is always less than V_0. This means that using income to protect the goal is not simply equivalent to transferring an amount equal to the present value of savings from the personal bucket to the market bucket. By accepting to rely on income, the investor does not free up as much wealth from this bucket as he would by selling a claim on future savings to turn it into liquid assets. It is worth noting that this non-equivalence occurs because liquid wealth must remain non-negative at all times: were negative values allowed, we would recover the equality between $\tilde{G}_0 - \tilde{H}_0$ and V_0, so the increase in market bucket value would be exactly equal to the present value of savings.

The success indicators reported in Figure 4.32 show that the main impact of the new approach to protect EG1 is on the aspirational

Figure 4.32. Investor 3 — Success indicators with strategy securing EG1 with income, assuming a zero re-investment rate for income.

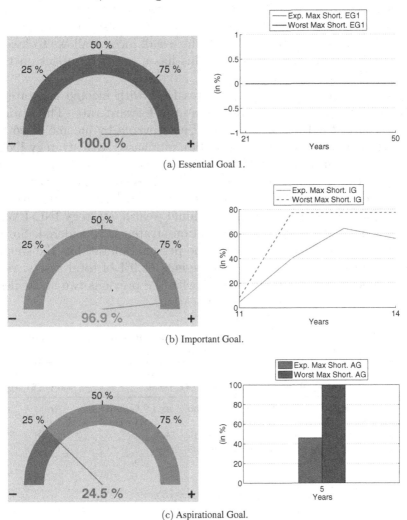

(a) Essential Goal 1.

(b) Important Goal.

(c) Aspirational Goal.

Notes: This figure shows the success probabilities (left column) and the expected and the worst maximum shortfalls (right column) for a strategy securing EG1 with income, assuming a zero re-investment rate for income. From year 1 to year 20, the portfolio is buy-and-hold in the MSR of stocks and bonds and the option that secures the fraction of EG1 not covered by income. After year 20, the option is replaced by the bond that pays the cash flows of EG1. (Success indicators are defined in the caption of Figure 4.30.)

goal. The probability of reaching IG is not substantially modified with respect to the strategy LIQ, but the success probability for AG rises from 1.5% to 24.5% and the expected shortfall is now 47.1%, which represents a substantial reduction with respect to the value reported in Figure 4.31. As usual, the use of income allows to invest more in performance assets, and this has a positive impact on the achievement for ambitious goals.

The second strategy that secures EG1 with income is strategy INC-FWD, which invests income at the forward rate. The option that secures the fraction of the goal not covered by income is worth $628,750, which is less than the option purchased with strategy INC-ZER-RET, which is a straightforward property since forward rates are positive. Assuming that income is re-invested at the forward rate is thus less conservative than assuming that it will produce no returns at all. In terms of usage of current liquid wealth, strategy INC-FWD is the cheapest of the three protection strategies considered. So, it is for this investment policy that the personal bucket has the smallest weight in the allocation: it represents 68.9% of total assets, versus, respectively, 73.7% and 76.9% with the previous two strategies. Table 4.20 summarises the risk allocation.

Table 4.20.   **Investor 3 — Initial risk allocation with strategy securing EG1 with income and forward contracts.**

	Value ($)	% of Total		Value ($)	% of Total		Value ($)	% of Total
Personal Bucket	688,750	68.9	Market Bucket	311,250	31.1	Aspirational Bucket	0	0
Residence	300,000	25.2	Equity	250,315	80.4			
Cash	10,000	0.8	US Fixed Income	60,935	19.6			
GHP EG1	628,750	52.9						
Adjustable Rate Mortgage	(250,000)	21.0						

Notes: This table shows the risk allocation at date 0 when the investor partially secures EG1 with income, when the income payments are re-invested at forward rates specified at time 0. The remaining fraction of the goal is secured by purchasing an option (GHP EG1). The personal bucket contains the assets that are used to finance investor's essential goals. The aspirational bucket is empty because income is entirely dedicated to the protection of an essential goal. The market bucket contains all other assets (equities and bonds here). The table displays the weights of the various assets within each bucket, as well as the relative weights of the buckets.

Figure 4.33 displays the success indicators. The essential goal is still secured with probability 1, but the protection with forward contracts has an ambiguous impact on the achievement of non-essential goals. On the one hand, the indicators for AG are improved: the success probability is significantly higher than it was with the strategy INC-ZER-RET since it is now 42% as opposed to 24.5%, and the expected shortfall has fallen down from 47.1% to 40.5%. On the other hand, the strategy performs less well with respect to IG: the success probability is now 83.9%, versus 96.9% with strategy INC-ZER-RET, and the expected and maximum shortfalls tend to be larger. This situation may be attributed to two competing effects. On the one hand, the investor initially holds a larger fraction of assets in the form of the MSR portfolio of stocks and bonds, and this leads to a greater expected wealth after 5 years. Thus, AG is reached with higher probability. On the other hand, there is a competition between AG and IG: since AG is paid for more often, there is less money after year 5 to finance IG in full.

4.3.2.3. *Introduction of a minimum wealth constraint*

We now introduce a new goal, which is to secure a minimum wealth level at the 50-year horizon. This minimum wealth can be interpreted as a minimum amount of money that the investor would like to leave to his children upon death. We refer to it as Goal 4 (G4), and we take the goal threshold to be the initial liquid wealth, \$940,000 capitalised at the 2.5% annual rate. This rate, which represents the expected annual inflation rate, is applied because the investor would like to protect the capital in real terms. The nominal goal threshold in year t is

$$G_t^4 = \begin{cases} A_0 \times 1.025^t & \text{for } t = 50 \\ 0 & \text{otherwise} \end{cases},$$

with $A_0 = \$940,000$.

Figure 4.34 shows how the previous strategies perform with respect to this new goal. The success probabilities are greater than 59%, but none of the strategies secures the goal with probability 1. It is therefore interesting to test strategies that secure the goal, provided it is feasible to construct such strategies. This is possible if the

Figure 4.33.   Investor 3 — Success indicators with strategy securing EG1 with income and forward contracts.

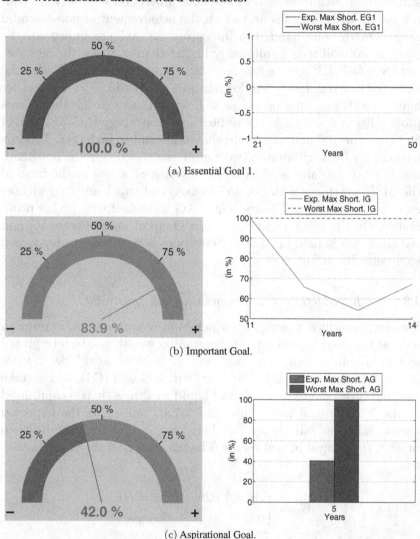

(a) Essential Goal 1.

(b) Important Goal.

(c) Aspirational Goal.

Notes: This figure shows the success probabilities (left column) and the expected and the worst maximum shortfalls (right column) for a strategy securing EG1 with income when the income payments are re-invested at forward rates specified at date 0. From year 1 to year 20, the portfolio is buy-and-hold in the MSR of stocks and bonds and the option that secures the fraction of EG1 not covered by income. After year 20, the option is replaced by the bond that pays the cash flows of EG1. (Success indicators are defined in the caption of Figure 4.30.)

Figure 4.34. Investor 3 — Success indicators for wealth-based goal with strategies securing EG1.

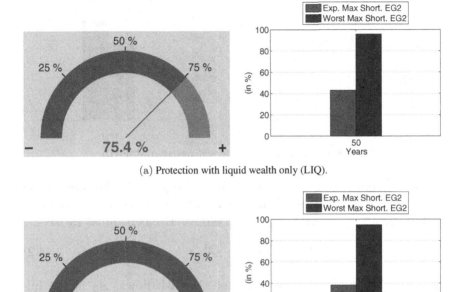

(a) Protection with liquid wealth only (LIQ).

(b) Protection with income, assuming a zero re-investment rate (INC-ZER-RET).

Notes: This figure shows the success probabilities (left column) and the expected and the worst maximum shortfalls (right column) with respect to the goal of protecting the initial liquid wealth ($940,000) plus inflation at the 50-year horizon. The strategy LIQ (Panel (a)) protects Essential Goal 1 by purchasing a bond that pays the cash flows for the goal. The strategy INC-ZER-RET (Panel (b)) protects EG1 with income, assuming that future income payments will be re-invested at a zero rate. The fraction of EG1 not covered by income is secured by purchasing an option. The strategy INC-FWD (Panel (c)) protects EG1 with income, and the re-investment rate for the income payments is fixed at date 0 by entering forward contracts. Again, the remaining fraction of EG1 is secured with an option.

goal is jointly affordable with other goals that have greater priority. In terms of priority, we treat the wealth-based goal as a goal of intermediate priority between Goal 1 (the retirement goal) and Goal 2 (the education goal): so, if the investor cannot secure G1 and G4 simultaneously, he will give up on the latter goal and only secure G1, but he attaches more importance to G4 than to G2.

Figure 4.34. (*Continued*)

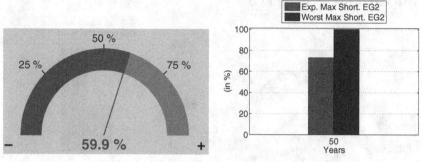

(c) Protection with income and forward contracts (INC-FWD).

So, we must first qualify the affordability of G4. By absence of arbitrage opportunities, if this goal and G1 are reached with certainty, then the liquid wealth just before retirement must satisfy

$$A_{21-} \geq \tilde{G}_{21-}^1 + G_{50}^4 \times b_{21,50}, \tag{4.2}$$

where $\tilde{G}_{21-}^1$ is the present value of G1 cash flows, A_0 is the initial wealth (\$940,000) and $b_{21,50}$ is the price of a zero-coupon bond maturing at date 50. Conversely, if inequality (35) holds, then the investor can afford both the bond paying the cash flows of G1 and a zero-coupon that will deliver A_0 on date 50. Hence, Equation (4.2) is a necessary and sufficient condition for the goals G1 and G4 to be jointly affordable.

Introducing a wealth-based goal is thus equivalent to raising the floor at date 21 with respect to the situation where no minimum wealth constraint is imposed. In order to secure this minimum wealth level, the investor can choose one of the following three approaches:

- Purchase a bond that will pay the floor on date 21: this is the strategy called LIQ, which relies on liquid wealth only;
- Use income assuming a zero re-investment rate: this is the strategy called INC-ZER-RET. The fraction of the goal not covered by income must be secured by purchasing an option maturing at date 21 with payoff

$$U_{\text{ret},21} = \left(\tilde{G}_{21-}^1 + G_{50}^4 \times b_{21,50} - \sum_{k=1}^{20} y_k \right)^+;$$

Table 4.21. Investor 3 — Funding status of goals in the presence of a minimum wealth goal.

(i) Value of assets (in $).

Market wealth	940,000
Present value of future savings	181,506
Total	**1,121,506**

(ii) Minimum capital required to secure one or more goal(s) (in $).

	Liquid wealth only	Income and zero re-investment rate	Income and forward contracts
Goal 1	810,256	709,181	628,750
Goal 4	106,733	106,733	106,733
G1 and G4	**916,989**	**815,914**	**735,482**
Goal 2	169,893	169,893	169,893
G1, G4 and G2	**1,086,882**	**985,807**	**905,376**
Goal 3	305,274	305,274	305,274
All goals	**1,392,156**	**1,291,081**	**1,210,650**

Notes: Panel (i) shows the value of investor's assets and Panel (ii) the minimum capital required to secure the various goals when the investor has a wealth-based goal (Goal 4), which is to preserve the initial liquid wealth plus expected inflation at the 50-year horizon. This goal has intermediate priority rank between EG1 and IG. In the second column of Panel (ii), the investor relies only on liquid wealth. In the third column, he uses income to secure EG1 and G4, assuming a zero re-investment rate for future income payments, and purchases an option to make up for the uncovered fraction of the goal. In the fourth column, he uses income assuming that future income will be re-invested at the forward rate fixed at date 0, and purchases an option to make up for the uncovered fraction.

- Re-invest income at the forward rates. This strategy, labelled INC-FWD, has a cost equal to the price of the payoff

$$W_{21} = \left(\tilde{G}^1_{21-} + G^4_{50} \times b_{21,50} - \sum_{k=1}^{20} y_k (1 + f_{k,21-k})^{21-k} \right)^+ .$$

Table 4.21 shows the minimum capital required to secure the goals, individually or jointly. It appears that the investor can afford as of date 0 both the bond that delivers the cash flows of G1 and the zero-coupon that delivers the minimum wealth level at date 50. Hence, G4 is jointly affordable with G1 whichever mode of protection is chosen. But of course, it is less costly in terms of liquid wealth to use income. In what follows, we test strategies that secure both G1 and G4, which means that both goals are treated as essential: the retirement goal is still referred to as EG1 and the bequest goal as EG2.

It also turns out that G2 (the education goal) cannot be secured together with G1 and G4, except if the investor can fix as of date 0 the re-investment rate of future income payments. Thus, except in this situation, G2 is no longer an affordable goal and it should be regarded as an aspirational goal. In what follows, we thus refer to it as AG1, and to the home goal (previously known as AG) as AG2.

We now compare the three strategies designed to secure EG1 and EG2 simultaneously. Each of them involves a buy-and-hold position in the MSR portfolio of the stock and the bond indices and a GHP that secures the two essential goals. This GHP is a bond in the case of strategy LIQ, and an option in strategies INC-ZER-RET and INC-FWD. It should be noted that unlike in Case 1, where there was a clear separation between the GHPs for the two essential goals, such a separation cannot be done for the two strategies relying on income. Indeed, both goals are protected with a single option.

Table 4.22 provides the initial risk allocation for the various strategies. Purchasing two bonds to protect the two goals is highly costly: the two bonds cost $916,989, which is about 98% of the investor's initial liquid wealth ($940,000). As a result, there remain only $23,011 available to invest in performance-seeking assets, and the market bucket represents a tiny 1.9% of the total allocation. In order to save space, we only report the success probabilities of the three strategies in the next figures. As appears from Figure 4.35, the strategy that only uses liquid wealth, while securing both essential goals as it should, has virtually zero chances to reach the non-essential ones. This is of course a consequence of the low allocation to the market assets.

If the investor relies on income to secure as much as possible of the two essential goals, he only has to purchase an option that is worth less than the two bonds. He must liquidate $815,924 of the initial market bucket, but there remain $124,086 available to invest in the

Table 4.22. Investor 3 — Initial risk allocations with strategies securing EG1 and EG2.

(a) Protection with liquid wealth only.

	Value ($)	% of Total		Value ($)	% of Total		Value ($)	% of Total
Personal Bucket	**976,989**	**82.7**	**Market Bucket**	**23,011**	**1.9**	**Aspirational Bucket**	**181,506**	**15.4**
Residence	300,000	20.3	Equity	18,506	80.4	Present value of savings	181,506	100
Cash	10,000	0.7	US Fixed-Income	4,505	19.6			
GHP EG1 and EG2	916,989	62.1						
Adjustable Rate Mortgage	(250,000)	16.9						

(b) Protection with income re-invested at zero rate.

	Value ($)	% of Total		Value ($)	% of Total		Value ($)	% of Total
Personal Bucket	**875,914**	**87.6**	**Market Bucket**	**124,086**	**12.4**	**Aspirational Bucket**	**0**	**0**
Residence	300,000	21.8	Equity	99,793	80.4			
Cash	10,000	0.7	US Fixed-Income	24,293	19.6			
GHP EG1 and EG2	815,914	59.3						
Adjustable Rate Mortgage	(250,000)	18.2						

(*Continued*)

MSR portfolio. As can be seen from Figure 4.36, this higher allocation to performance-seeking assets translates into a huge improvement in the probability of reaching AG1, which jumps from 0.7% to 74.8%. An increase is also observed for AG2, but it is less spectacular, with a probability that grows from 0% to 1.3%. Both probabilities are lower than with the strategy that secures only the retirement goal (see Figure 4.32), which reflects the opportunity cost associated with the protection of a second essential goal. Interestingly, the dollar allocation to the performance-seeking assets was higher with this strategy

Table 4.22. (*Continued*)

(c) Protection with income and forward contracts.

	Value ($)	% of Total		Value ($)	% of Total		Value ($)	% of Total
Personal Bucket	795,482	79.5	Market Bucket	204,518	20.5	Aspirational Bucket	0	0
Residence	300,000	23.2	Equity	164,478	80.4			
Cash	10,000	0.8	US Fixed-Income	40,040	19.6			
GHP EG1 and EG2	735,482	56.8						
Adjustable Rate Mortgage	(250,000)	19.2						

Notes: This table shows the risk allocation at date 0 for three strategies securing EG1 and EG2. In Panel (a), the investor purchases a bond that pays the cash flows of EG1 for years 21 to 50 and delivers the minimum wealth level of EG2 on year 50. This bond is referred to as "GHP EG1 and EG2" in the table. In Panel (b), the investor partially secures the two essential goals with income, assuming a zero re-investment rate for future income, and secures the uncovered fraction of the goals by purchasing an option. In Panel (c), he fixes at date 0 the re-investment rate by entering forward contracts and he purchases another option to complete the protection. The personal bucket contains the assets used to finance investor's essential goals. The aspirational bucket contains a claim on future savings except when income is dedicated to the protection of such essential goals. The market bucket contains all other assets (equities and bonds here). The table displays the weights of the various assets within each bucket, as well as the relative weights of the buckets.

(see Table 4.19), which points to the existence of an increasing relationship between the size of the market bucket and the probabilities of reaching the non-essential goals.

It is with the third strategy, which uses forward contracts, that the GHP is the least expensive and that the market bucket is the largest. In this context, it comes as no surprise that the success probabilities for both AG1 and AG2 are very significantly improved with respect to the case where protection relies on liquid wealth alone: As can be seen from Figure 4.37, for AG1, the probability is a large 70.9%, and for AG2, it is 9.6%, which is still low but not negligible.

The key points of the analysis of strategies protecting either one essential goal or both can be summarised as follows:

• A strategy that relies on liquid wealth only (LIQ) has a substantial opportunity cost in terms of the probability of reaching non-essential goals. The probabilities of reaching these goals are in

Figure 4.35. **Investor 3 — Success probabilities with strategy securing EG1 and EG2 with liquid wealth only.**

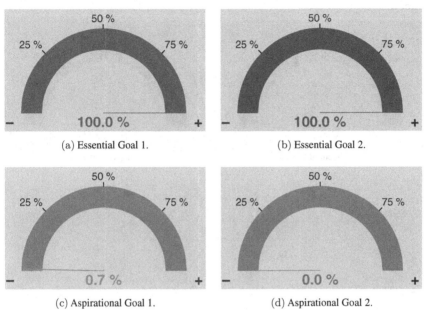

(a) Essential Goal 1.

(b) Essential Goal 2.

(c) Aspirational Goal 1.

(d) Aspirational Goal 2.

Notes: This figure shows the success probabilities for a strategy securing EG1 and EG2 with liquid wealth only. The portfolio is buy-and-hold in the MSR portfolio of stocks and bonds and the bond that pays the cash flows of EG1 for years 21 to 50 plus the minimum wealth level in year 50.

general disappointing, especially when there are more than one essential goals to protect, since the bond that secures both goals consumes most of the initial wealth and leaves little cash available to invest in a performance-seeking portfolio;

- The success probabilities for non-essential goals are significantly improved by using income to secure as much as possible of the essential goal(s) (strategies INC-ZER-RET and INC-FWD). Indeed, it is less costly to purchase an option to secure the fraction of the goal(s) that is not covered by income than to invest in a bond that delivers the cash flows of this (these) goal(s);

- There is no clear dominance of one of the strategies INC-ZER-RET and INC-FWD over the other: from the previous results, it appears that the former performs better with respect to the education goal while the latter displays better scores with respect to the home

Figure 4.36. Investor 3 — Success probabilities with strategy securing EG1 and EG2 with income, assuming a zero re-investment rate for income.

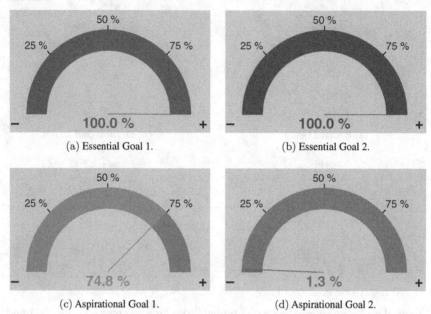

(a) Essential Goal 1. (b) Essential Goal 2.

(c) Aspirational Goal 1. (d) Aspirational Goal 2.

Notes: This figure shows the success probabilities for a strategy securing EG1 and EG2 with income, assuming a zero re-investment rate for future income. The fraction of the goals not covered by income is protected with an option maturing at date 21 (the retirement date). The portfolio is buy-and-hold in the MSR portfolio of stocks and bonds and the option.

goal. This suggests that there is a form of competition between the two goals: indeed, the home goal has shorter horizon, so that there is money available to finance the next goal if the property has been purchased before.

4.3.3. *Impact of taxes*

We now check the robustness of the previous results in the presence of a positive tax rate. The objective of this section is threefold. First, we present adjustments to the previous strategies intended to protect the retirement goal; second, we re-examine the funding status of each goal in the presence of taxes; third, we look at the properties of these strategies with respect to the other goals (education and home goals).

Figure 4.37. Investor 3 — Success probabilities with strategy securing EG1 and EG2 with income and forward contracts.

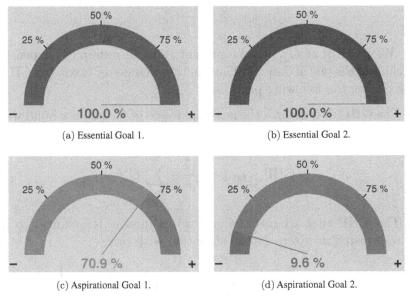

(a) Essential Goal 1. (b) Essential Goal 2.

(c) Aspirational Goal 1. (d) Aspirational Goal 2.

Notes: This figure shows the success probabilities for a strategy securing EG1 and EG2 with income, when the re-investment rate of income is fixed at date 0 by entering forward contracts. The fraction of the goals not covered by income is protected with an option maturing at date 21 (the retirement date). The portfolio is buy-and-hold in the MSR portfolio of stocks and bonds and the option.

As in Section 2.3, we apply a uniform tax rate ζ, which will be taken equal to 10% or 20%, and we adopt the LIFO convention to compute the taxable gains (see Appendix A.6.5 for mathematical details).

4.3.3.1. *Adjustment to GHP for goal 1*

In the context of this case study, taxes arise from the selling operations in the stock and the bond indices held within the PSP building block and from the coupons paid by the bond that secures EG1, coupons which equal the consumption expenses.

As explained in Section 3.3.3.1, the effect of taxes on coupons can be virtually removed by purchasing $1/(1 - \zeta)$ units of the bond. In other words, for the goal to be secured with certainty, the investor's wealth just before retirement (i.e. at date 21, just before the first payment) must satisfy

$$A_{21-} \geq \frac{1}{1-\zeta} \tilde{G}^1_{21-}.$$

We recall that $\tilde{G}^1_{21-}$ is the present value of retirement expenses, including the one of date 21. Thus, in the presence of taxes, the GHPs for G1 are the following portfolios:

- The GHP that secures the goal regardless of income is a bond with price

$$\mathrm{GHP}_{\mathrm{G1,tax},t} = \frac{1}{1-\zeta} \sum_{\substack{s=21 \\ s>t}}^{50} G^1_s b_{t,s}.$$

- The GHP that secures the goal when income is assumed to be re-invested at a zero rate is an option with price

$$U_{\mathrm{ret,tax},t} = \mathbb{E}_t \left[\frac{M_{21}}{M_t} \left(\frac{1}{1-\zeta} \tilde{G}^1_{21-} - \sum_{\substack{s=1 \\ s>t}}^{20} y_s \right)^+ \right].$$

- The GHP that secures the goal when income is invested at the forward rates is an option with price

$$W_{\mathrm{tax},t} = \mathbb{E}_t \left[\frac{M_{21}}{M_t} \left(\frac{1}{1-\zeta} \tilde{G}^1_{21-} - \sum_{\substack{s=1 \\ s>t}}^{20} y_s (1 + f_{s,21-s})^{21-s} \right)^+ \right].$$

These GHPs are clearly more expensive than the ones that secure the goal in the absence of taxes, which will have implications for the payment policy of non-essential goals: the minimum level of wealth required to pay for the education or home goal in full is higher than in the case without taxes.

A tax adjustment could also be performed for the bonds that protect the other two goals, namely G2 and G3. If the investor was to protect them, he would have to purchase $1/(1-\zeta)$ units of the bonds that pay the goal cash flows. This raises the minimum capital requirement for these goals.

By taking a buy-and-hold position in one of the three GHPs that protect the retirement goal, the investor can afford the retirement expenses. But the strategies that we implement also involve as a second building block the MSR portfolio of stock and bond indices: the periodical rebalancing generates taxes which are not hedged by the adjustment to the GHP value. In other words, this adjustment provides a hedge for only a fraction of the total taxes to be paid. Being not compensated by any inflow, the taxes generated by selling operations can cause violations of the essential goal, at least in theory.

4.3.3.2. *Affordability of goals*

We start by examining the funding status of the various goals in the presence of taxes. Table 4.23 shows the minimum capital requirements for two values of the tax rate. With a 10% rate, the investor can purchase the bond that delivers the cash flows of G1 (the retirement goal) adjusted for taxes. This does not suffice, however, to establish that G1 can be effectively secured because the adjustment to the GHP value does not recognise the presence of taxes on rebalancing operations within the PSP. Nevertheless, we say that Goal 1 is affordable, in the sense that the bond that pays the tax-adjusted cash flows is affordable. For a 20% rate, the bond cannot be purchased with liquid wealth alone, so that G1 (and subsequently the goals of lower priority) should be treated as aspirational. With such a tax rate, G1 can only be protected if the investor uses income to secure as much as possible of the goal. Alternatively, G1 may become affordable if the investor receives an additional endowment at date 0 to increase liquid wealth. For instance, a 10% increase results in an initial capital

$$1.1 \times \$940,000 = \$1,034,000,$$

which is sufficient to secure G1.

The other two goals are G2 (the education goal) and G3 (the home goal). The investor can never afford all of them. But G2 becomes jointly affordable with G1 if the tax rate is sufficiently low (10%) and the investor chooses to partially secure the goal with income invested at forward rates. Overall, taking as a reference the funding status with liquid wealth only:

- With a 10% tax rate, G1 can be treated as an essential goal so that it will still be referred to as EG1. G2 and G3 are aspirational and will be referred to as AG1 and AG2;
- With a 20% tax rate, all three goals are aspirational, except if the investor can increase the initial liquid wealth by 10%, in which case

Table 4.23.   Investor 3 — Funding status of goals in the presence of taxes.

(i) Value of assets (in $).

Market wealth	940,000
Present value of future savings	181,506
Total	**1,121,506**

(ii) Minimum capital required to secure one or more goal(s) (in $) – 10% tax rate.

	Liquid wealth only	Income and zero re-investment rate	Income and forward contracts
Goal 1	900,284	799,209	718,778
Goal 2	188,770	188,770	188,770
G1 and G2	**1,089,054**	**987,979**	**907,548**
Goal 3	339,194	339,194	339,194
G1, G2 and G3	**1,428,248**	**1,237,173**	**1,246,742**

(iii) Minimum capital required to secure one or more goal(s) (in $) – 20% tax rate.

	Liquid wealth only	Income and zero re-investment rate	Income and forward contracts
Goal 1	1,012,820	911,745	831,314
Goal 2	212,366	212,366	212,366
G1 and G2	**1,225,186**	**1,124,111**	**1,043,680**
Goal 3	381,593	381,593	381,593
G1, G2 and G3	**1,606,779**	**1,505,704**	**1,425,273**

Notes: Panel (i) shows the assets of the investor, which consist of liquid market assets and a claim on future savings. Panels (ii) and (iii) show the minimum liquid wealth required in order to secure one or more goal(s) for three modes of protection of G1 (the retirement goal): the investor relies only on liquid wealth; or he uses income assuming a zero re-investment rate; or he uses income re-invested at forward rates specified at date 0. G2 is the education goal and G3 is the home goal. The difference between Panels (ii) and (iii) is the tax rate applied to the coupons paid by bonds (10% or 20%). Goals are ranked by order of decreasing priority.

Goal 1 becomes affordable and can again be regarded as essential. G2 and G3 remain aspirational in all cases.

4.3.3.3. *Test of strategies securing essential goal 1*

As before, we simulate the three protection strategies as buy-and-hold portfolios where the "safe building block" is one of the three GHPs and the "performance building block" is the MSR portfolio of stock and bond indices.

Figure 4.38 shows that by purchasing 1/0.9 units of the bond that pays the retirement expenses, the investor secures the achievement of EG1. As explained above, this result is not trivial because the increase in the allocation to the GHP only compensates for the taxes on coupons, but does not recognise the existence of taxes on selling operations in stock and bond indices. The results suggest that these

Figure 4.38. **Investor 3 — Success probabilities with strategy securing EG1 with liquid wealth only; 10% tax rate.**

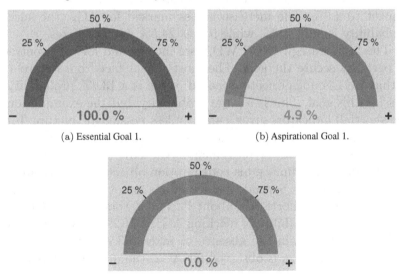

(a) Essential Goal 1.   (b) Aspirational Goal 1.

(c) Aspirational Goal 2.

Notes: This figure shows the success probabilities for a strategy securing EG1 with liquid wealth only when a 10% tax rate is applied to bond coupons and to selling operations in stock and bond indices. The portfolio is buy-and-hold in the MSR portfolio of stock and bond indices and the bond that pays the cash flows of EG1 for years 21 to 50, adjusted for the tax rate.

taxes can be paid by liquidating a fraction of the positions in stocks and bonds, without having to reduce the exposure to the GHP. But the probabilities of reaching the two aspirational goals are extremely low compared to the situation without taxes: they fall, respectively, to 4.9% for AG1 and even 0% for AG2, while they were 77.7% and 1.5% in the absence of taxes (see Figure 4.31). This severe reduction is explained by the huge cost of the bond that delivers the tax-adjusted cash flows. This bond is worth $900,284, which represents close to 96% of the initial endowment: thus, the investor can invest hardly 4% of his wealth in performance assets.

These disappointing scores make a strong case for the use of income to secure as much as possible of EG1. In Figure 4.39, we thus look at the success probabilities for strategy INC-ZER-RET: EG1 is still attained with probability 1, but the probabilities for the other two goals are higher than with the previous strategy. The increase is spectacular for AG1, with a success probability of 80.6%: this is still less than in the absence of taxes (the probability is 96.9% in Figure 4.32), but represents a very substantial improvement with respect to 4.9%. The increase is less marked for AG2: the success probability is only 1.9%, while it was 24.5% without taxes.

The last strategy, INC-FWD, uses income and forward contracts to partially secure the goal. The most salient fact from Figure 4.40 is that EG1 is not perfectly secured: there is a 13.4% probability of missing this goal. This is a large probability, but the examination of the shortfall indicators gives a slightly less pessimistic picture. First, it turns out that deviations from the consumption objective occur only in the last year of retirement (year 50): in other words, the investor can fully finance his consumption objectives for the first 29 years of retirement. Second, the deviations are of rather limited size, with an expected shortfall of about 1% and a worst case shortfall less than 5%. The probability of reaching AG1 is 71.2%, which falls below the value achieved in the absence of taxes (83.9% in Figure 4.33). A stronger reduction is observed for AG2: the probability falls from 42% to 12.9%.

Although the shortfall indicators for EG1 are not extremely bad, it is undisputable that the strategy has a substantial shortfall probability with respect to this goal. It turns out that in the simulations, the paths where EG1 is missed are exactly those where the allocation to the MSR portfolio falls to zero at some point. The risk budget allocated to the MSR portfolio is entirely consumed only when taxes

Figure 4.39. Investor 3 — Success probabilities with strategy securing EG1 with income re-invested at a zero rate; 10% tax rate.

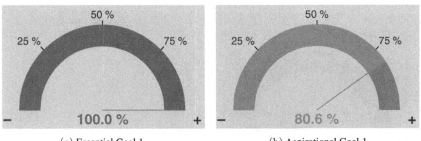

(a) Essential Goal 1.   (b) Aspirational Goal 1.

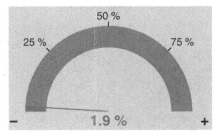

(c) Aspirational Goal 2.

Notes: This figure shows the success probabilities for a strategy securing EG1 with income assumed to be re-invested at a zero rate when a 10% tax rate is applied to bond coupons and to selling operations in stock and bond indices. The portfolio is buy-and-hold in the MSR portfolio of stock and bond indices and an option that secures the fraction of the goal value which is not covered by income.

are paid or a non-essential goal is paid for. The liquidation of the stock and bond positions gives rise to capital gains, and taxes, which will be paid at the end of the fiscal year. But because there are no more stock and bond indices in the portfolio, these taxes can only paid by decreasing the exposure to the GHP.

This mechanism is illustrated in Panel (a) of Figure 4.41, which shows the allocations (expressed as numbers of shares) to the MSR portfolio and the GHP in a scenario that saw a deviation from the goal.[6] At the end of year 5, the investor liquidates most of the position

---

[6]The number of shares of the MSR portfolio is computed as the dollar allocation to the MSR building block, divided by the value of the MSR portfolio, assuming an investment of $1 at date 0.

Figure 4.40. **Investor 3 — Success indicators with strategy aiming to secure EG1 with income re-invested at forward rates; 10% tax rate.**

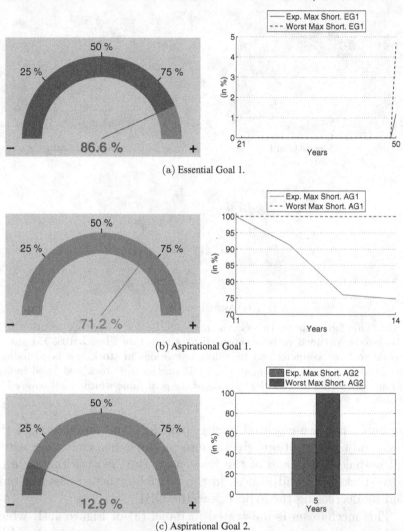

(a) Essential Goal 1.

(b) Aspirational Goal 1.

(c) Aspirational Goal 2.

Notes: This figure shows the success probabilities (left column) and the shortfall indicators (right column) for a strategy aiming to secure EG1 with income re-invested at forward rates when a 10% tax rate is applied to bond coupons and to selling operations in stock and bond indices. The portfolio is buy-and-hold in the MSR portfolio of stock and bond indices and an option that secures the fraction of the goal value which is not covered by income.

Figure 4.41. Investor 3 – Sample scenarios of allocations to MSR portfolio and GHP with strategy protecting Essential Goal 1 with income and forward contracts.

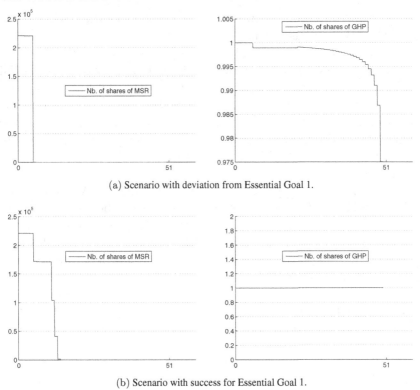

(a) Scenario with deviation from Essential Goal 1.

(b) Scenario with success for Essential Goal 1.

Notes: Panel (a) shows the time series of allocations to the MSR portfolio and the GHP in a scenario where EG1 is not reached. Panel (b) shows the allocations on a path where the goal is reached. Each allocation is expressed as a number of shares. The strategy implemented here uses income to secure the largest possible fraction of EG1, the re-investment rate of income being locked up at date 0 by the means of forward contracts. The fraction of the goal that is not covered by income is secured with an option.

in the MSR portfolio in order to make the non-financial payments of this date (taxes and payment of the home goal). The taxes generated by this liquidation are paid at the end of the following year, which is year 6. Since the value of the position in MSR portfolio does not cover them, the investor not only has to liquidate the remainder of the MSR portfolio but he must also sell shares of the GHP. This is why, after year 6, he holds less than one unit of the GHP, and wealth is less than the minimum capital requirement. As a result, EG1 is no longer secured with probability 1, and after a sufficiently long period, this lack of protection results in a failure to meet the consumption objective. By contrast, Panel (b) shows the allocations in a scenario where the allocation to the MSR portfolio remains positive, in spite of the payments made in years 1 to 20 to finance the non-essential goals: these payments are apparent on the picture, but they never lead to a zero allocation. In this context, the taxes generated by the transactions in stock and bond indices can be paid by decreasing the exposures to these assets, and there is no need to sell a fraction of the GHP: the number of shares of the GHP remains equal to 1, and the goal is fully secured.

This effect is not specific to strategy INC-FWD. With strategy INC-ZER-RET, the allocation to the MSR portfolio can also fall to zero. But the difference is that the former strategy allows a fraction of income to be re-invested in the MSR portfolio (see Section 4.3.1.3), while the latter invests the totality of income in a separate account, earning the forward rate. As a consequence, strategy INC-ZER-RET allows to recover a positive allocation to the MSR building block, which limits (and, in our simulations, completely avoids) the risk of having to partially liquidate the position in the GHP to pay taxes.

Chapter 5

Concluding Remarks

This book introduces a general operational framework, which formalises the goals-based risk allocation approach to wealth management introduced by Chhabra (2005), and which can be used by a financial advisor to allow individual investors to optimally allocate to the categories of risks they face across all life stages and wealth segments so as to achieve personally meaningful financial goals. Through a number of realistic case studies, we document the benefits of the approach, which secure the individual investor's essential goals with a high probability, while having the upside potential needed to reach ambitious aspirational goals.

In addition to developing and analysing optimal portfolio construction methodologies, this book also introduces robust heuristics, which can be thought of as reasonable approximations for optimal strategies that can accommodate a variety of implementation constraints, including the presence of transaction costs, the presence of short-sale constraints, the presence of parameter estimation risk, etc. One key feature that is explicitly discussed in this book is the constraint on limited customisation. While providing each individual investor with a dedicated investment solution precisely tailored to meet their goals and constraints would be desirable, it would not be consistent with the implementation constraints faced by financial advisors. The appropriate granularity in terms of numbers and types of underlying building blocks and allocation strategies will therefore have to be carefully assessed, with a key trade-off between increasing accuracy in implementing dedicated investment solutions and increasing costs of implementation.

After developing an implementable and robust approach to allocating across risk buckets so as to solve for investor-specific goals, while accounting for the key risks faced by an investor, and their interplay with the investor's goals, this book also presents a number of case studies which can be regarded as applications of the approach to various situations that are typical of individual investors' problems. In all cases, the proposed approach is shown to result in an implementable risk-based solution that dominates a standard mean–variance optimal portfolio in terms of the probability of achieving the respective goals and objectives, while taking into account the presence of a number of important practical dimensions such as taxes, illiquid assets and health contingencies, etc.

One dimension that is not addressed in this book but would be important in retirement planning is the presence of longevity risk, which requires dedicated hedging instruments and modelling techniques. With the need to supplement retirement savings via voluntary contributions, individuals will increasingly be responsible for their own saving and investment decisions. This global trend poses substantial challenges as individual investors not only face behavioural limitations, but also often lack the expertise needed to make educated investment decisions. In response to these concerns, a number of new investment products have been proposed over the past few years by the asset management industry, both with and without protection against longevity risk. However, there are reasons to believe that these products, known as target date funds and variable annuities, respectively, fall short of providing satisfactory solutions to the problems faced by individuals when approaching investment saving decisions. We leave for further research an in-depth analysis of the design of long-term retirement solutions in the presence of time-varying opportunity sets, multiple goals and uncertain lifetime.

Appendices

This appendix collects the proofs of the main results given in the book.

A.1. Affordability of Goals

A.1.1. *Proof of Proposition 3*

Assume first that the goal is affordable and consider a strategy of value A_t that reaches it with certainty. We show by induction that $A_{T_{p-j}} \geq K_{T_{p-j}}$ for all $j = 0, \ldots, p$. (In this inequality as well as in the subsequent ones, the expression "with probability 1" is implicit and is omitted for brevity).

- Since $K_{T_p} = G_{T_p}$ and $A_{T_p} \geq G_{T_p}$, the property is true for $j = 0$;
- Assume that $A_{T_{p-j}} \geq K_{T_{p-j}}$ for some $j \leq p - 1$. This implies, by absence of arbitrage opportunities:

$$A_{T_{p-j-1}} \geq E_{T_{p-j-1}} \left[\frac{M_{T_{p-j}}}{M_{T_{p-j-1}}} K_{T_{p-j}} \right].$$

Because the goal is secured, we thus have

$$A_{T_{p-j-1}} \geq \max \left[G_{T_{p-j-1}}, E_{T_{p-j-1}} \left[\frac{M_{T_{p-j}}}{M_{T_{p-j-1}}} K_{T_{p-j}} \right] \right].$$

The right-hand side is $K_{T_{p-j-1}}$ (we recall that $G_{T_0} = 0$ by definition).

241

Hence, we have $A_0 \geq K_0$. Observe that the implication "if the goal is affordable, then $A_0 \geq K_0$" does not require market completeness.

Assume now that $A_0 \geq K_0$. Because the market is complete, all the payoffs $K_{T_1}, \ldots, K_{T_p}$ are replicable. We let $(\underline{x}_{jt})_{0 \leq t \leq T_j}$ denote the weights of the dynamic strategy that replicates K_{T_j}. We consider the following strategy, which is a roll-over of the exchange options:

$$\underline{w}_t = \underline{x}_{j+1,t}, \quad \text{for } T_j \leq t < T_{j+1} \text{ and } j = 0, \ldots, p-1.$$

We now show by induction that $A_{T_j} \geq K_{T_j}$ for all $j = 0, \ldots, p$.

- The property is true for $j = 0$ by assumption;
- If it is true for some $j < p$, then we have

$$A_{T_j} \geq E_{T_j} \left[\frac{M_{T_{j+1}}}{M_{T_j}} K_{T_{j+1}} \right].$$

The right-hand side is the price at date T_j of the payoff $K_{T_{j+1}}$ to be paid at date T_{j+1}. Over the period $[T_j, T_{j+1}]$, the portfolio is fully invested in the strategy that replicates this payoff. Hence,

$$A_{T_{j+1}} \geq K_{T_{j+1}}.$$

Eventually, we have $A_{T_j} \geq K_{T_j}$ for all $j = 1, \ldots, p$, and these inequalities imply that

$$A_{T_j} \geq G_{T_j} \quad \text{for } j = 1, \ldots, p,$$

so the goal is secured.

A.1.2. *Proof of Corollary 1*

We show that $K_{T_{p-j}} = G_{T_{p-j}}$ by recursion on j.

- The property is true for $j = 0$, by definition of K_{T_p};
- Assume that it is true for some $j \leq p - 2$. Then,

$$\mathbb{E}_{T_{p-j-1}} \left[\frac{M_{T_{p-j}}}{M_{T_{p-j-1}}} K_{T_{p-j}} \right] = \mathbb{E}_{T_{p-j-1}} \left[\frac{M_{T_{p-j}}}{M_{T_{p-j-1}}} G_{T_{p-j}} \right] \leq G_{T_{p-j-1}},$$

hence,

$$K_{T_{p-j-1}} = G_{T_{p-j-1}}.$$

Hence, $K_{T_{p-j}} = G_{T_{p-j}}$ for all $j = 0, \ldots, p-1$. It follows that the present value of the goal is

$$\tilde{G}_t = \mathbb{E}_t \left[\frac{M_{T_{j+1}}}{M_t} G_{T_{j+1}} \right], \quad \text{for } T_j < t \le T_{j+1} \text{ and } j = 0, \ldots, p-1,$$

and

$$\tilde{G}_0 = K_0 = \mathbb{E}\left[M_{T_1} G_{T_1} \right].$$

A.1.3. *Equivalent form of Definition 4*

Consider the wealth process given by Equation (2.4). We have to show that if A_T is non-negative almost surely, then A_t is non-negative, too, for all t between 0 and T.

Wealth is discontinuous (on the consumption dates), but the state-price deflator M is continuous, so the standard version of Ito's formula applies

$$d\left(M_t A_t \right) = A_t dM_t + M_t dA_t - M_t \underline{q}_t' \underline{\sigma}_t' \lambda_t dt.$$

Substituting the dynamics of M and A and simplifying gives

$$d(M_t A_t) = M_t [\underline{\sigma}_t \underline{q}_t - A_t \lambda_t]' d\underline{z}_t - M_t \sum_{j=1}^{p} c_{T_j} dJ_{T_j, t}.$$

Because $dJ_{T_j, t}$ equals 1 if $t = T_j$ and 0 otherwise, the M_t in the second term of the right-hand side can be replaced by M_{T_j}, which gives

$$d(M_t A_t) = M_t [\underline{\sigma}_t \underline{q}_t - A_t \lambda_t]' d\underline{z}_t - \sum_{j=1}^{p} M_{T_j} c_{T_j} dJ_{T_j, t}.$$

Define now the right-continuous process

$$\hat{A}_t = A_t + \sum_{\substack{j=1 \\ T_j \le t}}^{p} \frac{M_{T_j}}{M_t} c_{T_j}.$$

We have

$$d\left(M_t \hat{A}_t \right) = d\left(M_t A_t \right) + \sum_{j=1}^{p} M_{T_j} c_{T_j} dJ_{T_j, t}.$$

Hence,

$$d(M_t \hat{A}_t) = M_t [\underline{\sigma}_t \underline{q}_t - A_t \underline{\lambda}_t]' d\underline{z}_t.$$

Thus, $M\hat{A}$ follows a martingale, and we have, for all t between 0 and T,

$$M_t \hat{A}_t = \mathbb{E}_t [M_T \hat{A}_T].$$

Re-arranging terms, we obtain

$$A_t = \mathbb{E}_t \left[\frac{M_T}{M_t} A_T \right] + \mathbb{E}_t \left[\sum_{\substack{j=1 \\ T_j > t}}^{p} \frac{M_{T_j}}{M_t} c_{T_j} \right], \quad \text{for all } t \text{ in } [0, T]. \quad (A.1)$$

Because consumption is non-negative, it follows that if A_T is non-negative, A_t is non-negative, too.

A.1.4. *Proof of Proposition 4*

It is shown in the main text that if the goal is affordable, then the initial wealth satisfies $A_0 \geq \tilde{G}_0$.

For the converse implication, suppose that $A_0 \geq \tilde{G}_0$, and consider the strategy fully invested in the coupon-paying bond, the coupons being re-invested in the bond. The equation that governs the evolution of wealth reads

$$dA_t = A_t \frac{d\hat{G}_t}{\hat{G}_t} - \sum_{j=1}^{p} c_{T_j} dJ_{T_j,t}.$$

Moreover, the differential of the total return index is

$$\frac{d\hat{G}_t}{\hat{G}_t} = \frac{d\tilde{G}_t}{\tilde{G}_t} + \sum_{j=1}^{p} \frac{c_{T_j}}{\tilde{G}_t} dJ_{T_j,t}.$$

Hence,

$$d(A_t - \tilde{G}_t) = \frac{A_t - \tilde{G}_t}{\hat{G}_t} d\hat{G}_t.$$

Integrating this equation, we obtain

$$A_t = \tilde{G}_t + \left(\frac{A_0}{\tilde{G}_0} - 1 \right) \hat{G}_t.$$

A.1.5. *Proof of Proposition 5*

Before proving the proposition, we start with a simple technical lemma, showing that the present value of a goal is not impacted if one introduces an additional horizon where the minimum wealth is zero.

Lemma. *Consider a wealth-based goal represented by the non-negative minimum wealth levels $(G_{T_1}, \ldots, G_{T_p})$ on dates $T_1 < \cdots < T_p$. Let τ be a date distinct from $T_1, \ldots, T_p$, and define the goal G^2 as*

$$G^2_{T_j} = G_{T_j}, \quad for\ j = 1, \ldots, p,$$
$$G^2_\tau = 0.$$

Then: $\tilde{G}^2_0 = \tilde{G}_0$.

Proof.   There are three cases to distinguish: $\tau < T_1$, $\tau > T_p$ or τ is between T_j and T_{j+1} for some j. We focus on the last one, because the first two are handled in a similar way. We define the payoffs K_{T_k} and $K^2_{T_k}$ and the prices $\tilde{K}_{T_k, T_{k+1}}$ and $\tilde{K}^2_{T_k, T_{k+1}}$ in the same way as in Proposition 3. We have

$$K^2_{T_k} = K_{T_k}, \quad \text{for } k = j+1, \ldots, p,$$
$$\tilde{K}^2_{T_k, T_{k+1}} = \tilde{K}_{T_k, T_{k+1}}, \quad \text{for } k = j, \ldots, p-1.$$

Then, $K^2_\tau = \max[0, \tilde{K}^2_{\tau, T_{j+1}}] = \tilde{K}^2_{\tau, T_{j+1}}$ so that

$$\tilde{K}^2_{T_j, \tau} = \mathbb{E}_{T_j}\left[\frac{M_{T_{j+1}}}{M_{T_{j+1}}} K^2_{T_{j+1}}\right] = \mathbb{E}_{T_j}\left[\frac{M_{T_{j+1}}}{M_{T_{j+1}}} K_{T_{j+1}}\right] = \tilde{K}_{T_j, T_{j+1}}.$$

Hence,

$$K^2_{T_j} = \max[G_{T_j}, \tilde{K}_{T_j, T_{j+1}}] = K_{T_j}.$$

Then, we obtain $K^2_{T_k} = K_{T_k}$ for all $k = 0, 1, \ldots, j$.

Let us return to the framework of the proposition. The lemma implies that one can introduce additional minimum levels equal to zero to a wealth-based goal without changing its present value. Hence, without loss of generality, one can assume that all goals have the same set of horizons $\mathcal{T} = \{T_1, \ldots, T_p\}$. We show by induction that $K_{T_{p-j}} \geq K^l_{T_{p-j}}$:

- This is true for $j = 0$, as $K_{T_p} = G_{T_p} \geq G^l_{T_p} = K^l_{T_p}$;
- Assume that the property is true for some j between 0 and $p - 1$. Then,

$$K_{T_{p-j-1}} = \max[G_{T_{p-j-1}}, \tilde{K}_{T_{p-j-1}, T_{p-j}}],$$

with

$$G_{T_{p-j-1}} \geq G^l_{T_{p-j}},$$

$$\tilde{K}_{T_{p-j-1}, T_{p-j}} = \mathbb{E}_{T_{p-j-1}} \left[\frac{M_{T_{p-j}}}{M_{T_{p-j-1}}} K_{T_{p-j}} \right]$$

$$\geq \mathbb{E}_{T_{p-j-1}} \left[\frac{M_{T_{p-j}}}{M_{T_{p-j-1}}} K^l_{T_{p-j}} \right] = \tilde{K}^l_{T_{p-j-1}, T_{p-j}}.$$

Hence,

$$K_{T_{p-j-1}} \geq \max \left[G^l_{T_{p-j}}, \tilde{K}^l_{T_{p-j-1}, T_{p-j}} \right] = K^l_{T_{p-j-1}}.$$

Eventually, we have $K_0 \geq K^l_0$ for $l = 1, \ldots, L$. As a result,

$$K_0 \geq \max[K^1_0, \ldots, K^L_0],$$

that is

$$\tilde{G}_0 \geq \max[\tilde{G}^1_0, \ldots, \tilde{G}^L_0].$$

$\square$

A.1.6. *Proof of Proposition 8*

Assume that the goal is affordable, and take a strategy that secures it, with wealth evolving as in Equation (2.5). Define the payoffs $(V_{T_j})_{j=1,\ldots,p}$ as in the proposition. We let by convention $A_{0-} = A_0$, and we show by induction that $A_{T_{p-j}-} \geq V_{T_{p-j}}$ for all $j = 0, \ldots, p$.

- The property is true for $j = 0$. Indeed, we have

$$A_{T_p} \geq c_{T_p},$$

hence,

$$A_{T_p-} + y_{T_p} \geq c_{T_p}.$$

Since the goal is affordable, we also have $A_{T_p-} \geq 0$, hence $A_{T_p-} \geq (c_{T_p} - y_{T_p})^+ = V_{T_p}$.

- Suppose that the property is true for some $j = 0, \ldots, p-1$, that is

$$A_{T_{p-j}-} \geq V_{T_{p-j}}.$$

Taking the present values on both sides, we obtain

$$A_{T_{p-j-1}} \geq \tilde{V}_{T_{p-j-1},T_{p-j}},$$

that is

$$A_{T_{p-j-1}-} \geq \tilde{V}_{T_{p-j-1},T_{p-j}} + c_{T_{p-j-1}} - y_{T_{p-j-1}}.$$

We also have $A_{T_{p-j-1}-} \geq 0$, hence,

$$A_{T_{p-j-1}-} \geq V_{T_{p-j-1}}.$$

Eventually, we obtain $A_0 \geq V_0$.

Conversely, suppose that $A_0 \geq V_0$, and consider a roll-over of exchange options, each of them paying off V_{T_j} at date T_j (these options exist because the market is complete). We let by convention $\tilde{V}_{T_p,T_{p+1}} = V_{T_p}$, and we show by induction that $A_{T_j} \geq \tilde{V}_{T_j,T_{j+1}}$ for all $j = 0, \ldots, p$.

- The property is true for $j = 0$, since $A_0 \geq V_0 = \tilde{V}_{0,T_1}$;
- Assume that the property is true for some $j = 0, \ldots, p-1$, that is

$$A_{T_j} \geq \tilde{V}_{T_j,T_{j+1}}.$$

Then, the wealth process remains non-negative between dates T_j and T_{j+1}, and the wealth just before income at date T_{j+1} is

$$A_{T_{j+1}-} = \frac{A_{T_j}}{\tilde{V}_{T_j,T_{j+1}}} V_{T_{j+1}} \geq V_{T_{j+1}} = \left(\tilde{V}_{T_{j+1},T_{j+2}} + c_{T_{j+1}} - y_{T_{j+1}}\right)^+,$$

so that

$$A_{T_{j+1}} \geq \tilde{V}_{T_{j+1},T_{j+2}}.$$

Eventually, we obtain $A_t \geq 0$ for all t, so the goal is secured.

Let us now establish the bounds for V_0. We show by induction that $\tilde{G}_{T_{p-j}-} - \tilde{H}_{T_{p-j}-} \leq V_{T_{p-j}} \leq \tilde{G}_{T_{p-j}-}$ for all $j = 0, \ldots, p$.

- The property is true for $j = 0$. Indeed, we have

$$V_{T_p} = (c_{T_p} - y_{T_p})^+ \geq c_{T_p} - y_{T_p},$$
$$V_{T_p} \leq c_{T_p},$$

and

$$\tilde{G}_{T_{p-j}-} = c_{T_p}, \quad \tilde{H}_{T_p-} = y_{T_p}.$$

- Assume that the property is true for some $j = 0, \ldots, p-1$, that is

$$\tilde{G}_{T_{p-j}-} - \tilde{H}_{T_{p-j}-} \leq V_{T_{p-j}} \leq \tilde{G}_{T_{p-j}-}.$$

Then, taking the present values of both sides, we obtain

$$\tilde{G}_{T_{p-j-1}} - \tilde{H}_{T_{p-j-1}} \leq \tilde{V}_{T_{p-j-1}, T_{p-j}} \leq \tilde{G}_{T_{p-j-1}},$$

hence,

$$V_{T_{p-j-1}} \geq \tilde{G}_{T_{p-j-1}} - \tilde{H}_{T_{p-j-1}} + c_{T_{p-j-1}} - y_{T_{p-j-1}}$$
$$= \tilde{G}_{T_{p-j-1}-} - \tilde{H}_{T_{p-j-1}-},$$

and

$$V_{T_{p-j-1}} \leq \tilde{G}_{T_{p-j-1}} + c_{T_{p-j-1}} - y_{T_{p-j-1}} \leq \tilde{G}_{T_{p-j-1}} + c_{T_{p-j-1}}$$
$$= \tilde{G}_{T_{p-j-1}-}.$$

Eventually, we obtain $\tilde{G}_0 - \tilde{H}_0 \leq V_0 \leq \tilde{G}_0$.

Suppose now that the goal and the income payments are such that $\tilde{G}_{T_j-} \geq \tilde{H}_{T_j-}$ for all $j = 1, \ldots, p$. The same backward induction as before shows that $V_0 = \tilde{G}_0 - \tilde{H}_0$.

A.1.7. *Proof of Proposition 9*

Assume that $A_0 \geq U_0$ and purchase the p options at date 0. We recall that $e_{T_j} = y_{T_j} - c_{T_j}$ denotes the net income and we define v_{T_j} as the income payment plus the excess of date T_{j-1} invested at a zero rate:

$$v_{T_j} = u_{T_{j-1}} + e_{T_j}, \quad \text{for } j = 1, \ldots, p.$$

Then, we have

$$u_{T_j} = v_{T_j}^+,$$

$$U_0 = \sum_{k=1}^{p} \mathbb{E}[M_{T_k}(-v_{T_k})^+].$$

More generally, we also define U_{T_j} as the price at date T_j of the remaining $p - j$ options, that is

$$U_{T_j} = \mathbb{E}_{T_j}\left[\sum_{k=j+1}^{p} \frac{M_{T_k}}{M_{T_j}}(-v_{T_k})^+ \right].$$

Assume that at some date T_j with $j = 1, \ldots, p-1$, we have $A_{T_j} \geq U_{T_j}$, and that u_{T_j} is invested in zero-coupons paying \$1 on date T_{j+1}. These zero-coupons have prices less than \$1 because nominal rates are non-negative. Then, just before income and consumption at date T_{j+1}, we have

$$A_{T_{j+1}-} \geq U_{T_{j+1}} + u_{T_j} = \mathbb{E}_{T_{j+1}}\left[\sum_{k=j+2}^{p} \frac{M_{T_k}}{M_{T_{j+1}}}(-v_{T_k})^+ \right]$$

$$+ (-v_{T_{j+1}})^+ + u_{T_j}.$$

By definition, $v_{T_{j+1}} = u_{T_j} + e_{T_{j+1}}$, hence,

$$u_{T_j} + (-v_{T_{j+1}})^+ + e_{T_{j+1}} \geq v_{T_j}^+ - v_{T_{j+1}} + e_{T_{j+1}} = 0.$$

Moreover, u_{T_j} and $(-v_{T_{j+1}})^+$ are non-negative, hence,

$$u_{T_j} + (-v_{T_{j+1}})^+ + e_{T_{j+1}} \geq e_{T_{j+1}}.$$

We thus have

$$u_{T_j} + (-v_{T_{j+1}})^+ + e_{T_{j+1}} \geq e_{T_{j+1}}^+,$$

so that

$$A_{T_{j+1}} \geq \mathbb{E}_{T_{j+1}} \left[\sum_{k=j+2}^{p} \frac{M_{T_k}}{M_{T_{j+1}}} (-v_{T_k})^+ \right] + e_{T_{j+1}}^+ = U_{T_{j+1}} + e_{T_{j+1}}^+.$$

This shows that $A_{T_{j+1}} \geq U_{T_{j+1}}$.

Hence, we have $A_{T_j} \geq U_{T_j}$ for all $j = 1, \ldots, p$. In particular, A_{T_j} is non-negative for all $j = 1, \ldots, p$, which implies that A_t is non-negative for all t. So, the goal is secured in the sense of Definition 8.

A.1.8.   *Proof of Proposition 9 bis*

Assume that $A_0 \geq U_{\text{ret},0}$. Then, at date 0, the option that pays $U_{\text{ret},T_{r+1},1}$ at date T_{r+1} is affordable. More generally, suppose that at some date T_j, where $j = 0, \ldots, r-1$, we have $A_{T_j} \geq U_{\text{ret},T_j,j}$. Then the option with payoff $U_{\text{ret},T_{r+1},j}$ is affordable. Purchasing this option and investing the remainder of wealth in any other portfolio strategy (with a non-negative payoff), we have

$$A_{T_{j+1}-} \geq U_{\text{ret},T_{j+1},j},$$

where

$$U_{\text{ret},T_{j+1},j} = \mathbb{E}_{T_{j+1}} \left[\frac{M_{T_r}}{M_{T_{j+1}}} U_{\text{ret},T_{r+1},j} \right].$$

Because the net income $e_{T_{j+1}} = y_{T_{j+1}} - c_{T_{j+1}}$ is non-negative, we have

$$U_{\text{ret},T_{r+1},j} = [U_{\text{ret},T_{r+1},j+1} - e_{T_{j+1}}]^+,$$

hence,

$$U_{\text{ret},T_{j+1},j} \geq \mathbb{E}_{T_{j+1}} \left[\frac{M_{T_{r+1}}}{M_{T_{j+1}}} [U_{\text{ret},T_{r+1},j+1} - e_{T_{j+1}}] \right]$$

$$= U_{\text{ret},T_{j+1},j+1} - e_{T_{j+1}} b_{T_{j+1},T_{r+1}},$$

where $b_{T_{j+1},T_{r+1}}$ is the price at date T_{j+1} of the zero-coupon bond maturing at date T_{r+1}. As long as nominal rates are non-negative, we have $b_{T_{j+1},T_{r+1}} \leq 1$, so that

$$U_{\text{ret},T_{j+1},j} + e_{T_{j+1}} \geq U_{\text{ret},T_{j+1},j+1}.$$

Hence,

$$A_{T_{j+1}} \geq U_{\text{ret},T_{j+1},j+1}.$$

This proves that the strategy is implementable since the wealth of date T_j (after income) is sufficient to purchase the option which pays $U_{\text{ret},T_{r+1},j}$ on date T_{r+1}. Moreover, with this strategy, we have $A_t \geq 0$ for all t. This means that the goal is secured in the sense of Definition 8.

A.2. Probability-Maximising Strategies

A.2.1. *Proof of Proposition 10*

Define $N_T = G_T - F_T$, and $\tilde{N}_t = \tilde{G}_t - \tilde{F}_t$: N_T is positive by the assumption that $G_T > F_T$ almost surely, and $\tilde{N}_t$ is positive, too, since $\tilde{N}_t = E_t\left[\frac{M_T}{M_t}N_T\right]$. Following El Karoui and Rouge (2000), we introduce the probability measure $\mathbb{Q}^N$ such that discounted prices expressed in the numeraire $\tilde{N}$ follow $\mathbb{Q}^N$-martingales. The conditional Radon–Nikodym density of $\mathbb{Q}^N$ with respect to $\mathbb{P}$ is

$$\left.\frac{d\mathbb{Q}^N}{d\mathbb{P}}\right|_t = \frac{M_T N_T}{M_t \tilde{N}_t}.$$

We then define the set

$$\tilde{R} = \{M_T N_T \leq K\tilde{N}_0\},$$

and assume that K can be chosen in such a way that $\mathbb{E}[M_T N_T I_{\tilde{R}}] = A_0 - \tilde{F}_0$, or equivalently that $\mathbb{Q}^N(\tilde{R}) = \frac{A_0 - \tilde{F}_0}{\tilde{N}_0}$.[1] We let $X^* = F_T +$

---

[1] A sufficient condition for the existence of K is that the cumulative distribution function of the random variable N_T under $\mathbb{Q}^N$ be continuous. This is the case if N_T has no atoms (i.e. for any real number x, the probability that $N_T = x$ is zero).

$N_T \mathbb{I}_{\tilde{R}}$, which is a replicable payoff since the market is complete. Note that since N_T is positive, we have

$$\{X^* \geq G_T\} = \{N_T \mathbb{I}_{\tilde{R}} \geq N_T\} = \tilde{R}.$$

Consider now any strategy with a terminal wealth A_T which satisfies $A_T \geq F_T$ almost surely, and define the "success region" $R = \{A_T \geq G_T\}$. We have

$$\mathbb{Q}^N(R) = \frac{1}{\tilde{N}_0}\mathbb{E}[M_T N_T I_R] \leq \frac{1}{\tilde{N}_0}\mathbb{E}[M_T(A_T - F_T)\mathbb{I}_R] \leq \frac{A_0 - \tilde{F}_0}{\tilde{N}_0},$$

hence, $\mathbb{Q}^N(R) \leq \mathbb{Q}^N(\tilde{R})$. By Neyman–Pearson lemma, it follows that

$$\mathbb{P}(R) \leq \mathbb{P}(\tilde{R}).$$

This inequality means that X^* is the probability-maximising payoff subject to the floor constraint. Using the equality $A_{\mathrm{go},T} = \frac{A_0}{M_T}$, this payoff can be rewritten as

$$A_T^* = F_T + (G_T - F_T) \times \mathbb{I}_{\left\{\frac{A_{\mathrm{go},T}}{N_T} \geq \frac{A_0}{KN_0}\right\}}.$$

The optimal wealth process is given by

$$A_t^* = \tilde{F}_t + \tilde{N}_t \mathbb{Q}_t^N(\tilde{R}).$$

(The second term in the right-hand side is the price of the digital option which pays 1 upon realisation of the event $\tilde{R}$.) Assume that $\tilde{F}_t = \alpha \tilde{G}_t$, which implies that $\underline{w}_{\mathrm{GHP},s} = \underline{w}_{\mathrm{FHP},s}$. Then, if $\underline{\sigma}_{Fs} = \underline{\sigma}_s \underline{w}_{Gs}$ denotes the volatility vector of $\tilde{G}$, we have

$$N_T = \tilde{N}_t \times \exp\left[\int_t^T \left(r_s + \underline{\sigma}_{Gs}'\underline{\lambda}_s - \frac{1}{2}\|\underline{\sigma}_{Gs}\|^2\right) ds + \int_t^T \underline{\sigma}_{Gs}'d\underline{z}_s\right],$$

and

$$M_T N_T = M_t \tilde{N}_t \times \exp\left[-\frac{1}{2}\int_t^T \|\underline{\lambda}_s - \underline{\sigma}_{Gs}\|^2 ds - \int_t^T [\underline{\lambda}_s - \underline{\sigma}_{Gs}]'d\underline{z}_s\right].$$

By Girsanov's theorem, the process $\underline{z}_t^N = \underline{z}_t + \int_0^t [\underline{\lambda}_s - \underline{\sigma}_{Gs}]ds$ is a $\mathbb{Q}^N$-Brownian motion. It follows that

$$\frac{A_{\mathrm{go},T}}{N_T} = \frac{A_{\mathrm{go},t}}{\tilde{N}_t} \times \exp\left[-\frac{1}{2}\int_t^T \|\underline{\lambda}_s - \underline{\sigma}_{Gs}\|^2 ds + \int_t^T [\underline{\lambda}_s - \underline{\sigma}_{Gs}]'d\underline{z}_s^N\right].$$

If $\underline{\lambda}_s$ and $\underline{\sigma}_{Fs}$ are deterministic functions of time, then $A_{\text{go},T}/N_T$ is log-normally distributed conditional on $\mathcal{F}_t$. This implies that, if $\kappa_{t,T} = \sqrt{\int_t^T \|\underline{\lambda}_s - \underline{\sigma}_{Gs}\|^2 ds}$, we have

$$Q_t^N(\tilde{R}) = \mathcal{N}\left(\frac{-\ln\frac{A_0}{KN_0} + \ln\frac{A_{\text{go},t}}{N_t} - \frac{1}{2}\kappa_{t,T}^2}{\kappa_{t,T}}\right).$$

Therefore,

$$A_t^* = \tilde{F}_t + \tilde{N}_t\mathcal{N}(W_t),$$

with $W_t = \dfrac{-\ln\frac{A_0}{KN_0} + \ln\frac{A_{\text{go},t}}{N_t} - \frac{1}{2}\kappa_{t,T}^2}{\kappa_{t,T}}$. By Ito's lemma,

$$dA_t^* = d\tilde{F}_t + \mathcal{N}(W_t)d\tilde{N}_t + \tilde{N}_t n(W_t)dW_t + (\cdots)dt,$$

which implies that

$$dA_t^* = \tilde{F}_t\underline{\sigma}_{Gt}'d\underline{z}_t + \mathcal{N}(W_t)\tilde{N}_t\underline{\sigma}_{Gt}'d\underline{z}_t + \frac{\tilde{N}_t n(W_t)}{\kappa_{t,T}}[\underline{\lambda}_t - \underline{\sigma}_{Gt}]'d\underline{z}_t + (\cdots)dt.$$

Matching the diffusion terms of both sides, we obtain the optimal vector of dollar amounts to be invested in the risky assets

$$A_t^*\underline{w}_t^* = \tilde{F}_t\underline{w}_{\text{GHP},t} + (A_t^* - \tilde{F}_t)\underline{w}_{\text{GHP},t} + \frac{\tilde{N}_t n(W_t)}{\kappa_{t,T}}[\underline{w}_{\text{go},t} - \underline{w}_{\text{GHP},t}].$$

Let $\varphi_t = \dfrac{\tilde{N}_t n(W_t)}{\kappa_{t,T}A_t^*}$. Then,

$$\underline{w}_t^* = \varphi_t\underline{w}_{\text{go},t} + (1 - \varphi_t)\underline{w}_{\text{GHP},t}.$$

Because $\underline{w}_{Gs} = \underline{w}_{Fs}$, the coefficient $\kappa_{t,T}$ can be rewritten as

$$\kappa_{t,T} = \sqrt{\int_t^T \|\underline{\lambda}_s - \underline{\sigma}_{Fs}\|^2 ds}.$$

The allocation to the growth-optimal portfolio can be rewritten as

$$\varphi_t = \frac{1}{\kappa_{t,T}}\frac{\tilde{N}_t}{A_t^*} n\left[\mathcal{N}^{-1}\left(\frac{A_t^* - \tilde{F}_t}{\tilde{N}_t}\right)\right].$$

If A_t^* approaches $\tilde{F}_t$ from above (respectively, $\tilde{G}_t$ from below), then the ratio $(A_t^* - \tilde{F}_t)/\tilde{N}_t$ approaches 0 (respectively, 1). Hence, the quantity $\mathcal{N}^{-1}(\frac{A_t^* - \tilde{F}_t}{\tilde{N}_t})$ diverges to minus infinity (respectively, plus infinity), so that φ_t shrinks to zero.

A.3. Utility-Maximising Strategies

A.3.1. *Proof of Proposition 11*

A.3.1.1. *Optimal payoff*

Assume that the financial market is dynamically complete, so there exists a unique state-price deflator. We follow the martingale approach of Cox and Huang (1989). Consider the following candidate optimal payoff for Program (3.11):

$$X^* = G_T U'^{-1}(\eta_1 M_T G_T),$$

where the constant η_1 is adjusted in such a way that the budget constraint $\mathbb{E}[M_T X^*] = A_0$ is satisfied. Such a constant does exist, because we have

$$X^* = \eta_1^{-\frac{1}{\gamma}} G_T^{1-\frac{1}{\gamma}} M_T^{-\frac{1}{\gamma}},$$

so it suffices to take

$$\eta_1 = \frac{A_0^{-\gamma}}{\mathbb{E}\left[(M_T G_T)^{1-\frac{1}{\gamma}}\right]^{-\gamma}}.$$

(If U was not specified as the CRRA function, the constant η_1 might not be calculable in closed form, and conditions would have to be imposed on U' to ensure the existence and the uniqueness of η_1.)

Consider now any portfolio strategy that yields a positive terminal wealth A_T. Because U is concave, we have

$$U\left(\frac{A_T}{G_T}\right) \leq U\left(\frac{X^*}{G_T}\right) + \frac{A_T - X^*}{G_T} U'\left(\frac{X^*}{G_T}\right),$$

so that

$$U\left(\frac{A_T}{G_T}\right) \le U\left(\frac{X^*}{G_T}\right) + (A_T - X^*)\eta M_T.$$

Because A_T is the terminal value of a self-financing portfolio strategy, we have $\mathbb{E}\left[M_T A_T\right] = A_0 = \mathbb{E}[M_T X^*]$, hence,

$$\mathbb{E}\left[U\left(\frac{A_T}{G_T}\right)\right] \le \mathbb{E}\left[U\left(\frac{X^*}{G_T}\right)\right].$$

This shows that X^* achieves the highest expected utility. Moreover, because the market is complete, X^* is attainable. Hence, it is the optimal terminal wealth, so we denote it with A_T^{*G}.

To solve Program (3.7), it suffices to note that it is equivalent to Program (3.11), with the random variable G_T being replaced by the constant 1. Hence, the optimal terminal wealth in Program (3.7) has the form

$$A_T^{*0} = U'^{-1}(\eta_0 M_T).$$

Using the expression for the inverse marginal utility, we get

$$A_T^{*G} = \eta_1^{-\frac{1}{\gamma}} G_T^{1-\frac{1}{\gamma}} M_T^{-\frac{1}{\gamma}}, \tag{A.2}$$

$$A_T^{*0} = \eta_0^{-\frac{1}{\gamma}} M_T^{-\frac{1}{\gamma}}, \tag{A.3}$$

with $\eta_0 = \dfrac{A_0^{-\gamma}}{\mathbb{E}[M_T^{1-\frac{1}{\gamma}}]^{-\gamma}}$.

Hence,

$$A_T^{*G} = \nu_1 A_T^{*0} G_T^{1-\frac{1}{\gamma}},$$

with

$$\nu_1 = \left(\frac{\eta_1}{\eta_0}\right)^{-\frac{1}{\gamma}} = \frac{\mathbb{E}\left[M_T^{1-\frac{1}{\gamma}}\right]}{\mathbb{E}\left[(M_T G_T)^{1-\frac{1}{\gamma}}\right]}.$$

A.3.1.2. *Optimal strategy*

The optimal wealth on date t for Program (3.11) is given by

$$A_t^{*G} = \mathbb{E}_t\left[\frac{M_T}{M_t}A_T^{*G}\right] = \eta_1^{-\frac{1}{\gamma}}\mathbb{E}_t\left[\left(\frac{M_T G_T}{M_t \tilde{G}_t}\right)^{1-\frac{1}{\gamma}}\right]M_t^{-\frac{1}{\gamma}}\tilde{G}_t^{1-\frac{1}{\gamma}}.$$

Let Z_{Gt} denote the conditional expectation in the right-hand side, and write its dynamics as

$$\frac{dZ_{Gt}}{Z_{Gt}} = \mu_{ZGt}dt + \underline{\sigma}'_{ZGt}d\underline{z}_t.$$

Apply now Ito's lemma to A_t^{*G} and match the diffusion terms of both sides of the equality, to obtain

$$\underline{\sigma}_t\underline{w}_t^{*G} = \frac{1}{\gamma}\underline{\lambda}_t + \underline{\sigma}_{ZGt} + \left(1 - \frac{1}{\gamma}\right)\underline{\sigma}_{Gt},$$

so the optimal strategy is

$$\underline{w}_t^{*G} = \frac{1}{\gamma}\underline{w}_{go,t} + \underline{\Sigma}_t^{-1}\underline{\sigma}_t'\underline{\sigma}_{ZGt} + \left(1 - \frac{1}{\gamma}\right)\underline{w}_{Gt}.$$

A similar derivation can be made for Program (3.7), provided the present value of the goal is replaced by the zero-coupon price. The optimal strategy is

$$\underline{w}_t^{*0} = \frac{1}{\gamma}\underline{w}_{go,t} + \underline{\Sigma}_t^{-1}\underline{\sigma}_t'\underline{\sigma}_{Z0t} + \left(1 - \frac{1}{\gamma}\right)\underline{w}_{bt},$$

where Z_{0t} is the random variable

$$Z_{0t} = \mathbb{E}_t\left[\left(\frac{M_T}{M_t b_{t,T}}\right)^{1-\frac{1}{\gamma}}\right],$$

and $\underline{w}_{bt}$ is the portfolio that replicates the zero-coupon bond maturing on date T. The optimal weights in the presence of the goal can thus be written as

$$\underline{w}_t^{*G} = \underline{w}_t^{*0} + \Sigma_t^{-1}\underline{\sigma}_t' [\underline{\sigma}_{ZGt} - \underline{\sigma}_{Z0t}] + \left(1 - \frac{1}{\gamma}\right)[\underline{w}_{Gt} - \underline{w}_{bt}].$$

The deflated goal and zero-coupon values can be expressed as

$$M_T G_T = M_t \tilde{G}_t \times \exp\left[-\int_t^T \|\underline{\lambda}_s - \underline{\sigma}_{Gs}\|^2 ds - \int_t^T [\underline{\lambda}_s - \underline{\sigma}_{Gs}]' d\underline{z}_s\right],$$

$$M_T = M_t b_{t,T} \times \exp\left[-\int_t^T \|\underline{\lambda}_s - \underline{\sigma}_{b,s,T}\|^2 ds - \int_t^T [\underline{\lambda}_s - \underline{\sigma}_{b,s,T}]' d\underline{z}_s\right].$$

Thus, if $\underline{\lambda}_t$, $\underline{\sigma}_{Gt}$ and $\underline{\sigma}_{b,t,T}$ are deterministic functions of time, the random variables $(\frac{M_T G_T}{M_t \tilde{G}_t})^{1-\frac{1}{\gamma}}$ and $(\frac{M_T}{M_t b_{t,T}})^{1-\frac{1}{\gamma}}$ are independent from $\mathcal{F}_t$, so the conditional expectations equal the unconditional expectations. Hence, Z_{Gt} and Z_{0t} are deterministic functions of time, so their volatility vectors are zero. It follows that

$$\underline{w}_t^{*G} = \underline{w}_t^{*0} + \left(1 - \frac{1}{\gamma}\right)[\underline{w}_{Gt} - \underline{w}_{bt}].$$

A.3.2.   *Proofs of Proposition 12 and Corollary 2*

A.3.2.1.   *Optimal payoff*

Consider the following candidate optimal payoff for Program (3.12):

$$X^* = \max(F_T, \nu_2 A_T^{*G}).$$

First, we look for a value of ν_2 such that $\mathbb{E}[M_T X^*] = A_0$. We let $f(\nu_2) = \mathbb{E}[M_T X^*]$, so that $f(0) = \tilde{F}_0$, which by assumption is less than A_0. By the dominated convergence theorem, f is continuous. We also have $f(1) \geq A_0$. Hence, by the intermediate value theorem, there exists a solution for the equation $f(\nu_2) = A_0$ in the range $[0, 1]$.

To see that the solution is unique when $A_0 > \tilde{F}_0$, consider two candidate solutions $\nu_{21} \leq \nu_{22}$. Because

$$\max(F_T, \nu_{21} A_T^{*G}) \leq \max(F_T, \nu_{22} A_T^{*G}). \tag{A.4}$$

Both solutions are necessarily positive since $A_0 > \tilde{F}_0$. There is a positive probability that $\nu_{21} A_T^{*G} > F_T$, otherwise we would have

$f(\nu_{21}) = \tilde{F}_0$, hence, $f(\nu_{21}) < A_0$. Taking a ω such that $\nu_{21} A_T^{*G}(\omega) > F_T(\omega)$ and (A.4) holds, we obtain

$$\nu_{21} A_T^{*G}(\omega) = \nu_{22} A_T^{*G}(\omega),$$

hence, $\nu_{21} = \nu_{22}$ since $A_T^{*G}(\omega) > 0$.

Let A_T be the terminal value of a strategy that satisfies $A_T \geq F_T$ almost surely. By the concavity of U, we have

$$U\left(\frac{A_T}{G_T}\right) \leq U\left(\frac{X^*}{G_T}\right) + \frac{A_T - X^*}{G_T} U'\left(\frac{X^*}{G_T}\right).$$

Because U' is strictly decreasing, we obtain

$$U\left(\frac{A_T}{G_T}\right) \leq U\left(\frac{X^*}{G_T}\right) + \frac{A_T - X^*}{G_T} \min\left[U'\left(\frac{\nu_2 A_T^{*G}}{G_T}\right), U'\left(\frac{F_T}{G_T}\right)\right],$$

which can equivalently be written as

$$U\left(\frac{A_T}{G_T}\right) \leq U\left(\frac{X^*}{G_T}\right) + \frac{A_T - X^*}{G_T}$$

$$\times \left\{ U'\left(\frac{\nu_2 A_T^{*G}}{G_T}\right) - \left[U'\left(\frac{\nu_2 A_T^{*G}}{G_T}\right) - U'\left(\frac{F_T}{G_T}\right)\right]^+ \right\}.$$

By (A.2), we have $A_T^{*G} = \eta^{-\frac{1}{\gamma}} G_T^{1-\frac{1}{\gamma}} M_T^{-\frac{1}{\gamma}} = U'^{-1}(\eta M_T G_T) G_T$ for some constant η. Hence,

$$U'\left(\frac{\nu_2 A_T^{*G}}{G_T}\right) = \eta \nu_2^{-\frac{1}{\gamma}} M_T G_T.$$

Because $\mathbb{E}[M_T X^*] = \mathbb{E}[M_T A_T]$, it follows that

$$\mathbb{E}\left[U\left(\frac{A_T}{G_T}\right)\right] \leq \mathbb{E}\left[U\left(\frac{X^*}{G_T}\right)\right]$$

$$- \mathbb{E}\left[(A_T - X^*)\left[U'\left(\frac{\nu_2 A_T^{*G}}{G_T}\right) - U'\left(\frac{F_T}{G_T}\right)\right]^+\right].$$

The positive part in the right-hand side is non-zero only when $\nu_2 A_T^{*G} < F_T$, in which case X^* equals F_T, and is therefore less than A_T. Hence, the expectation in the right-hand side is non-negative, so that

$$\mathbb{E}\left[U\left(\frac{A_T}{G_T}\right)\right] \leq \mathbb{E}\left[U\left(\frac{X^*}{G_T}\right)\right].$$

So, X^* is utility-maximising. Moreover, it is an attainable payoff by the market completeness, so it is the optimal terminal wealth.

For Corollary 2, note that the optimal terminal wealth satisfies

$$A_T^{*F} \leq \nu_2 A_T^{*G} + F_T.$$

Taking the present values on both sides, we obtain

$$A_0 \leq \nu_2 A_0 + \tilde{F}_0.$$

hence,

$$1 - \frac{\tilde{F}_0}{A_0} \leq \nu_2.$$

Assume now that $\nu_2 = 1$. Then, by definition of ν_2,

$$\mathbb{E}[M_T \max(F_T, A_T^{*G})] = A_0 = \mathbb{E}[M_T A_T^{*G}],$$

which implies that $M_T \max(F_T, A_T^{*G}) = M_T A_T^{*G}$, hence, that $\max(F_T, A_T^{*G}) = A_T^{*G}$, hence, that $A_T^{*G} \geq F_T$. By contraposition, if $\mathbb{P}(A_T^{*G} < F_T) > 0$, then it must be the case that $\nu_2 < 1$.

A.3.2.2. *Optimal strategy*

The optimal wealth process for Program (3.12) can be written as

$$A_t^{*F} = \nu_2 A_t^{*G} + \tilde{F}_t \mathbb{E}_t \left[\frac{M_T F_T}{M_t \tilde{F}_t}\left[1 - \frac{\nu_2 A_T^{*G}}{F_T}\right]^+\right].$$

Let $\mathbb{Q}^F$ be the probability measure whose Radon–Nikodym density with respect to $\mathbb{P}$ is

$$\left.\frac{d\mathbb{Q}^F}{d\mathbb{P}}\right|_t = \frac{M_T F_T}{M_t \tilde{F}_t}.$$

Under this measure, asset prices expressed in the numeraire $\tilde{F}$ follow martingales. We have

$$A_t^{*F} = \nu_2 A_t^{*G} + \tilde{F}_t \mathbb{E}_t^{\mathbb{Q}^F}\left[\left[1 - \frac{\nu_2 A_T^{*G}}{F_T}\right]^+\right].$$

By Girsanov's theorem, the process $\underline{z}_t^F = \underline{z}_t + \int_0^t [\underline{\lambda}_s - \underline{\sigma}_{Fs}] ds$ is a $\mathbb{Q}^F$-Brownian motion. The dynamics of the ratio $R^{*G} = A^{*G}/\tilde{F}$ under $\mathbb{Q}^F$ can be written as

$$\frac{dR_t^{*G}}{R_t^{*G}} = [\underline{\sigma}_t \underline{w}_t^{*G} - \underline{\sigma}_{Ft}]' d\underline{z}_t^F.$$

If the vectors $\underline{\sigma}_{Gt} = \underline{\sigma}_t \underline{w}_{Ft}$ and $\underline{\sigma}_t^{*G} = \underline{\sigma}_t \underline{w}_t^{*G}$ are deterministic functions of time, then the Black–Scholes formula implies that

$$\mathbb{E}_t^{\mathbb{Q}^F} \left[\left[1 - \frac{\nu_2 A_T^{*G}}{F_T} \right]^+ \right] = -\frac{\nu_2 A_t^{*G}}{\tilde{F}_t} \mathcal{N}(-d_{1t}) + \mathcal{N}(-d_{2t}),$$

with

$$d_{1t} = \frac{1}{\zeta_{t,T}} \left[\ln \frac{\nu_2 A_t^{*G}}{\tilde{F}_t} + \frac{1}{2} \zeta_{t,T}^2 \right],$$

$$d_{2t} = d_{1t} - \zeta_{t,T},$$

$$\zeta_{t,T} = \sqrt{\int_{tT} \| \underline{\sigma}_{s^{*G}} - \underline{\sigma}_{Fs} \|^2 ds}.$$

Note that $\mathcal{N}(-d_{2t})$ equals $\mathbb{Q}_t^F(\nu_2 A_T^{*G} \le F_T)$, which is the probability that the insurance put ends up in the money.

Therefore,

$$A_t^{*F} = \nu_2 A_t^{*G} \mathcal{N}(d_{1t}) + \tilde{F}_t \mathcal{N}(-d_{2t}).$$

Note that this can be rewritten as

$$A_t^{*F} = \tilde{F}_t + \tilde{F}_t \left[\frac{\nu_2 A_t^{*G}}{\tilde{F}_t} \mathcal{N}(d_{1t}) - \mathcal{N}(d_{2t}) \right],$$

where the term in the brackets can be identified with the Black–Scholes price of a call expressed in the numeraire $\tilde{F}$

$$\frac{\nu_2 A_t^{*G}}{\tilde{F}_t} \mathcal{N}(d_{1t}) - \mathcal{N}(d_{2t}) = \mathbb{E}_t^{\mathbb{Q}^F} \left[\left[\frac{\nu_2 A_T^{*G}}{F_T} - 1 \right]^+ \right].$$

The expression for the diffusion term in the dynamics of the ratio $R^{*F} = A^{*F}/\tilde{F}$ follows from the textbook expression for the delta of a call option in the Black–Scholes model. We obtain

$$\frac{dR_t^{*F}}{R_t^{*F}} = (\cdots)dt + \nu_2 R_t^{*G} \mathcal{N}(d_{1t})[\underline{\sigma}_t^{*G} - \underline{\sigma}_{Ft}]' d\underline{z}_t^F.$$

But by Ito's lemma, this diffusion term can also be written as

$$R_t^{*F}[\underline{\sigma}_t \underline{w}_t^{*F} - \underline{\sigma}_{Ft}]' d\underline{z}_t^F.$$

Matching the two expressions, we get

$$\underline{w}_t^{*F} = \underline{w}_{\text{FHP},t} + \frac{\nu_2 A_t^{*G} \mathcal{N}(d_{1t})}{A_t^{*F}}[\underline{w}_t^{*G} - \underline{w}_{\text{FHP},t}],$$

hence,

$$\underline{w}_t^{*F} = \underline{w}_{\text{FHP},t} + \frac{A_t^{*F} - \tilde{F}_t \mathcal{N}(-d_{2t})}{A_t^{*F}}[\underline{w}_t^{*G} - \underline{w}_{\text{FHP},t}].$$

If A_t^{*F} is close to $\tilde{F}_t$, then the call is deeply out of the money, which means that the current underlying price, $\nu_2 A_t^{*G}/\tilde{F}_t$, is small compared to the strike, 1. In this situation, d_{2t} goes to minus infinity, so that $\mathcal{N}(-d_{2t})$ converges to 1. Thus, the risk budget $[A_t^{*F} - \tilde{F}_t \mathcal{N}(-d_{2t})]$ shrinks to 0.

If A_t^{*F} grows to infinity, then the call is deeply in the money, so $\nu_2 A_t^{*G}/\tilde{F}_t$ is much larger than 1. Hence, d_{2t} diverges to plus infinity, and $\mathcal{N}(-d_{2t})$ shrinks to zero. Thus, the risk budget $[A_t^{*F} - \tilde{F}_t \mathcal{N}(-d_{2t})]$ coincides with A_t^{*F}.

A.3.3. *Proofs of Proposition 13 and Corollary 3*

Define

$$X^{**} = \min[C_T, \max(F_T, \nu_3 A_T^{*G})],$$

and let $f(\nu_3) = E[M_T X^{**}]$. By the monotone convergence theorem, f is increasing and satisfies $f(+\infty) = \tilde{C}_0$. Moreover,

$$f(\nu_2) \leq \mathbb{E}[M_T X^*] = A_0,$$

where $X^* = \max(F_T, \nu_2 A_T^{*G})$. Finally, f is continuous by the dominated convergence theorem. Because $A_0 < \tilde{C}_0$, the intermediate value theorem implies that there exists a value ν_3 in $[0, \infty[$ such that $f(\nu_3) = A_0$. The uniqueness of the solution when $A_0 > \tilde{F}_0$ is proven by the same arguments as in Appendix A.3.2.

The optimality of X^{**} follows from the same concavity arguments as in Appendix A.3.3. The derivation of the optimal strategy is also done by applying the same techniques. We do not repeat these calculations here. The reader can find a detailed proof in Deguest *et al.* (2014).

Assume that $\nu_3 = \nu_2$. Then,

$$\mathbb{E}[M_T \min[C_T, X^*]] = A_0 = \mathbb{E}[M_T X^*],$$

which implies that

$$\min[C_T, X^*] = X^*,$$

hence, that $X^* \leq C_T$. By contraposition, if $X^* > C_T$ holds with positive probability, it must be the case that $\nu_3 > \nu_2$.

A.3.4.   *Proof of Proposition 14*

In the presence of consumption, the budget constraint reads (see (A.1))

$$\mathbb{E}[M_T A_T] = A_0 - \tilde{G}_0.$$

Suppose first that $A_0 > \tilde{G}_0$, and consider the following candidate optimal payoff for Program (3.8):

$$X^* = U'^{-1}(\eta_3 M_T).$$

The constant η_3 is chosen so as to make the budget constraint hold. The only possible choice is

$$\eta_3 = \frac{(A_0 - \tilde{G}_0)^{-\gamma}}{E\left[M_T^{1-\frac{1}{\gamma}}\right]^{-\gamma}}.$$

The same arguments as in Appendix A.3.1 show that X^* is utility-maximising.

Note that by (A.3), X^* can be rewritten as

$$X^* = \left(\frac{\eta_3}{\eta_0}\right)^{-\frac{1}{\gamma}} A_T^{*0} = \frac{A_0 - \tilde{G}_0}{A_0} A_T^{*0}.$$

This payoff can be replicated by taking a long position (of value $\tilde{G}_0$) in the coupon-paying bond, plus a long position (of value $[A_0 - \tilde{G}_0]$) in the strategy which is optimal for Program (3.7). Thus, X^* is the optimal terminal wealth, and the optimal wealth process is given by

$$A_t^* = \mathbb{E}_t[M_T X^*] + \tilde{G}_t = \left(1 - \frac{\tilde{G}_0}{A_0}\right) A_t^{*0} + \tilde{G}_t.$$

The optimal weight vector is obtained by matching the diffusion terms in both sides of the equation:

$$A_t^* \underline{\sigma}_t \underline{w}_t^* = \left(1 - \frac{\tilde{G}_0}{A_0}\right) A_t^{*0} \underline{\sigma}_t \underline{w}_t^{*0} + \tilde{G}_t \underline{\sigma}_t \underline{w}_{\mathrm{GHP},t}.$$

It follows that

$$A_t^* \underline{w}_t^* = (A_t^{*c} - \tilde{G}_t) \underline{w}_t^{*0} + \tilde{G}_t \underline{w}_{\mathrm{GHP},t}.$$

A.4. Goals-Based Investing Strategies

A.4.1. *Proof of Proposition 15*

Consider a wealth-based goal with the horizons $T_1, \ldots, T_p$ and the minimum wealth levels $G_{T_1}, \ldots, G_{T_p}$, and the strategy defined by (3.20). The notations K_{T_j} (option payoff) and $\tilde{K}_{T_j,T_{j+1}}$ (option price) are defined in Proposition 3. The weights (3.20) can be rewritten as

$$\underline{w}_t^{\mathrm{GBI,MH}} = m\left(1 - \frac{\tilde{G}_t}{A_t}\right) \underline{w}_{\mathrm{PSP},t} + \left[1 - m\left(1 - \frac{\tilde{G}_t}{A_t}\right)\right] \underline{w}_{\mathrm{GHP},t},$$

for $T_{j-1} < t \leq T_j$ and $j = 1, \ldots, p$.

We show by induction on j that $A_{T_j} \geq K_{T_j}$.

- The property is true for $j = 0$, since $A_0 \geq K_0$ and $K_0 = \tilde{K}_{0,T_1}$ by definition;
- Assume that the property is true at the rank $j{-}1$, where j is between 1 and p. We let

$$RB_t = A_t - \tilde{K}_{t,T_j}$$

denote the risk budget.

Let $A_{\mathrm{GHP},t}$ be the value of the GHP with an initial investment of $\tilde{G}_0$. We have, for $T_{j-1} < t \le T_j$ (see (2.6)),

$$A_{\mathrm{GHP},t} = \left[\prod_{k=1}^{j-1} \frac{\tilde{G}_{T_k}}{\tilde{G}_{T_k+}} \right] \times \tilde{K}_{t,T_j},$$

the coefficient within the bracket being constant with respect to t. Let $A_{\mathrm{PSP},t}$ be the value of the PSP with an initial investment of A_0. By definition of the strategy, we have

$$dA_t = m \frac{RB_t}{A_{\mathrm{PSP},t}} dA_{\mathrm{PSP},t} + \frac{A_t - mRB_t}{A_{\mathrm{GHP},t}} dA_{\mathrm{GHP},t},$$

hence,

$$dRB_t = m \times RB_t \frac{dA_{\mathrm{PSP},t}}{A_{\mathrm{PSP},t}} + (1 - m) \times RB_t \frac{d\tilde{K}_{t,T_j}}{\tilde{K}_{t,T_j}}$$

Let

$$df_t = \frac{m(m-1)}{2} \frac{d\langle A_{\mathrm{PSP},t} \rangle}{A_{\mathrm{PSP},t}^2} - \frac{m^2}{2} \frac{d\langle \tilde{K}_{t,T_j} \rangle}{\tilde{K}_{t,T_j}^2}.$$

$$Z_t = A_{\mathrm{PSP},t}^m \tilde{K}_{t,T_j}^{1-m}.$$

Applying Ito's lemma, we arrive, after a bit of algebra, at

$$RB_t = \frac{RB_{T_{j-1}}}{Z_{T_{j-1}}} \times Z_t \times \exp\left[\int_{T_{j-1}}^t df_s \right].$$

By assumption, $A_{T_{j-1}} \ge K_{T_{j-1}}$. Because $K_{T_{j-1}} = \max(F_{T_{j-1}}, \tilde{K}_{T_{j-1},T_j})$, it follows that $A_{T_{j-1}} \ge \tilde{K}_{j,T_{j-1}}$, hence, $RB_{T_{j-1}} \ge 0$. So RB_t is non-negative too; in particular

$$RB_{T_j} - = A_{T_j} - \tilde{K}_{T_j,T_j} = A_{T_j} - K_{T_j} \ge 0.$$

Hence, we have $A_{T_j} \ge K_{T_j}$ for all $j = 1, \ldots, p$. Since $K_{T_j} \ge F_{T_j}$, it follows that $A_{T_j} \ge F_{T_j}$.

A.4.2. *Proof of Proposition 16*

We recall that $\tilde{G}_t$ is the price of the bond whose cash flows match the consumption expenses, while $\hat{G}_t$ is the total return index, that is, the price of the bond with coupons re-invested. The dynamics of $\hat{G}$ can be written as

$$\frac{d\hat{G}_t}{\hat{G}_t} = \frac{d\tilde{G}_t}{\tilde{G}_t} + \sum_{j=1}^{p} \frac{c_{T_j}}{\tilde{G}_t} dJ_{jt}.$$

The dynamics of the risk budget, $(A_t - \tilde{G}_t)$, reads

$$d(A_t - \tilde{G}_t) = A_t[(r_t + \underline{w}'_t\underline{\mu}_t)dt + \underline{w}'_t\underline{\sigma}'_t d\underline{z}_t]$$

$$- \sum_{j=1}^{p} c_{T_j} dJ_{jt} - \left[\tilde{G}_t \frac{d\hat{G}_t}{\hat{G}_t} - \sum_{j=1}^{p} c_{T_j} dJ_{jt} \right],$$

hence,

$$d(A_t - \tilde{G}_t) = A_t[(r_t + \underline{w}'_t\underline{\mu}_t)dt + \underline{w}'_t\underline{\sigma}'_t d\underline{z}_t] - \tilde{G}_t \frac{d\hat{G}_t}{\hat{G}_t}.$$

The dynamics of the total return index can also be written as

$$\frac{d\hat{G}_t}{\hat{G}_t} = (r_t + \underline{w}'_{\mathrm{GHP},t}\underline{\mu}_t)dt + \underline{w}'_{\mathrm{GHP},t}\underline{\sigma}'_t d\underline{z}_t.$$

Hence, with Strategy (3.21), the risk budget evolves as

$$d(A_t - \tilde{G}_t)$$
$$= (A_t - \tilde{G}_t)\{r_t dt + [m\underline{w}_{\mathrm{PSP},t} + (1 - m)\underline{w}_{\mathrm{PSP},t}]'[\underline{\mu}_t dt + \underline{\sigma}'_t d\underline{z}_t]\}.$$

Moreover, we have, by Ito's lemma,

$$\frac{d(A_{\mathrm{PSP},t}^m \hat{G}_t^{1-m})}{A_{\mathrm{PSP},t}^m \hat{G}_t^{1-m}} = m\frac{dA_{\mathrm{PSP},t}}{A_{\mathrm{PSP},t}}$$

$$+ (1 - m)\frac{d\hat{G}_t}{\hat{G}_t} + \frac{1}{2}m(m - 1)\|\underline{\sigma}_{\mathrm{PSP},t} - \underline{\sigma}_{Gt}\|^2 dt,$$

with $\underline{\sigma}_{\text{PSP},t} = \underline{\sigma}_t \underline{w}_{\text{PSP},t}$ and $\underline{\sigma}_{Gt} = \underline{\sigma}_t \underline{w}_{Gt}$. Hence,

$$A_t - \tilde{G}_t = \frac{A_0 - \tilde{G}_0}{A_{\text{PSP},0}^m \hat{G}_0^{1-m}} \times A_{\text{PSP},t}^m \hat{G}_t^{1-m}$$

$$\times \exp\left[-\frac{1}{2}m(m-1) \int_0^t \|\underline{\sigma}_{\text{PSP},s} - \underline{\sigma}_{Gs}\|^2 ds \right].$$

If $A_0 \geq \tilde{G}_0$, we thus have that $A_t \geq \tilde{G}_t$ for all t in $[0, T]$. In particular, wealth remains non-negative, so the goal is affordable.

A.5.   Monte-Carlo Simulation Model

This section describes the various stochastic processes involved in the Monte-Carlo simulation model, as well as the base case values parameter values. We also provide a detailed description of the rebalancing rules applied in our simulations, as well as the formal definition of the various success indicators for the goals and the algorithm for computing taxes.

A.5.1.   *Stochastic processes and parameter values*

A.5.1.1.   *Asset prices*

We model asset prices as Geometric Brownian motions. This dynamics is a special case of (2.1) where the drift and the volatility are constant. For instance, the stock index (S) evolves as

$$\frac{dS_t}{S_t} = e_S dt + \underline{\sigma}_S' d\underline{z}_t,$$

where e_S is the expected arithmetic return and $\underline{\sigma}_S$ is the volatility vector. The dimension d of the Brownian motion is taken equal to the number of stochastic processes to simulate. We postulate similar dynamics for the bond index (B), the illiquid stock (X), the real estate (Y) and the alternative investment (Z).

We fix the expected return and the volatility of the stock and bond indices to the values estimated by Dimson, Marsh and Staunton (2002) for the US market over the 1900–2000 period (see p. 306 of their book). Such a long dataset is not available for real estate and alternative investment, so we simply set the risk and return parameters to "reasonable" values. For the illiquid stock, we take the same expected return as for the broad index, but we set its volatility twice as high, in order to reflect the amount of idiosyncratic risk, which is larger in an individual stock than in an index. The risk and return parameters for the various asset classes are summarised in Table 4.24.

To estimate the maximum Sharpe allocation to the stock and the bond indices, we need the expected excess returns of these assets, μ_S and μ_B. Since we assume constant expected returns and a stochastic interest rate (see Section A.5.1.2), the actual expected excess return is stochastic

$$\mu_{St} = e_S - r_t.$$

Nevertheless, we take constant values to compute the weights of the MSR portfolio. This is done primarily for simplicity, but it can also be noted that this apparent inconsistency reflects the situation of an investor who does not know the true parameter values. We fix the expected excess returns to the long-term values reported in Dimson *et al.* (2002, p. 36).

A.5.1.2. *Term structure*

The nominal short-term rate follows the Vasicek (1977) model:

$$dr_t = a(\bar{r} - r_t)dt + \underline{\sigma}_r' d\underline{z}_t.$$

Here, a is the speed of mean reversion, b is the long-term mean and $\underline{\sigma}_r$ is the volatility vector. We assume a constant price of interest rate risk, λ_r. The price at date t of a zero-coupon bond paying \$1 on date T is then

$$b_{t,T} = \exp\left[-D(T-t)r_t + E_B(T-t)\right],$$

with

$$D(s) = \frac{1 - e^{-as}}{a},$$

$$E_B(s) = \left(\bar{r} - \frac{\sigma_r \lambda_r}{a}\right)[D(s) - s] + \frac{\sigma_r^2}{2a^2}\left[s - 2D(s) + \frac{1 - e^{-2as}}{2a}\right].$$

Table 4.24. Base case parameter values.

(i) Univariate parameters.

Asset expected returns and volatilities	
Parameter	**Base case value**
e_S	0.12
e_B	0.051
e_X	0.012
e_Y	0.062
e_Z	0.012
μ_S	0.0782
μ_B	0.0108
σ_S	0.199
σ_B	0.083
σ_X	0.398
σ_Y	0.141
σ_Z	0.398

Continuous-time processes for short-term rate and price index	
Parameter	**Base case value**
a	0.0668
$\bar{r}$	0.0353
σ_r	0.0168
λ_r	−0.3340
π	0.025
σ_Φ	0.0134
λ_Φ	0

(ii) Correlations.

	Stock	Bond	Illiquid stock	Real estate	Alternative investment	Short-term rate	Price index
Stock	1						
Bond	0.237	1					
Illiquid stock	0.500	0.237	1				
Real estate	0.567	0.273	0.567	1			
Alternative investment	0.132	0.226	0.132	0.513	1		
Short-term rate	0.014	−0.044	0.014	0.094	−0.132	1	
Price index	−0.09	−0.21	−0.09	−0.04	0.05	−0.44	1

Notes: This table summarises the base case parameter values assumed for the simulation of the various stochastic processes introduced in Section 4. The stock and bond expected excess returns (μ_S and μ_B) are not used for simulation purposes but to compute the weights of the MSR portfolio.

This expression for the zero-coupon price is used to discount cash flows that are fixed in nominal terms.

Note that in this model, the Sharpe ratio of a zero-coupon is $-\lambda_r$. For the term premium to be positive, it is necessary to take a negative value for λ_r. The parameters of the model are borrowed from Martellini, Milhau and Tarelli (2013), who estimate them from monthly series of US sovereign zero-coupon yields over the period from August 1971 to August 2012.

To discount cash flows fixed in real terms, we use a stochastic model for inflation. The price index is modelled as a Geometric Brownian motion. We assume

$$\frac{d\Phi_t}{\Phi_t} = e_\Phi dt + \underline{\sigma}_{\Phi'} d\underline{z}_t,$$

where e_Φ represents expected inflation. The price of an inflation-indexed zero-coupon which pays Φ_T/Φ_0 on date T is

$$I_{t,T} = \frac{\Phi_t}{\Phi_0} \exp\left[-D(T-t)r_t + E_I(T-t)\right],$$

with

$$E_I(s) = E_B(s) + (\pi - \sigma_\Phi \lambda_\Phi)s + \frac{1}{2}\sigma_\Phi^2 s - \frac{\sigma_r \sigma_\Phi \rho_{r\Phi}}{a}[s - D(s)].$$

We set the expected inflation and the volatility of realised inflation to reasonable values, and we take the price of inflation risk, λ_Φ, to be zero. In theory, this parameter could be estimated from the real yield curve, but the estimation will be largely imprecise because only a relatively small dataset is available.[2] That is why we set λ_Φ to a neutral value. Note that real yields are increasing in λ_Φ: a higher value would make real yields lower, and even possibly negative.

So as to avoid negative 1-year real rates in the simulations for Case Study 1 (see Section 4.1 of Chapter 4), we impose a floor equal to $E_I(1)/D(1)$ to the nominal short-term rate in the simulations. This lower bound is equal to 2.20% given our parameter values (see Table 24), so the requirement of a non-negative real rate is stronger than the requirement of a non-negative nominal short-term rate.

---

[2]See Gürkaynak, Sack and Wright (2010) for the construction of a zero-coupon yield curve starting from 1999.

In the other two case studies (Sections 4.2 and 4.3 of Chapter 4), real interest rates are not used, so we impose a floor equal to zero to the nominal short-term rate.

A.5.1.3. *Correlations*

We set the correlations between the stock, the bond and the real estate class to reasonable values. We fix the correlation between the stock index and the illiquid stock by imposing that the beta of the latter stock with respect to the index be equal to 1. This condition implies that the correlation is

$$\rho_{SX} = \frac{\sigma_S}{\sigma_X} \times \beta_{S/X} = \frac{\sigma_S}{\sigma_X} = 0.5.$$

The correlations of the illiquid stock with the other processes are set to the same values as the correlations of the stock index.

The correlations of the various asset classes with the price index are set to reasonable values. In order to fix the correlations between the processes and the short-term rate, we use the approximation of a bond return as the negative of duration times the interest rate change. Considering a roll-over of bonds with a "short" maturity h (h must be short for the bond yield to be close to the short-term rate), we obtain the following approximation to the realised return:

$$R_{t,t+h} \approx -\mathrm{Dur} \times (r_{t+h} - r_t).$$

Hence, the correlation between a given stochastic process and changes in the short-term rate is close to the negative of the correlation between the process and the returns on a roll-over of short bonds. Thus, we start by estimating realistic values for the correlations between the various processes and a roll-over, and we take the negatives as estimates of the correlations with the short-term rate. The complete list of correlation values is given in Table 4.24.

A.5.2. *Constant-annuity mortgage amortisation*

In this appendix, we derive the expression for the annuity in a mortgage with constant annuities and constant interest rate. We use the following notations:

Notation	Meaning
L_t	Capital due at date t before annual payment.
L	Principal of loan.
$\updownarrow$	Constant annuity.
r	Borrowing rate.
T	Initial maturity of loan.
k_t	Capital repaid on date t.
i_t	Interest paid on date t.

We assume that the annuities are paid on dates $t = 1, \ldots, T$. It follows from the above definitions that, for $t = 1, \ldots, T$,

$$i_t = r L_t,$$

$$l = k_t + i_t,$$

and that for $t = 1, \ldots, T{-}1$,

$$k_t = L_t - L_{t+1}.$$

For $t = T$, we have $k_T = L_T$, a condition which means that all of the principal is redeemed after the last payment has taken place.

Hence, for $t = 1, \ldots, T{-}1$,

$$\ell = (1 + r)L_t - L_{t+1}.$$

Dividing both sides by $(1 + r)^{t+1}$, we obtain

$$\frac{\ell}{(1+r)^{t+1}} = \frac{L_t}{(1+r)^t} - \frac{L_{t+1}}{(1+r)^{t+1}}.$$

Summing up from $t = 1$ to $t = T$, we get

$$\sum_{t=1}^{T} \frac{\ell}{(1+r)^{t+1}} = \frac{L_1}{(1+r)^1} - 0.$$

The capital due before the first payment equals the loan principal value, so that $L_1 = L$. Hence, the present value of all annuities discounted at the borrowing rate must equal the principal

$$L = \sum_{t=1}^{T} \frac{\ell}{(1+r)^t}.$$

Calculating the geometric sum in the second term, we obtain the value of the constant annuity

$$\ell = \frac{r}{1 - (1+r)^{-T}} \times L.$$

A.6. Budget Equations and Definitions of Analytics

This appendix contains a description of the generic budget equations used in the simulations (for all strategies) and the detailed expressions for the weights of the GBI strategies. We next give the definitions of the success indicators that are computed for the various investment strategies considered in this book.

A.6.1. *Notations*

We use the following notations:

Notation	Meaning
Wealth processes	
$A_{btax,t}$	Before-tax wealth at date t (i.e. before taxes and non-portfolio gains and payments).
$A_{atax,t}$	After-tax wealth at date t (i.e. after taxes and before non-portfolio gains and payments).
$A_{anpf,t}$	Wealth after non-portfolio flows (gains and payments) at date t.
Non-portfolio inflows/outflows	
Θ_t	Amount of taxes due at date t.
l_t	"Constrained consumption" stream (e.g. mortgage), net of income.
c_t	"Flexible consumption" stream, i.e. any consumption expenditure at date t not already included in constrained consumption.
Asset prices and dividends	
$\underline{S}_{bdiv,t}$	Vector of asset prices at date t, before dividend and coupon payments.
$\underline{S}_{adiv,t}$	Vector of asset prices at date t, after dividend and coupon payments.
$\underline{D}_t$	Vector of dividend and coupon payments at date t.

(*Continued*)

Notation	Meaning
Portfolio composition	
$\underline{N}_{bdiv,t}$	Vector of numbers of shares held at date t before dividend and coupon payments, taxes and any other non-portfolio inflow or outflow.
$\underline{N}_{btax,t}$	Vector of numbers of shares held at date t after dividend and coupon payments, before taxes and non-portfolio gains and payments.
$\underline{N}_{atax,t}$	Vector of numbers of shares held at date t after dividend and coupon payments and taxes, and before non-portfolio flows (gains and payments).
$\underline{N}_{anpf,t}$	Vector of numbers of shares held at date t after dividend and coupon payments, taxes and non-portfolio gains and payments, and before rebalancing.
$\underline{N}_{areb,t}$	Vector of numbers of shares held at date t after rebalancing.
$\underline{q}$	Vector of sums invested in constituents (same subscripts as $\underline{N}$).
$\underline{w}$	Vector of constituent weights (same subscripts as $\underline{N}$).

A.6.2. *Generic budget equations*

In this section, we write the budget equations, which apply to all case studies and strategies. The timing of payments on a given date t is as follows:

1. Get dividends and coupons, and re-invest them in constituents;
2. Pay taxes;
3. Make all other payments (mortgage, consumption) and cash in non-portfolio income;
4. Rebalance.

1. Dividend and coupon payments

These payments cause no discontinuity to wealth, but they imply a change in the numbers of shares held in the portfolio. Since the dividend paid by each constituent is re-invested in the constituent itself, the number of shares held after the dividend is paid is

$$[\underline{N}_{btax,t}]_i = [\underline{N}_{bdiv,t}]_i \times \left(1 + \frac{[\underline{D}_t]_i}{[\underline{S}_{adiv,t}]_i}\right).$$

Note that this implies no change in portfolio weights. Indeed, the weights before and after the dividend payments are defined as

$$\underline{w}_{bdiv,t} = \frac{\underline{N}_{bdiv,t} \odot \underline{S}_{bdiv,t}}{A_{btax,t}}, \quad \underline{w}_{btax,t} = \frac{\underline{N}_{btax,t} \odot \underline{S}_{adiv,t}}{A_{btax,t}},$$

and a straightforward computation shows that

$$\underline{w}_{btax,t} = \underline{w}_{bdiv,t}.$$

2. **Tax payments**

These payments cause a downwards jump in wealth, since

$$A_{atax,t} = A_{btax,t} - \Theta_t.$$

The number of shares in each asset is recalculated in such a way that the relative weights after taxes have been paid are the same as before (that is, the tax payment is "evenly widespread" across the constituents). Thus, we have

$$\left[\underline{N}_{atax,t}\right]_i = \left[\underline{N}_{btax,t}\right]_i \times \frac{A_{atax,t}}{A_{btax,t}}.$$

3. **Other non-portfolio flows (gains and payments)**

The effect of these payments is similar to that of taxes (except that the net effect of consumption and income on wealth may be positive), so that

$$A_{anpf,t} = A_{atax,t} - l_t - c_t$$

$$\left[\underline{N}_{anpf,t}\right]_i = \left[\underline{N}_{atax,t}\right]_i \times \frac{A_{anfs,t}}{A_{atax,t}}.$$

(We recall that l_t is net of income payments.)

4. **Rebalancing**

This causes no discontinuity to wealth, but of course, the numbers of shares can be modified by this operation. By convention, if no rebalancing takes place on date t, we let

$$\underline{N}_{areb,t} = \underline{N}_{anpf,t}.$$

The evolution of wealth and portfolio composition between dates t and $t + h$ is governed by the following equations:

$$A_{btax,t+h} = \underline{N}'_{areb,t} \underline{S}_{bdiv,t+h},$$

$$\underline{N}_{bdiv,t+h} = \underline{N}_{areb,t}.$$

A.6.3. Dollar allocations and risk budgets for GBI strategies

In this appendix, we give the detailed expressions for the allocations to the locally risky assets by the GBI strategies described in Section 3.3.2 of Chapter 3. These expressions differ from the theoretical equations written in Section 3.3.2 of Chapter 3 through the imposition of no short-sales constraints in the building blocks.

A.6.3.1. GBI strategy securing a single essential goal

The essential goal (EG) can be wealth-based with a single horizon or with multiple horizons, or consumption-based. The weights of the corresponding GBI strategies without short-sales constraints are given in Equations (3.19)–(3.21). Ruling out short positions, we obtain the following expressions:

Equation	Description
$\underline{q}_t^{\mathrm{GBI}} = q_{\mathrm{PSP},t}\underline{w}_{\mathrm{PSP},t} + q_{\mathrm{FHP},t}\underline{w}_{\mathrm{FHP},t}$	Vector of dollar allocations to locally risky assets with GBI strategy.
$q_{\mathrm{PSP},t} = \min[A_{\mathrm{liq},t}, m \times RB_t]$	Dollar allocation to PSP.
$q_{F,t} = A_{\mathrm{liq},t} - q_{\mathrm{PSP},t}$	Dollar allocation to "floor-hedging portfolio" (portfolio super-replicating the goal).
$RB_t = \max[0, A_{G,t} - \tilde{F}_t]$	Risk budget.
$A_{G,t}$	Reference wealth for the goal (see the definition that follows).
$A_{\mathrm{liq},t}$	Liquid wealth.
$\tilde{F}_t$	Floor value, equal to goal present value for exogenous goals and drawdown floor for drawdown goal.

The reference wealth depends on the goal:

- In Case Study 1, the reference wealth for EG1 is the sum of liquid wealth and aspirational wealth, because the goal is to protect a minimum value for this total wealth. It coincides with liquid wealth when aspirational assets are liquidated;

- In Case Study 1, the reference wealth for EG2 is the liquid wealth because the goal is to protect the liquid investments from large drawdowns;
- In Case Studies 2 and 3, the reference wealth for the consumption-based goals is the liquid wealth because consumption expenses are financed with money withdrawn from the liquid bucket.

A.6.3.2. *GBI strategy securing two essential goals*

The two EGs can be wealth-based or consumption-based goals. The weights of the GBI strategy protecting the two goals without short-sales constraints are given in Equation (3.22). The following table describes the strategy with short-sales constraints applied.

Equation	Description
$q_t^{\text{GBI}} = q_{\text{PSP},t}\underline{w}_{\text{PSP},t} +$ $\quad q_{\text{FHP1},t}\underline{w}_{\text{FHP1},t} +$ $\quad q_{\text{FHP2},t}\underline{w}_{\text{FHP2},t}$	Vector of dollar allocations to locally risky assets with GBI strategy.
$q_{\text{PSP},t} = \min[A_{\text{liq},t}, m \times RB_t]$	Dollar allocation to PSP.
$q_{\text{FHP1},t} = (A_{\text{liq},t} - q_{\text{PSP},t}) \times$ $\quad \mathbb{I}_{\{RB_{1t} < RB_{2t}\}}$	Dollar allocation to FHP1 (portfolio super-replicating the first goal).
$q_{\text{FHP2},t} = (A_{\text{liq},t} - q_{\text{PSP},t}) \times$ $\quad \mathbb{I}_{\{RB_{1t} \geq RB_{2t}\}}$	Dollar allocation to FHP2 (portfolio super-replicating the second goal).
$RB_t = \max[RB_{1t}, RB_{2t}]$	Risk budget.
$RB_{it} = \max[0, A_{Gi,t} - \tilde{F}_{it}]$	Risk budget associated with ith goal $(i = 1, 2)$.
$A_{Gi,t}$	Reference wealth for ith goal $(i = 1, 2)$.
$A_{rmliq,t}$	Liquid wealth.
$\tilde{F}_{it}$	Floor value associated with ith goal $(i = 1, 2)$.

A.6.3.3. *GBI strategy with a cap*

The following table adapts the definition of the GBI strategy with a cap (see Equation (3.23)) to the case where short-sales constraints are imposed.

Equation	Description
$\underline{q}_t^{\text{GBI}} = q_{\text{PSP},t}\underline{w}_{\text{PSP},t} + q_{Ft}\underline{w}_{\text{FHP},t} + q_{Ct}\underline{w}_{\text{CHP},t}$	Vector of dollar allocations to locally risky assets with GBI strategy.
$q_{\text{PSP},t} = \min[A_{\text{liq},t}, m \times RB_t]$	Dollar allocation to PSP.
$RB_t = $	Risk budget.
$\quad RB_{Ft} \times \mathbb{I}_{\{A_t \le \xi_t\}} + RB_{Ct} \times \mathbb{I}_{\{A_t > \xi_t\}}$	
$\xi_t = \frac{\tilde{F}_t + \tilde{C}_t}{2}$	Threshold.
$RB_{Ft} = \max[0, A_t - \tilde{F}_t]$	Risk budget associated with floor.
$RB_{Ct} = \max[0, \tilde{C}_t - A_t]$	Risk budget associated with cap.
$x_{Ft} = (1 - x_{\text{PSP},t}) \times \mathbb{I}_{\{A_t \le \xi_t\}}$	Dollar allocation to FHP.
$x_{Ct} = (1 - x_{\text{PSP},t}) \times \mathbb{I}_{\{A_t > \xi_t\}}$	Dollar allocation to CHP.
A_t	Reference wealth for floor and cap.
$A_{\text{liq},t}$	Liquid wealth.
$\tilde{F}_t$	Floor value.
$\tilde{C}_t$	Cap value.

A.6.3.4. *GBI strategy with a single floor and a short position (Case Study 1)*

Equation	Description
$\underline{q}_t^{\text{GBI}} = q_{\text{PSP},t}\underline{w}_{\text{PSP},t} + q_{Ft}\underline{w}_{\text{FHP},t} + q_{\text{short},t}\underline{w}_{\text{short},t}$	Vector of dollar allocations to locally risky assets with GBI strategy.
$\underline{w}_{\text{short},t}$	Portfolio invested at 100% in the shortable asset.
$q_{\text{PSP},t} = \max[0, \min(A_{\text{liq},t}, m \times RB_t - A_{\text{asp},t})] \times \mathbb{I}_{\{m \times RB_t \ge A_{\text{asp},t}\}}$	Dollar allocation to PSP.
$q_{\text{short},t} = -\min[A_{X,t}, A_{\text{asp},t} - m \times RB_t] \times \mathbb{I}_{\{A_{\text{asp},t} > m \times RB_t\}}$	Dollar allocation to shortable asset (non-positive by definition).
$q_{Ft} = A_{\text{liq},t} - q_{\text{PSP},t} - q_{\text{short},t}$	Dollar allocation to FHP.
RB_t	Risk budget.
$A_{X,t}$	Value of position in illiquid stock within the aspirational bucket.
$A_{\text{asp},t}$	Aspirational wealth.
$A_{\text{liq},t}$	Liquid wealth.

A.6.4. *Success indicators for goals*

In this section, we define the "success indicators", which measure the degree of achievement of the goals. These definitions apply to affordable and non-affordable goals, whichever portfolio strategy is implemented.

A.6.4.1. *Wealth-based goals with a single horizon*

We use the framework of Section 2.2.1.1, where the wealth-based goal is represented by a payoff G_T on date T. The success indicators must quantify the likelihood of reaching the goal, and the size of deviations from the goal in case it is mixed. For the likelihood, it is natural to look at the success probability, defined as the probability that $A_T \geq G_T$. Formally,

$$sp = \mathbb{P}(A_T \geq G_T).$$

The size of deviations from the goal can be measured as the (relative) loss

$$\text{Loss}_T = \left[1 - \frac{A_T}{G_T}\right]^+.$$

It is zero if the goal is reached, and positive otherwise, but remains less than 100% as long as wealth remains non-negative. The expected relative shortfall is the expectation of $Loss_T$ conditioned on the event of a loss:

$$es = \mathbb{E}[\text{Loss}_T \,|\, \text{Loss}_T > 0].$$

By Bayes's formula, we have ($\mathbb{I}$ denoting an indicator function)

$$es = \frac{\mathbb{E}[\text{Loss}_T \times \mathbb{I}_{\{\text{Loss}_T > 0\}}]}{\mathbb{P}(\text{Loss}_T > 0)}.$$

Because the loss is always non-negative, the numerator equals the expected loss. Moreover, the denominator is 1 minus the success probability. Hence,

$$es = \frac{\mathbb{E}[\text{Loss}_T]}{1 - sp}.$$

By convention, the expected shortfall is set to 0 if the success probability is 1.

One may also look at the worst case, that is, the worst relative loss. Mathematically, the worst shortfall is defined as the "essential supremum" of the loss. For any random variable Y, the essential supremum is defined as the infimum of the values y such that the probability that Y exceeds y is zero:

$$\operatorname{ess\,sup} Y = \inf \{y; \mathbb{P}\,(Y > y) = 0\}.$$

(If Y has always a non-zero probability of exceeding any arbitrarily high threshold, the essential supremum is infinity.) Hence, the worst shortfall is defined as

$$\mathrm{ws} = \operatorname{ess\,sup} \mathrm{Loss}_T.$$

The following definition summarises the three success indicators for wealth-based goals.

Definition 11 (Success Indicators for a Wealth-Based Goal with a Single Horizon). Consider a wealth-based goal represented by the payoff G_T. The success indicators are defined as follows:

- The success probability: $\mathrm{sp} = \mathbb{P}(A_T \geq G_T)$;
- The expected shortfall: $\mathrm{es} = \frac{\mathbb{E}[\mathrm{Loss}_T]}{1-sp}$;
- The worst shortfall: $\mathrm{ws} = \operatorname{ess\,sup} \mathrm{Loss}_T$.

According to this terminology, a replicable goal is affordable if there exists a portfolio strategy $\underline{w}$ such that the success probability starting from the investor's initial wealth equals 100%.

A.6.4.2. *Wealth-based goals with multiple horizons*

A wealth-based goal with multiple horizons $T_1, \ldots, T_p$ is represented by the minimum wealth levels $(G_{T_1}, \ldots, G_{T_p})$. The definitions of the success indicators are similar to those for a single horizon, but an adaptation is needed to account for the fact that this goal is represented by multiple floors. The success probability is naturally defined as the probability that wealth is greater than or equal to the floor on each date

$$sp = \mathbb{P}(A_{T_j} \geq G_{T_j}; \forall j = 1, \ldots, p).$$

A deviation from the goal can potentially arise on each of the dates $T_1, \ldots, T_p$. We define the (relative) loss on date T_j as the gap between wealth and the goal value if the former is lower, that is

$$\text{Loss}_{T_j} = \left[1 - \frac{A_{T_j}}{G_{T_j}}\right]^+.$$

The quantity of interest is the maximum of losses over all horizons:

$$\max \text{Loss} = \max[\text{Loss}_{T_1}, \ldots, \text{Loss}_{T_p}].$$

The expected maximum shortfall is then defined as the expectation of this maximum, conditioned on the event that at least one of the losses is positive (which is equivalent to saying that the maximum is positive)

$$\text{ems} = \mathbb{E}\left[\max \text{Loss} \,|\, \max \text{Loss} > 0\right].$$

Again, an application of Bayes's formula shows that this indicator can be expressed as a function of the expected maximum loss and the success probability

$$\text{ems} = \frac{\mathbb{E}[\max \text{Loss}]}{1 - \text{sp}}.$$

Finally, the worst maximum shortfall is the essential supremum of maximum losses: thus, it represents the largest deviation from the consumption objective, across all dates and states of the world:

$$\text{wms} = \text{ess}\sup \max \text{Loss}.$$

For the drawdown goal, we will replace the expected and the worst maximum shortfalls by the expected and the worst maximum drawdowns. The drawdown is defined in terms of the current wealth (A_{T_j}) and the maximum-to-date of wealth $(\overline{A}_{T_j})$:

$$\text{DD}_{T_j} = \frac{\overline{A}_{T_j} - A_{T_j}}{\overline{A}_{T_j}}.$$

By definition, the drawdown is non-negative, and is less than 1 (as long as wealth remains positive).

The following definition summarises the mathematical expressions for the success indicators.

Definition 12 (Success Indicators for a Wealth-Based Goal with Multiple Horizons). Consider a wealth-based goal represented by the minimum wealth levels $(G_{T_1}, \ldots, G_{T_p})$. The success indicators are defined as follows:

- The success probability: $\text{sp} = \mathbb{P}(A_{T_j} \geq G_{T_j}; \forall j = 1, \ldots, p)$;
- The expected maximum shortfall: $\text{ems} = \frac{\mathbb{E}[\max \text{Loss}]}{1 - \text{sp}}$;
  or the expected maximum drawdown: $\text{emd} = \mathbb{E}[\max DD_{T_p}]$;
- The worst maximum shortfall: $\text{wms} = \text{ess sup} \max \text{Loss}$;
  or the worst maximum drawdown: $\text{wmd} = \text{ess sup} \max \text{LossDD}_{T_p}$.

A.6.4.3. *Consumption-based goals*

A consumption-based goal is represented by a consumption stream $(c_{T_1}, \ldots, c_{T_p})$. The success probability is defined as the probability that on each consumption date, the available wealth covers the consumption payment, that is

$$\text{sp} = \mathbb{P}(A_{T_j-} \geq c_{T_j}; \forall j = 1, \ldots, p).$$

This is identical to the probability that the wealth after consumption, i.e. the quantity $A_{T_j} = A_{T_j-} - c_{T_j}$, is non-negative. Effective consumption at date T_j, denoted by c_{eff, T_j}, is defined as the minimum between the target consumption level and wealth right before consumption. The loss with respect to the goal is defined as the difference between effective consumption and the target, that is

$$\text{Loss}_{T_j} = \left[1 - \frac{c_{\text{eff}, T_j}}{c_{T_j}} \right]^+.$$

The expected maximum shortfall and the worst maximum shortfall are then defined in the same way as for a wealth-based goal with multiple horizons.

Definition 13 (Success Indicators for a Consumption-Based Goal). Consider a consumption-based goal represented by the payments $(c_{T_1}, \ldots, c_{T_p})$. The success indicators are defined as follows:

- The success probability: $\text{sp} = \mathbb{P}(A_{T_j-} \geq c_{T_j}; \forall j = 1, \ldots, p)$;
- The expected maximum shortfall: $\text{ems} = \frac{\mathbb{E}[\max \text{Loss}]}{1 - \text{sp}}$;
- The worst maximum shortfall: $\text{wms} = \text{ess sup} \max \text{Loss}$.

A.6.5. *Taxes*

The sequence of operations on a given month t is as follows:

- If t is the end of the year, pay taxes first: included are transactions and roll-over operations performed since the last tax payment date (included) and before the current date (excluded);
- Then, rebalance the portfolio: weights of dynamic GBI strategies based on after-tax wealth;
- Then, compute the taxes generated by operations of date t: included are the selling operations, and, if t is the end of the year, the roll-over operations.

A.6.5.1. *Taxes on selling operations*

We now give the detailed expressions for the taxes generated by the selling operations on the constituents of a portfolio. We take the notations of Table 4.25.

For $l = 1, 2, 3, \ldots$, the amount of taxes generated by the selling operations in asset i on date lh is

$$
\theta_{i,lh} = \zeta \times \left[\sum_{m=n_l}^{l-1} u_{ilm} \times (S_{i,lh} - S_{i,mh}) + \sum_{m=0}^{n_l-1} u_{ilm} \times (S_{i,lh} - S_{i,mh})^+ \right],
$$

Table 4.25.   Symbols for tax calculation.

Symbol	Definition
N	Number of constituents.
$S_{i,t}$	Asset price.
$N_{i,t}$	Number of shares of asset i held on date t.
h	Rebalancing period, expressed as a fraction of year.
ζ	Tax rate (20% in base case).
$\theta_{i,t}$	Amount of taxes generated by the selling operations in asset i on date t.
$\tilde{\theta}_{i,t}$	Amount of taxes generated by the roll-over operation for asset i on date t.
u_{ilm}	Number of shares of asset i purchased at date mh and sold at rebalancing of date lh.
v_{ilm}	Number of shares of asset i purchased at date mh and sold at roll-over of date lh.
Θ_n	Amount of taxes to be paid at the end of year n.
$A_{liq,t}$	Liquid wealth of date t.

Note: This table contains the definitions of the symbols that appear in the tax formulas.

with

$$n_l = \frac{\lfloor lh \rfloor}{h}$$

being the previous year end. Observe that $\theta_{i,lh}$ is the sum of two contributions: one from the transactions within the year, for which compensations between gains and losses are possible, and the other one from the older transactions, for which compensations are not possible. The positive part is taken only for price changes within the year.

According to the LIFO rule, the number of shares purchased at date mh and sold at date lh is recursively computed as

$$u_{ilm} = \min \left[\left\{ (N_{i,(l-1)h} - N_{i,lh})^+ - \sum_{j=m+1}^{l-1} u_{ilj} \right\}^+ \right.$$
$$\left. (N_{i,mh} - N_{i,(m-1)h})^+ \right], \quad \text{for } 1 \le m \le l - 1;$$

$$u_{il0} = \min \left[\left\{ (N_{i,(l-1)h} - N_{i,lh})^+ - \sum_{j=1}^{l-1} u_{ilj} \right\}^+ , N_{i,0} \right],$$

for $m = 0$ or $l = 1$.

It can be mathematically verified that the sum of these numbers is equal to the number of shares to sell on date lh, as follows:

$$\sum_{m=0}^{l-1} u_{ilm} = (N_{i,(l-1)h} - N_{i,lh})^+, \quad \text{for } l \ge 1.$$

A.6.5.2. *Taxes on a roll-over of bonds*

Consider now an asset which is an annual roll-over of bonds (as in Case 1). The taxation mechanism is similar, with the following modifications:

- On a given date, only the selling operations done within the year are taken into account (with compensations allowed);
- At the end of each year, we force the liquidation of the position in bonds, and taxes are paid on this operation.

The amount of taxes generated by the liquidation of the portfolio at the end of year $n = 1, 2, 3, \ldots$ is

$$\bar{\theta}_{i,n} = \zeta \times \sum_{m=l-\frac{1}{h}}^{l} v_{ilm} \times (S_{i,n} - S_{i,mh}),$$

with

$$l = \frac{n}{h},$$

and v_{ilm} is recursively computed as

$$v_{ill} = \min \left[N_{i,n}, (N_{i,n} - N_{i,n-h})^+ \right] = (N_{i,n} - N_{i,n-h})^+, \quad \text{for } m = l;$$

$$v_{ilm} = \min \left[\left\{ N_{i,n} - \sum_{j=m+1}^{l} v_{ilj} \right\}^+, (N_{i,mh} - N_{i,(m-1)h})^+ \right],$$

$$\text{for } l + 1 - \frac{1}{h} \le m \le l - 1,$$

$$v_{il,l-\frac{1}{h}} = \min \left[\left\{ N_{i,n} - \sum_{j=m+1}^{l} v_{ilj} \right\}^+, N_{i,n-1} \right], \quad \text{for } m = l - \frac{1}{h}.$$

A.6.5.3. *Annual tax payment*

Compensations across assets are possible, and the tax payment is floored at zero and capped at the value of liquid wealth. Thus, the amount of taxes to be paid at the end of year n is

$$\Theta_n = \min \left[A_{liq,t}, \left\{ \sum_{i=1}^{N} \sum_{l=0}^{\frac{1}{h}-1} \theta_{i,n-lh} + \bar{\theta}_{i,n} \right\}^+ \right].$$

Glossary

Achievement (of a Goal*)

Definition. The definition depends on the nature of the **goal***. A wealth-based **goal*** represented by minimum wealth levels to be attained at specified dates is said to be achieved if investor's wealth is greater than or equal to the prescribed minimum at each of the dates. A consumption-based **goal*** represented by expenses (not necessarily consumption expenses, despite the name) to be made at specified dates is said to be achieved if the investor remains solvent (i.e. if his/her wealth remains non-negative) at each point in time when the investor makes the payments.

Abbreviation. *None.*

Examples. An investor starts with $10,000 and targets $15,000 in 5 years. He invests the $10,000 in a cash account that earns 1.5% per year, so he ends up with $10,000 \times 1.015^5 = \$10,772$ 5 years after. The goal is not achieved.

Assume now that he invests in a stock index that earns on average 9% per year during the 5 years. Final wealth is $10,000 \times 1.09^5 = \$15,386$, so the goal is achieved.

Affordable Goal

Definition. A **goal*** whose achievement can be secured given investor's current and possibly future resources. For a fixed schedule of future resources, a goal is affordable if, and only if, current wealth is greater than or equal to the **minimum required capital***.

Abbreviation. *None.*

Examples. An investor starts with $70,000 and targets $100,000 in 10 years from now. Assuming that the current 10-year zero-coupon rate is 3%, the **minimum required capital** is $100,000 \times \exp[-0.03 \times 10] = \$74,082$. It is greater than $70,000, so the goal is not affordable.

Assume now that the investor receives $6,000 for sure in 3 years, and that the 7-year zero-coupon rate in 3 years, which is not yet known, is known to be non-negative for sure. Then, the $6,000 generate at least $6,000 in 10 years. The present value of $100,000-6,000 = \$94,000$ is $94,000 \times \exp[-0.03 \times 10] = \$69,637$, which is less than $70,000. The goal is now affordable.

Reference. Section 2.2.

Aspirational Goal

Definition. Any goal that is not affordable, and cannot therefore be secured.

Abbreviation. AG.

Examples. If a defined-benefit pension fund starts with a funding ratio of 98% and targets a ratio of 100% by the end of the year, this goal is aspirational because the present value of future assets (today's asset value) is less than the present value of future liabilities (today's liability market value). This means that no investment strategy can increase the funding ratio from 98% to 100% with certainty. Then, the choice is between strategies that have different success probabilities.

Reference. Section 2.4.1.

Essential Goal

Definition. An **affordable goal*** that an investor wants to achieve in all market conditions, without relying on assumptions of expected returns, correlations and volatilities. It can be secured with a **goal-based investing strategy***.

Abbreviation. EG.

Examples. Consider a defined-benefit pension fund that starts with a funding ratio of 113% and is subject to a minimum funding requirement of 110%. This constraint is an essential goal because if the fund fails to comply with the rule, then proper course of action is required, which is potentially costly (e.g. raise contributions levied from workers).

An individual estimates that he/she needs at least $1,500 per month in retirement to finance essential expenses (home, heating, car, etc.). This is an essential goal if his/her current wealth is at least equal to the **minimum capital requirement*** for this goal, which is the sum of the discounted values of income cash flows.

Reference. Section 2.4.1.

Floor

Definition. In a **goal-based investing strategy***, the floor is a minimum value that the portfolio must respect at all times. It is often taken to be the present value of an **essential goal***, that is a goal that the investor wants to reach with certainty at a given horizon: with this definition, wealth must be greater than or equal to the present value of the goal at the initial date, for otherwise the goal is not affordable and cannot be regarded as essential.

Abbreviation. *None.*

Examples. Suppose that initial wealth is $100,000, that the goal is to reach $150,000 in 10 years and that the current 10-year zero-coupon rate is 4.2%. The present value of the $150,000 is $150,000 \times \exp[-0.042 \times 10] = \$98,557$, which is less than current wealth. So, the goal is affordable and can be regarded as essential if the investor decides to secure it. At any point in time, the value of the floor is $150,000 \times \exp[-0.042 \times t]$, where t is the time-to-horizon, which is 10 years at the beginning and shrinks to zero as the investor nears horizon.

Goal

Definition. A level of wealth that an investor (individual or institutional) wants to attain in the future, or a series of expenses that he/she wants to make. Thus, a distinction is usually made between *wealth-based* and *consumption-based* goals. The latter category encompasses all goals involving expenses, even though these expenses do not necessarily correspond to consumption. A more formal definition is with a list of dates at which the minimum wealth levels must be attained or the expenses must be made, and a list of values representing the wealth levels or the expenses. The level of the goal on a date in the list does not need to be known in advance, but it must be the result of a rule that allows it to be calculated based on the information available at this date.

Abbreviation. *None.*

Examples. A defined-benefit pension fund must pay pensions to beneficiaries every month. The payments in a given month depend on the number of beneficiaries and their accrued rights, as well as realised inflation if pensions are indexed. None of these parameters is known in advance, but all of them are revealed at the payment date, so the goal level at the payment date is a function of the information available at this date, according to a fixed formula (by definition of a defined-benefit fund). The goal to pay pensions is a consumption-based goal for the pension fund, and the goal dates are the monthly payment dates.

An individual does not want to lose more than 5% every year for the next 10 years. This goal is a wealth-based goal, the dates are the calendar year ends, and the level of the goal on one of these dates is 95% of the wealth level attained at the previous year end.

Goal-Based Investing Strategy

Definition. A rule-based investment strategy that secures all **essential goals*** and has non-zero probability of reaching **aspirational goals***. In most practical examples, a goal-based investing strategy focuses on a single essential goal.

Abbreviation. GBI strategy.

Examples. GBI strategies are often designed as extended forms of portfolio insurance strategies, by taking a floor equal to the **minimum capital required*** to secure all essential goals, and a "safe asset" that super-replicates all goal-hedging portfolios. In the case of a single essential goal, the floor is the **minimum capital required*** to secure the goal, and the safe asset is the goal-hedging portfolio.

Goal-Hedging Portfolio

Definition. A portfolio that guarantees the achievement of a goal regardless of assumptions on expected returns, correlations and volatilities, as long as the investor invests at least the **minimum capital requirement*** in it. The composition of the goal-hedging portfolio depends on the investment universe at hand, and the rebalancing rule within it is possibly dynamic.

Abbreviation. GHP.

Examples. An individual targets fixed replacement income, equal to $10,000 per year, for the first 20 years of retirement. The GHP is a fixed-income portfolio that pays $10,000 per year for 20 years, as of the expected retirement date. Usually, there is no such bond in financial markets, so the GHP is a cash-flow-matching portfolio made with existing coupon-paying bonds.

An individual targets fixed capital, say 150% of his/her current wealth, in 10 years from now. The GHP is a zero-coupon bond that pays 150% of current wealth in 10 years if this zero-coupon exists. If not, the GHP is a cash-flow-matching portfolio for the zero-coupon bond.

Important Goal

Definition. An **affordable goal*** that the investor decides not to secure in order to increase the risk-taking, thus to increase the probability of reaching **aspirational goals***.

Abbreviation. IG.

Examples. An individual is endowed with $50,000 today and has a 10-year horizon. The 10-year zero-coupon rate is 3%, so the maximum level of wealth in 10 years that can be secured is $50,000 \times \exp[0.03 \times 10] = \$67,493$. The individual may decide to secure only $60,000 with a **goal-based investing strategy***, as opposed to $67,493, in order to have chances to reach non-affordable levels, e.g. $70,000. Then, the $60,000 are an **essential goal***, while the $67,493 are an important goal.

Reference. Section 2.4.1.

Liability-Hedging Portfolio

Definition. In asset–liability management, the liability-hedging portfolio is a portfolio made with the available assets and aiming to replicate the present value of liabilities. In this book, it is often assumed that replication is perfect, but to make a distinction between a portfolio that perfectly replicates and a portfolio that has some replication error, one can specify that the liability-hedging portfolio is "perfect". In practice, perfect replication is often impossible and replication methods like duration matching or duration-convexity matching are employed. The liability-hedging portfolio is the **goal-hedging portfolio*** when the investor wants to secure a minimum funding level.

Abbreviation. LHP.

Examples. A defined-benefit pension fund is committed to pay benefits to retired workers. If benefits are fixed in nominal terms, the present value of liabilities is the sum of future benefits discounted with the nominal zero-coupon rates of maturities equal to the horizons of the payments. In practice, the imperfect LHP is a portfolio of nominal bonds that matches the duration, and possibly the convexity, of the present value of liabilities.

If benefits are indexed on realised inflation, the discount rates are *real* zero-coupon rates, and the LHP uses inflation-indexed bonds together with nominal bonds to replicate the present value.

Maximum Drawdown

Definition. The largest drawdown recorded by a portfolio over a given period, where the drawdown on a date is the positive part of the difference between the maximum value recorded by the portfolio until this date and the current value, divided by the maximum. Taking the positive part means that if the current value is greater than or equal to the maximum-to-date, the drawdown is zero.

Abbreviation. Max DD.

Examples. The value of a cash account, in which funds are periodically re-invested at the prevailing short-term interest rate, is non-decreasing over time, as long as short-term rates remain non-negative. Thus, the drawdown of the cash account is zero at any point in time, and the maximum drawdown over a period of non-negative short-term rates is zero too.

Consider a portfolio with values $[100; 99.2; 95; 95.2; 94; 98.3; 101.5; 93]$. The calculation of the maximum drawdown can be decomposed as shown in the following table:

Date	0	1	2	3	4	5	6	7	8
Portfolio value ($)	100	99.2	95	95.2	94	98.3	101.5	93	96.8
Maximum-to-date ($)	100	100	100	100	100	100	101.5	101.5	101.5
Drawdown (%)	0	$100 \times (1 - 99.2/ 100) = 0.8$	5	4.8	6	1.7	0	$100 \times (1 - 93/ 101.5) = 8.37$	4.63
Maximum drawdown (%)								**8.37**	

The maximum drawdown is recorded over the period that ranges from date 6 to date 7 and is equal to 8.37%.

Maximum Sharpe Ratio Portfolio

Definition. The portfolio of risky assets that maximises the Sharpe ratio, defined as the expected return in excess over the risk-free rate, divided by the volatility. In the Capital Asset Pricing Model, the maximum Sharpe ratio is the slope of the capital market line. The maximum Sharpe ratio is an example of **performance-seeking portfolio**∗.

Abbreviation. MSR portfolio.

Minimum Capital Requirement for a Goal

Definition. The minimum amount of capital that an investor must have to secure the achievement of a goal without making assumptions on expected returns, correlations and volatilities. Starting from a capital equal to the minimum, not any strategy secures the goal: investing in the **goal-hedging portfolio**∗ does so, but other strategies may fail to do so. The two characteristics of the goal that impact the minimum required capital are its level and its horizon: high target consumption or wealth levels are more expensive to secure, and a longer horizon reduces the required capital, due to discounting effects. The main market parameter that affects the minimum required capital is the level of interest rates. The minimum capital required may also depend on the set of financial securities available for investment.

Abbreviation. *None.*

Examples. An individual targets fixed capital equal to $100,000 in 10 years from now. Assuming that the 10-year zero-coupon rate today is 3%, the minimum capital to invest is $100,000 \times \exp[-0.03 \times 10] = \$74,082$.

Assume now that the investor receives $30,000 for sure in 4 years, and that the 6-year zero-coupon rate in 4 years is non-negative with 100% probability. Then, the $30,000 generate at least $30,000 in

10 years, so the minimum capital to invest today is no more than the present value of $100,000$–$30,000 = \$70,000$, which is $70,000 \times \exp[-0.03 \times 10] = \$51,857$. The minimum required capital is less than or equal to \$51,857. It is in fact even less than this value if the investor has access to bond options.

Multiplier

Definition. In a **goal-based investing strategy***, the multiplier is a number greater than or equal to 1 that is applied as a scaling factor to the difference between the portfolio value and the **floor***. The multiplier is generally taken to be greater than 1 because this implies an allocation to the **performance-seeking portfolio*** greater than in a buy-and-hold strategy.

Abbreviation. *None.*

Examples. The multiplier is often taken to be an integer greater than 1 and less than 10, though it is perfectly possible to deviate from these conditions. It can also be specified as a time-varying quantity that depends on market conditions, so as to take into account the current expected return and volatility of the **performance-seeking portfolio***.

Performance-Seeking Portfolio

Definition. A portfolio *intended* to outperform the goal-hedging portfolio by the investment horizon, but that does not outperform it in all market conditions. This portfolio is used because it allows an investor to reach **aspirational goals*** when it sufficiently outperforms the goal-hedging portfolio, but it compromises the achievement of **essential goals***, unless a **goal-based investing strategy*** is employed to secure essential goals while preserving chances to reach aspirational goals. In fund separation theorems proved within modern portfolio theory, the performance-seeking portfolio is often identified with the **maximum Sharpe ratio*** portfolio.

Abbreviation. PSP.

294 *Glossary*

Examples. Equity portfolios are usual examples of performance-seeking portfolios, because goal-hedging portfolios are usually mostly invested in bonds, and equities are expected to outperform bonds in the long run.

Pricing Kernel

Definition. A stochastic process, that is a sequence of random variables indexed by time, that serves to calculate the price of future payoffs. Following the no-arbitrage pricing theory, the price to pay today to receive a payoff X at some future date t is the mathematical expectation of $M_t \times X$, where M_t is the pricing kernel for date t. Informally speaking, the pricing kernel measures, in each future state of the world, how a dollar received in this state is valued today. A future dollar is more valued today if it occurs in a future state of the world where the pricing kernel is high than if it is received in a state where the pricing kernel is low. Consumption-based asset pricing theory precisely shows that the pricing kernel is proportional to the "marginal utility of consumption": when marginal utility is high (respectively, low), the investor has high (respectively, low) utility from receiving one additional dollar, so this additional dollar is highly (respectively, lowly) valued. Other standard names for the pricing kernel are *stochastic discount factor* and *state-price deflator*.

Abbreviation. None.

Technical references. Chapter 6 in Duffie, D. *Dynamic Asset Pricing Theory*. 2002. Princeton University Press: Princeton, New Jersey.

Cochrane, J. *Asset Pricing*. 2005. Princeton University Press: Princeton, New Jersey.

References

Amenc, N., F. Goltz, A. Lodh, and L. Martellini. "Diversifying the Diversifiers and Tracking the Tracking Error: Outperforming Cap-Weighted Indices with Limited Risk of Underperformance." *Journal of Portfolio Management* 38, no. 3 (2012): 72–88.

Amenc, N., L. Martellini, V. Milhau, and V. Ziemann. "Asset-Liability Management in Private Wealth Management." *Journal of Portfolio Management* 36, no. 1 (2009): 100–120.

Amenc, N., F. Goltz, L. Martellini, and V. Milhau. *New Frontiers in Benchmarking and Liability-Driven Investing.* EDHEC-Risk Institute Publication, 2010.

Ang, A., W. Goetzmann, and S. Schaefer. "Evaluation of Active Management of the Norwegian Government Pension Fund - Global." *Technical Report* 2009.

Aucamp, D. "An Investment Strategy with Overshoot Rebates Which Minimizes the Time to Attain a Specified Goal." *Management Science* 23, no. 11 (1977): 1234–1241.

Barberis, N. "Investing for the Long Run when Returns Are Predictable." *Journal of Finance* 55, no. 1 (2000): 225–264.

Black, F., and A. Perold. "Theory of Constant Proportion Portfolio Insurance." *Journal of Economic Dynamics and Control* 16, no. 3 (1992): 403–426.

Black, F., and R. Jones. "Simplifying Portfolio Insurance." *Journal of Portfolio Management* 14, no. 1 (1987): 48–51.

Black, F., and M. Scholes. "The Pricing of Options and Corporate Liabilities." *The Journal of Political Economy* 81, no. 3 (1973): 637–654.

Brennan, M., and Y. Xia. "Dynamic Asset Allocation under Inflation." *Journal of Finance* 57, no. 3 (2002): 1201–1238.

Brown, J.R., and A. Finkelstein. "Why is the Market for Long-Term Care Insurance So Small?" *Journal of Public Economics* 91, no. 10 (2007): 1967–1991.

Browne, S. "Reaching Goals By a Deadline: Digital Options and Continuous-Time Active Portfolio Management." *Advances in Applied Probability* 31, no. 2 (1999): 551–577.

Campbell, J., and L. Viceira. "Consumption and Portfolio Decisions When Expected Returns are Time Varying." *Quarterly Journal of Economics* 114, no. 2 (1999): 433–495.

CDI Advisors Research. "Commitment Driven Investing: The Essentials." 2014.

Chhabra, A. "Beyond Markowitz: A Comprehensive Wealth Allocation Framework For Individual Investors." *The Journal of Wealth Management* 7, no. 5 (2005): 8–34.

Cox, J.C., J.E. Ingersoll, and S.A. Ross. "A Theory of the Term Structure of Interest Rates." *Econometrica* 53, no. 2 (1985): 385–408.

Cox, J.C., and C.F. Huang. "Optimal Consumption and Portfolio Policies when Asset Prices Follow A Diffusion Process." *Journal of Economic Theory* 49, no. 1 (1989): 33–83.

Cvitanic, J. "Minimizing Expected Loss of Hedging in Incomplete and Constrained Markets." *SIAM Journal on Control and Optimization* 38, no. 4 (2000): 1050–1066.

Deguest, R., A. Meucci, and A. Santangelo. "Measuring Portfolio Diversification Based on Optimized Uncorrelated Factors." Working Paper, 2013.

Deguest, R., L. Martellini, and V. Milhau. "Hedging Versus Insurance: Long-Horizon Investing with Short-Term Constraints." *Bankers, Markets and Investors*, no. Special Issue March–April 2014 (2014): 33–47.

Detemple, J., and M. Rindisbacher. "Dynamic Asset Allocation: Portfolio Decomposition Formula and Applications." *Review of Financial Studies* 23, no. 1 (2010): 25–100.

Dimson, E., P. Marsh, and M. Staunton. *Triumph of the Optimists: 101 Years of Global Investment Returns*. Princeton: Princeton University Press, 2002.

Duffee, G. "Term Premia and Interest Rate Forecasts in Affine Models." *Journal of Finance* 57, no. 1 (2002): 405–443.

Duffee, G., and R. Stanton. "Estimation of Term Structure Models." *Quarterly Journal of Finance* 2, no. 2 (2012).

Duffie, D. *Dynamic Asset Pricing Theory*. Princeton: Princeton University Press, 2001.

Dybvig, P. H., and C. Huang. "Nonnegative Wealth, Absence of Arbitrage and Feasible Consumption Plans." *Review of Financial Studies* 1, no. 4 (1988): 377–401.

El Karoui, N., and R. Rouge. "Pricing Via Utility Maximization and Entropy." *Mathematical Finance* 10, no. 2 (2000): 259–276.

El Karoui, N., M. Jeanblanc, and V. Lacoste. "Optimal Portfolio Management with American Capital Guarantee." *Journal of Economic Dynamics and Control* 29, no. 3 (2005): 449–468.

Fabozzi, F., L. Martellini, and P. Priaulet. "Hedging Interest Rate Risk with Term Structure Factor Models." In *The Handbook of Fixed-income Securities*, edited by F. Fabozzi. New York: J. Wiley, 2005.

Fama, F., and K. French. "The Cross-Section of Expected Stock Returns." *Journal of Finance* 47, no. 2 (1992): 427–465.

Föllmer, H., and M. Schweizer. *Hedging of Contingent Claims Under Incomplete Information*, edited by M. Davis and R. Elliot. London: Gordon and Breach, 1990.

Föllmer, H., and P. Leukert. "Efficient Hedging: Cost Versus Shortfall Risk." *Finance and Stochastic* 4, no. 2 (2000): 117–146.

Föllmer, H., and P. Leukert. "Quantile Hedging." *Finance and Stochastics* 3, no. 3 (1999): 251–273.

Goltz, F., and V. Le Sourd. *Does Finance Theory Make the Case for Capitalisation-Weighted Indexing?* EDHEC-Risk Institute Publication, 2011.

Gürkaynak, R., B. Sack, and J. Wright. "The TIPS Yield Curve and Inflation Compensation." *American Economic Journals: Macroeconomics* 2, no. 1 (2010): 70–92.

Harrison, J.M., and S.R. Pliska. "Martingales and Stochastic Integrals in the Theory of Stochastic Trading." *Stochastic Processes and Their Applications* 11 (1981): 215–260.

Harrisson, J.M., and D.M. Kreps. "Martingales and Arbitrage in Multiperiod Securities Markets." *Journal of Economic Theory* 20 (1979): 381–408.

He, H., and N. Pearson. "Consumption and Portfolio Policies with Incomplete Markets and Short-Sale Constraints: The Infinite Dimensional Case." *Journal of Economic Theory* 54 (1991): 259–304.

Heath, D., and W. Sudderth. "Continuous-Time Portfolio Management: Minimizing the Expected Time to Reach a Goal." *IMA Preprint Series*, 1984: 74.

Jagannathan, R., and T. Ma. "Risk Reduction in Large Portfolios: Why Imposing the Wrong Constraints Helps." *Journal of Finance* 58, no. 4 (2003): 1651–1683.

Karatzas, I., and S. Shreve. *Brownian Motion and Stochastic Calculus.* Springer, 2000.

Kardaras, C., and E. Platen. "Minimizing the Expected Market Time to Reach a Certain Wealth Level." *SIAM Journal on Financial Mathematics* 1, no. 1 (2010): 16–29.

Kim, T., and E. Omberg. "Dynamic Nonmyopic Portfolio Behavior." *Review of Financial Studies* 9, no. 1 (1996): 141–161.

Liu, J. "Portfolio Selection in Stochastic Environments." *Review of Financial Studies* 20, no. 1 (2007): 1–39.

Long, J. B. "The Numeraire Portfolio." *Journal of Financial Economics* 26 (1990): 29–69.

Maillard, S., T. Roncalli, and J. Teïletche. "The Properties of Equally Weighted Risk Contribution Portfolios." *Journal of Portfolio Management* 36, no. 4 (2010): 60–70.

Markowitz, H. "Portfolio Selection." *Journal of Finance* 7, no. 1 (1952): 77–91.

Markowitz, H. "The Optimization of a Quadratic Function Subject to Linear Constraints." *Naval Research Logistics Quarterly* 3, no. 1–2 (1956): 111–133.

Martellini, L., and V. Milhau. "An Empirical Analysis of the Benefits of Inflation-Linked Bonds, Real Estate and Commodities for Long-Term Investors with Inflation-Linked Liabilities." *Bankers, Markets and Investors*, no. 124 (2013): 4–18.

Martellini, L., and V. Milhau. "Dynamic Allocation Decisions in the Presence of Funding Ratio Constraints." *Journal of Pension Economics and Finance* 11, no. 4 (2012): 549–580.

Martellini, L., and V. Milhau. "Towards the Design of Improved Forms of Target-Date Funds." *Bankers, Markets and Investors* 109 (2010): 6–24.

Martellini, L., V. Milhau, and A. Tarelli. "Capital Structure Decisions and the Optimal Design of Corporate Market Debt Programs". *Journal of Corporate Finance* 49, issue C (2018): 141–167.

Merton, R. "An Intertemporal Capital Asset Pricing Model." *Econometrica* 41, no. 5 (1973): 867–887.

Merton, R. *Continuous-Time Finance.* Oxford: Blackwell Publishers, 1992.

Merton, R. "On Estimating the Expected Return on the Market: An Exploratory Investigation." *Journal of Financial Economics* 8, no. 4 (1980): 323–361.

Merton, R. "Optimal Portfolio and Consumption Rules in a Continuous-Time Model." *The Journal of Economic Theory* 3, no. 4 (1971): 373–413.

Mindlin, D. "A Tale of Three Epiphanies That Happened and One That Did Not." *Unpublished Working Paper* 2013.

Munk, C., and C. Sorensen. "Optimal Consumption and Investment Strategies with Stochastic Interest Rates." *Journal of Banking and Finance* 28, no. 8 (2004): 1987–2013.

Munk, C., C. Sorensen, and T. Vinther. "Dynamic Asset Allocation under Mean-Reverting Returns, Stochastic Interest Rates and Inflation Uncertainty: Are Popular Recommendations Consistent with Rational Behavior?" *International Review of Economics and Finance* 13 (2004): 141–166.

Nelson, C., and A. Siegel. "Parsimonious Modeling of Yield Curves." *The Journal of Business* 60, no. 4 (1987): 473–489.

Nielsen, L., and M. Vassalou. "The Instantaneous Capital Market Line." *Economic Theory* 28, no. 3 (2006): 651–664.

Reichenstein, W. "After-Tax Asset Allocation." *Financial Analysts Journal* 62, no. 4 (2006): 14–19.

Reichenstein, W., and W. Jennings. *Integrating Investments and the Tax Code.* Hoboken, NJ: John Wiley & Sons, 2003.

Roncalli, T. *Introduction to Risk Parity and Budgeting.* Chapman & Hall, CRC Financial Mathematics Series, 2013.

Ross, S. "The Arbitrage Theory of Capital Asset Pricing." *Journal of Economic Theory* 13, no. 3 (1976): 341–360.

Samuelson, P. "Lifetime Portfolio Selection by Dynamic Stochastic Programming." *Review of Economics and Statistics* 51, no. 3 (1969): 239–246.

Sangvinatsos, A., and J. Wachter. "Does the Failure of the Expectations Hypothesis Matter for Long-Term Investors?" *Journal of Finance* 60, no. 1 (2005): 179–230.

Tepla, L. "Optimal Investment with Minimum Performance Constraints." *Journal of Economic Dynamics and Control* 25, no. 10 (2001): 1629–1645.

Tobin, J. "Liquidity Preference as Behavior Towards Risk." *The Review of Economic Studies* 25, no. 2 (1958): 65–86.

Vasicek, O. "An Equilibrium Characterization of the Term Structure." *Journal of Financial Economics* 5, no. 2 (1977): 177–188.

Wachter, J. "Optimal Consumption and Portfolio Allocation under Mean-Reverting Returns: An Exact Solution for Complete Markets." *Journal of Financial and Quantitative Analysis* 37 (2002): 63–91.

Wachter, J. "Risk Aversion and Allocation to Long-Term Bonds." *Journal of Economic Theory* 112, no. 2 (2003): 325–333.

Wang, H., A. Suri, D. Laster, and H. Almadi. "Portfolio Selection in Goals-Based Wealth Management." *Journal of Wealth Management* 14, no. 1 (2011): 55–65.

Wilcox, J., J. Horvitz, and D. DiBartolomeo. *Investment Management for Taxable Private Investors*. Charlottesville, VA: Research Foundation of CFA Institute, 2006.

Index